Abiding Faith

ALSO BY SCOTT COWDELL

The Ten Commandments and Ethics Today

God's Next Big Thing: Discovering the Future Church

A God for This World

Is Jesus Unique? A Study of Recent Christology

Atheist Priest? Don Cupitt and Christianity

Abiding Faith

Christianity Beyond Certainty, Anxiety, and Violence

SCOTT COWDELL

CASCADE *Books* • Eugene, Oregon

ABIDING FAITH
Christianity Beyond Certainty, Anxiety, and Violence

Copyright © 2009 Scott Cowdell. All rights reserved. Except for brief quotations in critical publications or reviews, no part of this book may be reproduced in any manner without prior written permission from the publisher. Write: Permissions, Wipf & Stock, 199 W. 8th Ave., Suite 3, Eugene, OR 97401.

Cascade Books
A Division of Wipf and Stock Publishers
199 W. 8th Ave., Suite 3
Eugene, OR 97405

www.wipfandstock.com

ISBN 13: 978-1-60608-223-2

Cataloging-in-Publication data:

Cowdell, Scott.

    Abiding faith: Christianity beyond certainty, anxiety, and violence / Scott Cowdell.

    x + 232 p. ; 23 cm. —Includes bibliographical references and index.

    ISBN 13: 978-1-60608-223-2

    1. God (Christianity). 2. Christian life—Anglican authors. 3. Faith. 4. Girard, René. 5. Apologetics. I. Title.

BT1102 C60 2009

Manufactured in the U.S.A.

Bible quotations are from the *New Revised Standard Version* Bible, copyright © 1989, Division of Christian Education of the National Council of the Churches of Christ in the United States of America. Used by permission. All rights reserved.

Dedicated to

Gregory J. Burke, OCD

The Gospel is the only "twilight of the gods."

Henri de Lubac, *The Discovery of God*

Contents

Acknowledgments / ix
Introduction / 1

PART I Faith in the Crucible of Modernity

1. Homeless Hearts: Faith and the Modern Self / 7

2. Faith in "the System": The Modern Captivity of God / 48

3. The False Sacred: Modernity and Its Victims / 75

PART II Belonging, Believing, and Behaving

4. At Home in Jesus Christ: Abiding Faith / 103

5. Faith's Knowledge: Abiding Faith and Modern Doubt / 137

6. Behold, I Make All Things New: Vision, Self, Spirituality / 178

Conclusion / 205
Bibliography / 211
Index / 221

Acknowledgments

This book has been a long time coming, in the sense that I began taking an interest in the nature of belief as long ago as 1997. But only after being introduced to the work of René Girard and James Alison in 2004 did I really begin to understand what faith is, and what it is not. For opening my mind and heart to Girard and Alison, also for being the wise guide to whom I refer in Chapter 6, I thank my friend and mentor Bishop Bruce Wilson.

The book is dedicated to Fr Greg Burke, OCD, in the year we mark a quarter-century of friendship. Greg helped keep me sane in the mid-1980s when I was an intense young theological student in Brisbane and avid reader of skeptical English theology, always making me welcome at St. Teresa's Priory. He was my first and best teacher about the immense spiritual value of *ordinariness*. That is, the stable wisdom of inhabiting life undramatically, and finding God in the willing embrace of its demands, its continuities, and its aridities. Greg continues to be a fine role model in spiritual wisdom and easy, embodied Christian ministry.

I thank my publishers at Wipf and Stock (Cascade Books), and my editor, Dr. K. C. Hanson, for their belief in this project, and their friendly professionalism. I also thank my friend Revd Canon Dr Ivan Head, Warden of St. Paul's College at the University of Sydney, for four productive months spent in residence in the second half of 2004 as Visiting Scholar and for making my wife and me so very welcome. I acknowledge Charles Sturt University for the award of a one-year Research Fellowship, from mid-2007, during which time I completed the reading and wrote most of the text.

I thank Revd Dr James Alison for his interest and support, also Revd Dr Matthew Anstey for the trouble he took reading the manuscript in full, and for many helpful suggestions. My wife, Lisa Carley, has yet again supported the distracted boor that replaces a spouse in the writing phase of a book project, and I thank her from the bottom of my heart.

Scott Cowdell
Canberra, Australia
September 12, 2008

Introduction

This is a book about the nature of Christian faith. In our anxious age of violent certainties, it offers a holistic understanding of faith that I intend to be timely and liberating, orthodox, and critical. Today's widespread spiritual yearning for inclusion and deep re-connection with others and the world is shown to characterize Christian faith as it is presented here: as an abiding faith in Jesus Christ, of mystical flavor, worked out through the Eucharistic community.

I argue for a self-involving, spiritual-not-just-rational understanding of faith based on personal participation and transformation. Such faith is evident when certainty-craving *individuals* who are anxious and ultimately violence-prone toward the threatening "other"—all of which is shown to be typical of modern culture in the West—come to abide in Christ and his Eucharistic body. Hence we become relational *persons* freed to embrace the other.

Abiding faith is not to be confused with the tribal faith of more undifferentiated, pre-modern times. This book is not an exercise in nostalgic medievalism. But neither is it satisfied with the individualized faith typical of today's secularized West. Beyond tribal faith and individualized faith, then, abiding faith is identified as the classic understanding of intentional Christian faith from the New Testament and the Fathers. It was displaced by tribal faith in the period of Christendom, which in turn began to give way from the later Middle Ages. Thereafter individualized faith emerged with the agenda of modernity. Abiding faith then went underground and was redescribed as mysticism. It is now re-emerging as a post-modern theological and ecclesial option.

This book differs from others addressing the nature of faith because it brings together a range of normally separate discussions, also tackling the problem from a distinctive standpoint. It draws the lived reality of faith into conversation with philosophy of religion. It adopts sharp contemporary analysis of the violence inherent in modern culture as a background to understanding the distinctive nature of Christian faith. It sets out to explore faith against the backdrop of secularity, and modern Western experience more generally, without defensiveness. Its distinctive standpoint is Catholic-minded, ecclesial, and Eucharistic. Faith is presented in terms of liberating, inclusive, ecclesial praxis, beyond the anxious individualism and structural violence implicated in non-ecclesial, non-Eucharistic, non-inclusive definitions of faith.

The book is in two parts and six chapters. Part I explores how faith has fared in the crucible of modernity. Part II is a history, intellectual defense and reflection on the contemporary outworking of abiding faith, under a title taken from Australian Church historian Tom Frame and his book *Anglicans in Australia*, referring to the axes along which Australian Church life needs to be renewed. I have changed Bishop Frame's order, however, putting "belonging" before "believing," for reasons that will become obvious.

Chapter 1 is about the modern Western self and how it *feels*, in particular with regard to faith. A world of religious belonging has gone from the West, and faith has become a matter of individual choice and bricolage. This condition is explored under the headings of secularization, loss of community, the rise to cultural dominance of consumerism, and the annexation of faith by consumer culture. Various standard forms of post-modern faith are then considered: conservative Christianity, consumer spirituality, and atheism—the latter in two forms that I call *atheist chic* and *atheism-lite*.

Chapter 2 is about how our sense of God came to be reshaped by the culture of modernity. First, the roots of modernity are identified with a theological vision of power and control, from the rise of nominalism in the late Middle Ages, which inadvertently spawned the drive to autonomy characteristic of modern atheism. Modernity is then analyzed, drawing on Stephen Toulmin and his important book *Cosmopolis*. This title refers to a system of meaning offering certainty to a troubled Europe, from the early seventeenth century. Modernity's breakdown is charted against the post-modern mood of deregulation and volatilization of truth and power.

Chapter 3 explores the anxious roots and regularly violent consequences of human system building. "The system" of modernity is analyzed in terms of René Girard's theory of the false sacred. A range of deviant and foreign manifestations of "the other" become scapegoats, helping the modern West manage its anxiety and uncertainty. Here the discussion engages Michel Foucault on deviance and foreignness, looking also to post-colonial theory, environmentalism, feminism, and Queer theory. This chapter is a precursor to the Girardian account of modernity that I hope to provide in my next book.

In chapter 4, what I am calling abiding faith is defined, and its fortunes throughout Christian history are traced. This is an understanding of faith beyond tribalism and individualism, also beyond modernity's agenda of control and certainty. Abiding in Christ is identified as the typical understanding of faith from St. Paul to the monastic theology of the Middle Ages, whereupon the rational certainties of Scholasticism drove this classical, participatory approach to faith underground as mysticism. There it has remained as a reminder and a corrective to controlling theological rationalism. Ellen T. Charry, Michel de Certeau, Grace Jantzen, Andrew Louth, Denys Turner, and Mark McIntosh are the theologians who have helped me to understand mysticism more as a theological style than as a type of experience. In seeking to reappropriate St. Paul's mysticism for today, I indicate a Girardian path beyond the debate that passed from Albert Schweitzer to Rudolf Bultmann to E. P. Sanders in twentieth-century New Testament studies.

Chapter 5 is an apologetic account of abiding faith. Modern rationalism and its skeptical assessment of faith is given a run for its money by the more participatory, self-authenticating version of abiding faith identified in chapter 4—a faith that is not objectively verifiable nor subject to complete rational closure, but which is certainly intellectually compatible with the holistic epistemology that has emerged in post-modern times. The key ideas here are "participatory knowing" and "paradigmatic imagination." This chapter centers on a conversation with mid-to-late twentieth-century philosophies of religion and science, demonstrating that abiding faith need not entail a retreat from public meaningfulness. Among those I touch on are the later Ludwig Wittgenstein, W. V. Quine, and Thomas Kuhn in philosophy, also John Henry Newman, Nancey Murphy, George Lindbeck, and Garrett Green in theology. But the chapter hinges on a clear statement of the cumulative nature of abiding faith from the memoirs of Bishop David Jenkins, also a harrowing fictional story of conversion by contemporary Australian writer Tim Winton.

Chapter 6 offers an exposition of abiding faith and its implications for Christian life today under the headings of vision, self, and spirituality. I argue that faith does not necessarily entail a comprehensive system of belief, and I consider some Girardian implications of faith beyond the metaphysical agenda of modernity in conversation with the philosopher Gianni Vattimo. I discuss how faith is and is not passed on, engaging with Edith Wyschogrod and her theory of post-modern sanctity but opting for a Girardian account of how we become selves. Rather than *anxious individuals* defining themselves against "the other," the Church emerges in this chapter as a pacific community of *ecclesial persons* whose being is understood as fully relational, dwelling peacefully in the Trinitarian life. This transformation frees us from certainty, anxiety, and violence so we can embrace the other. The important theologians I touch on in this chapter are D. M. MacKinnon, Rowan Williams, John Zizioulas, and especially James Alison.

This is a wide-ranging discussion and its appeal might well depend on the reader's openness to René Girard and his account of human culture and religion. My hope, however, is that I might commend that account by showing something of its range and power. I also hope to commend faith's reconnection with participation in the Christian form of life, beyond the compromised understanding of faith that both religious skeptics and anxious believers take to be the genuine article.

PART I

Faith in the Crucible of Modernity

1

Homeless Hearts

Faith and the Modern Self

In 2007 many wondered why anyone would sit in a near-silent cinema for nearly three hours to watch a documentary film about Carthusian monks. *Into Great Silence* (in German, *Die Grosse Stille*) took us inside the mother house of this most austere of the Catholic orders, La Grande Chartreuse, over six months. A community of two dozen contemplatives live as hermits, spending up to eighteen hours a day in their self-contained hermitage (or cell), aside from daily mass and strenuous night offices together in the Abbey Church. Carthusians gather only on Sundays for a fixed period of relaxation and chatting, and on Mondays for a long ramble together during which they alternate talking in pairs. Meals are shared like other monks only on Sundays and feast days of the Church year and only then in silence, with a reader. Once a year there is a full-day community hike with a picnic lunch. No wonder the Carthusian website makes clear that no one really chooses this life, but that it chooses them.[1]

The film was profound and moving, and I know I was not the only one who saw it twice. The faces of the monks, on which the camera dwelt from

---

1. See the Carthusian Web site, with photographs and details of each Charterhouse. A link to the remote Vermont Charterhouse, of striking modernist design, is worth following for more detail about the spirituality. Online: http://www.chartreux.org/en/frame.html/. For removing the gloss from this potentially romantic-seeming life, see Maguire, *An Infinity of Little Hours*. For an account of how the Carthusians look post–Vatican II, see Skinner, *Hear Our Silence*.

time to time, were serene and hence beautiful, even the less photogenic ones. The patience, deliberateness, and collectedness of the life were plain, evoked by the loving attention of the camera to minutiae of the daily round, also the external elements. Long takes of the monks praying and reading, also still-life scenes lingering on the few items in a monk's fruit bowl, or the dish draining on his sink in a shaft of sunlight, recalled the intensity of the Dutch painter Vermeer's simple interiors, while the heavy snow of these remote, high alps starkly set off the wood fire-heated cells, and the inconceivable spiritual adventure taking place within them.

Thomas Merton, the Trappist, wrote about Christian faith today from the perspective of a strict monastic life in his poem "The Quickening of St John the Baptist," and his words came to mind as I sat in the dark and took in the even stricter vision of his Carthusian cousins.

> Beyond the scope of sight or sound we dwell upon the air,
> Seeking the world's gain in an unthinkable experience.
> We are exiles in the far end of solitude, living as listeners,
> With hearts attending to the skies we cannot understand,
> Waiting upon the first far drums of Christ the Conqueror,
> Planted like sentinels upon the world's frontier.[2]

But not all were moved by *Into Great Silence*. Some Protestant friends of mine refused to see it, while David Stratton, Australia's leading film critic, referred in his review to the monks' "wasted lives." Stratton is certainly agnostic if not atheist. He was struck by the film at the level of cinematography (certainly) and curiosity (probably), but at bottom he just could not fathom it. Clearly these men "planted like sentinels upon the world's frontier" ought to be doing something more useful—more self-justifying perhaps. Stratton was disappointed that "what the monks really did," *obviously* the manufacture of their signature green Chartreuse liqueur, was not on show—apart from a glimpse of the Prior handling an invoice at one point![3] Here I detect the imaginative patrimony of Richard Dawkins—and Ebenezer Scrooge. Here is the brave new world of our modern West standing before the mystery of faith with incomprehension, and a measure of frustrated annoyance.

Many others were intrigued and affected by this film, however, drawn through it to a sense of something that is presently "an unthinkable experi-

---

2. In Merton, *Tears of the Blind Lions*.

3. David Stratton and Margaret Pomeranz, "Into Great Silence." Stratton's comment about "wasted lives" was broadcast but not transcribed on the Web site.

ence." *Into Great Silence* challenges our modern, secularized Western self. This is a self that began to emerge from the late Middle Ages, and especially since the Enlightenment, which nowadays is ill at ease before the horizon of mystery—a little irritated, perhaps, but maybe also a little fascinated.

In this chapter I am going to begin exploring the religious and spiritual transformations that have brought us to this state of affairs—transformations that have given us a modern world vastly better that what went before in so many ways, yet at the expense of leaving many of us with what I am calling homeless hearts. I will focus on a tight cluster of related trends. First, and most obviously, there is *secularization*, understood as the disembedding of faith from an encompassing religious culture. Second, in tandem with secularization, we experience a widespread and fundamental *loss of community*. Third, the rise of *consumer culture* to become the imaginative horizon of our late-modern West has significantly shaped human identity and aspiration. Then, fourth, we will consider the profound impact consumer culture has had on religion and spirituality, shaping certain *standard options for faith*. From these beginnings I want to go on in chapter 2 to consider how God has been culturally annexed by the agenda of secular modernity. And from there, in chapter 3, I consider how modernity's drive toward certainty and closure has become a new sacred reality requiring the repression or exclusion of whatever is unsure and errant.

The monks of *Into Great Silence* make a highly contemporary statement. They demonstrate an abiding faith that is more personal than the undifferentiated religious belonging of pre-modern Western life, but also more integrated than the religious individualism to which modern Westerners have become accustomed. But before we seek the roots, test the intellectual credentials, and draw the consequences of that abiding faith in part 2 of the book, we need first to understand how faith is faring in the crucible of modernity.

SECULARIZATION AND THE DISEMBEDDING OF FAITH

Our story begins with the break up of an integrated religious civilization and the emergence of religion as a discrete category among other social institutions and private lifestyle options, in modern Western nations committed as never before to the life of this world. This break up has a technical name: *secularization*. And it could be said to have begun with a democratizing of the monastic ideal.

Even before Martin Luther left the cloister to marry and unleash the great secularizing flood of Protestantism, the Catholic reformer Erasmus was calling every Christian to be as serious as the monks of his day were supposed to have been. In *The Manual of a Christian Knight* (his *Enchiridion*, of 1501), Erasmus—himself an Augustinian priest—chides a layman for excusing himself by saying "I am not a priest, I am not a monk." "Yes," comes the retort, "but are you not a Christian?" Erasmus commends to the laity a measure of detachment towards personal property and a generous spirit, seeing this as the properly universal meaning of monastic poverty.[4] In this sober and serious spirit the early-modern European turn toward everyday life began with its universal trend towards responsible "individualized faith," away from a less-differentiated "tribal faith."

A century ago, Max Weber famously identified secularization with the passing of a baton from monasticism to Calvinism. The monks' rational asceticism was effectively handed on in new, Protestant dress to become the basis of a disciplined, secular workforce serving a this-worldly human good, and focused on the creation of wealth. In the booming economies of new nation-states, this became the spirit of modern capitalism. There were more pious Methodist, Baptist, and Quaker versions, with some Protestant groups adapted to lowlier niches in the economy, along with the more assertive Calvinistic mood of Puritanism, all of which gave rise to a widespread, purposeful, unostentatious vocation in the realm of business and affairs. This redefined sense of a calling in life further secularized into a conception of innate "sacred" order and obligation to be found in society, business, and family, though no longer with any necessary place for God, grace, Church, or worship. Weber points to the "utilitarian prudentialism" of Benjamin Franklin, for instance, secure in his own moral superiority, as a type still clearly recognizable in our own day.[5]

Franklin's Enlightenment contemporary, the Scots philosopher David Hume (1711–1776), was explicit in his condemnation of other-worldliness in religion, and "the monkish virtues" in particular. The great historian of ideas Charles Taylor helpfully points out just how

> much of the historical practice of Christianity ran afoul of the new ethic of purely immanent human good: all striving for something beyond this, be it monasticism, or the life of contemplation, be it Franciscan spirituality or Wesleyan dedication, everything which took us out of the path of ordinary human enjoyments and productive activity, seemed a threat to the good life, and was condemned under the names of "fanaticism" or "enthusiasm." Hume distin-

---

4. Cited in Bainton, *Erasmus of Christendom*, 90.
5. Weber, *The Protestant Ethic and the Spirit of Capitalism*.

guishes the genuine virtues (which are qualities useful to others and to oneself) from the "monkish virtues" ("celibacy, fasting, penance, mortification, self-denial, humility, silence, solitude"), which contribute nothing to, even detract from human welfare. These are rejected by "men of sense," because they serve no manner of purpose; neither advance one's fortune, nor render one more valuable to society, neither entertain others nor bring self-enjoyment.[6]

Here is the imaginative (or *un*imaginative) root of film guru David Stratton's problem with *Into Great Silence*. His disapproving bewilderment captures the social, cultural, economic, but also religious and spiritual, realignment that is secularization.

Unpacking Secularization: From Tribal Faith to Individualized Faith

I would like to offer an example to try and set the scene, as I begin to tease out what secularization means, how it *feels*, and from whence it comes. A short while ago—at lunchtime, on the day of writing—I took my sandwich and apple down to a shady spot by the lake here at St. Mark's National Theological Centre in Australia's national capital. On the way back to my office, I stopped in at an outdoor chapel that we have tucked away among the eucalyptus trees to sit quietly for a short while. On arriving, however, I was greeted cheerily by a woman sitting on the altar. This altar is rough-hewn from a huge log, and situated in front of a tall, freestanding cross. I smiled awkwardly and said hello back, then I sat on one of the benches ringing the open space to pray, but I found myself preoccupied. "Surely she knows it's an altar, and that you don't sit on altars," I thought. "You wouldn't try something like that in a mosque," I thought.

The woman, one of the many lunching government workers and day walkers who pass through our site, was middleaged and what you might call "alternative" in appearance. I found myself rehearsing in my mind a familiar assessment of New Age spirituality: that its exponents concoct a private spiritual perspective based on bricolage, utilizing resources from various religious traditions to cobble together a cosmology and spiritual practice suiting their own individual experience and preferences. And if that is your spiritual profile, then why not sit on an altar? All such sacramental symbols are at best props nowadays, rather than authoritative signs marking out the sacred in which we are bound up as part of a community. I could even imagine an

6. Taylor, *A Secular Age*, 263.

active Christian member of the St. Mark's community, perhaps a younger student, either not knowing or not caring that an altar was something special. And, of course, for many Protestant Christians there are no special places or sacred objects.

I suspected that were I to have said, "Excuse me, but I'm a priest on the staff here, and this is a Christian chapel, and you're not supposed to sit on the altar," the woman might have climbed down. But that would have been a more or less gracious response to a concerned individual, rather than the startled recognition of ecclesial authority or even of sacred epiphany: "surely the Lord is in *this* place—and I did not know it" (Gen 28:16). And what of my own response? I did not rush forward in unreflective reaction, as I might have done to put out a fire or to rescue someone from harm. Instead, by sitting and saying nothing, I affirmed, ultimately, that it did not matter enough to make an issue of it—that the woman's right to her own private spiritual expression was at least comparable with that of my own catholic preferences, and that I accept the inevitability of such relativism in a secular age.

In light of all this, what about my own personal religious convictions as a catholic-minded Anglican? I have to acknowledge that I am in the minority among my fellow Anglicans in holding such catholic views. They are essentially private religious opinions, albeit ones of which I have become rationally and imaginatively persuaded. I have sought to commend these convictions liturgically, theologically, and pastorally in parish appointments over the years, though usually with limited success. They are not an unquestioned part of Anglican identity in general, and they certainly cannot represent the same quality of conviction that would once have emerged from being soaked in a community of catholic belonging since infancy. So for me to have approached the woman on the basis of my catholic convictions would, by comparison with the embedded faith of pre-modern times, have represented one abstraction being challenged by another abstraction.

In tacit acknowledgement of this whole state of affairs, what is called being "pastoral" now takes the place of religious conviction in the mainstream Western Churches. We clergy nowadays are supposed to be *nice* to people, probably to ensure that we do not risk any more of our fast-collapsing market share. Since our clientele is now entirely voluntary, we cannot afford to *upset* anyone. Whereas in a more traditional religious society a priest would not have hesitated—like the leading nineteenth-century high-churchman John Keble, who, despite being an assiduous pastor (and especially attentive to the parish children), "never hesitated to put his stick across the shoulders of any boy who neglected to touch his cap to the Vicar."[7]

So it is no longer obviously inappropriate to sit on an altar, and such restrictions are policed (if at all) more with a view to issues of decorum in a social context rather than any visceral instinct or taboo. Charles Taylor reminds us that in medieval Europe the Blessed Sacrament was perceived to be charged with sacred power. It was regularly and reverently viewed in *Corpus Christi* processions, but actually receiving the sacrament was widely considered to be risky. Hence real unease greeted the Reformation novelty of frequent communion, *and* in both kinds (i.e. bread *and* wine). Being near the sacrament in those days was like our approaching live electric wires today.[8] But for us, while we might still sing the fourth century words of that Anglo-Catholic hymn to the real presence, "Let all mortal flesh keep silence," we will not *feel* about the Blessed Sacrament as our ancient or medieval forebears did. If we are accustomed to receive communion in a mood of recollection, and approach the wider sacramental action with reverence for its rituals, vessels, and furnishings, we are unlikely to do so in the unreflective blush of a taken-for-granted, tribal faith. Today, on the contrary, many Anglicans dunk their host in the chalice like a pastry in coffee because it offends their sensibilities to drink from the common cup. This is a telling instance of God having to fit into existing priorities about health, decorum, and, I suggest, religious privacy, accompanying an associational rather than organic view of Church and worship. This is individualized rather than tribal faith—but so is mine, too. I am as much the dweller in a secularized world and a representative of its characteristically individualized faith as the woman sitting on the altar.

How are we best to understand these religious transformations that the Western self has undergone? Charles Taylor talks about the replacement of yesterday's "porous self" with today's "buffered self." The "porous self" of pre-modern times was open to the sacred mediated through participation in a unified vision and a set of ritual practices at the heart of social life. This is what I am calling tribal faith. It gave way before the "buffered self" of modernity —an independent, even sovereign self that *chooses*, including the choice of an individualized faith. God is no longer the embracing context of life but simply an entity one might reason towards out of a pre-formed self operating in a purely natural, secular context.

---

7. Battiscombe, *John Keble*, 178.
8. Taylor, *A Secular Age*, 73.

Taylor acknowledges that this "buffered self" can be a quite satisfactory self, sharing the modern goal of finding closure and control in the face of life's unwelcome elements (more of this in the next two chapters). Many are sustained in an in-between state of half-belief by their involvement with nature, the arts, and music.[9] The cause of human rights also galvanizes many against the ready catharsis of violence. There is a healthier body-consciousness, too, and the wellness movement, all constituting gains for the "buffered self"[10] against often-harsher religious claims of the past. So the "buffered self" offers a metaphysically neutral chill-out zone that many are unwilling to relinquish, resisting any pull of mystery back toward some form of more "porous self." It represents a tolerable materialism, and perhaps a hard-won self-acceptance, with little sense of loss. Secularization has acted as a ratchet for these "buffered selves" who cannot imagine going backwards, to before the individualizing turn.[11]

If many find this to be a liberating and empowering way of being, however, others find it isolating and narrowing. For these homeless hearts, as I am calling them, a kind of melancholy or accidie (Greek *akēdia* registers this whole state of affairs as limiting and impoverishing. Taylor argues that it represents a malaise to do with meaning and purpose.[12] Despite the way that many cope and others even seem to thrive in such conditions, he points to the difficulty many have in maintaining a meaningful sense of the whole of life in the face of aging, death, and the loss of loved ones. This is not averted by the endless lifestyle variations available to explore in what Taylor calls our "Nova world," or entirely dulled by the consumer-driven pursuit of individual happiness that is today's main official agenda. Consequently, many still feel the pressure of something more in life, demanding their attention in joy and sorrow. "Our age is very far from settling in to a comfortable unbelief,"[13] Taylor concludes, noting today's widespread experience of what he calls "cross pressure" from belief and unbelief.

In an extended discussion of what I am calling the homeless heart, Dutch theorist Peter Sloterdijk explores thoroughly the sense of alienation and the yearning that emerges for secular selves "that are not really touched by the vitalism of consumption, sport, disco fever, and free sexuality." Sloterdijk

9. Ibid., 360.
10. Ibid., 676.
11. Ibid., 289.
12. Ibid., 303.
13. Ibid., 727.

concludes that "[t]his inner level of death is what was earlier called 'nihilism,' disillusionment and violent despair stemming from the feeling of emptiness and arbitrary craving." The posture of skepticism and irony in life that is his prescription for coping with these trends—a posture that he traces in its various manifestations since the ancient cynics—represents a powerful protest against the emptiness and chronic dissatisfaction registered by many homeless hearts today. Yet Sloterdijk, the skeptic, nevertheless has to admit that faith achieves the same end. "Religion is not primarily the opiate of the people but the reminder that there is more life in us than this life lives. The function of faith is an achievement of devitalized bodies that cannot be completely robbed of the memory that in them much deeper sources of vitality, strength, pleasure, and of the enigma and intoxication of 'being there' must lie hidden than can be seen in everyday life."[14]

I assume that the woman sitting on the altar was a post-religious spiritual *bricoleur* of the New Age variety, fully secularized in her attitude toward religious authority while unwilling to settle for the complete worldliness of atheistic materialism. She felt there was something more going on than that. As for me, the affronted Anglo-Catholic, my own religious perspective is equally a personal choice, shaped by a mixture of life experience, learning, and personal disposition, against a (typically Anglo-Catholic) background of dissatisfaction with the radically secular option. We were birds of a feather, really.

Now, this is a very interesting state of affairs. I want to explore it a little more deeply, drawing some insights from three disciplines in the human sciences.

Unpacking Secularization: Sociology, History of Ideas, and Anthropology

From *sociology* we draw four key themes that help explain this state of affairs. The *history of ideas* provides two linked accounts of what drives secularization, from the late-Middle Ages onwards. From *anthropology* we discover how the scope of our felt experience in life and faith changes as the society around us tightens or loosens its grip on us, hence diminishing or enlarging our options for self-expression.

I begin here with the leading sociologist of religion, José Casanova, who identifies three aspects of secularization, which he describes as a sociological

---

14. Sloterdijk, *Critique of Cynical Reason*, 277.

theory of how societies modernize.[15] The first, employing the key sociological concept of *differentiation*, refers to the increasing diversification of modern Western social structures and groups. This is seen in the separating-out of religion from spheres of life with which it was once intertwined, chiefly the state, the economy, and science—all of which become increasingly independent, while religion itself becomes what it has never been before: a separate sphere of life. This phenomenon of differentiation is also evident in the way religions themselves diversify and specialize. Different ethnic or class groups gravitate to having their own religions, likewise states and geographical regions. It happens even within religions, as we see for instance with the main Anglican parties of "high," "low" and "broad Church." So out of a religio-political-economic-cultural matrix emerges a differentiated modern world with many centers, only one of which is the new type of thing called "religion." The Protestant Reformation, the rise of the modern nation state, the market economy of the new middle classes flourishing thanks to trade with Europe's colonial empires, and the rise of science as an independent authority structure—the real bite in Galileo's controversy with Rome—all variously express this fact of *differentiation*.

Second, Casanova points to the collapse of religion's claim on individual allegiance. This refers to the much-vaunted statistics revealing a decline in churchgoing throughout the modern West. It also encompasses challenges to faith posed by the emergence of atheism, which in modern times became a widespread possibility for the first time among Christian rank and file. There is also the annexation, hence the dilution and deadening of religion by its formal association with modern states—an association representing a stage on the way to a more fully differentiated secular world. Secularization has advanced further, however, and now the social glue that religions once provided is no longer needed. Today the global economy and the priorities of consumer culture provide sufficient social glue, while the surviving state Churches (like the Churches of England and Sweden) are the ones hemorrhaging the worst, and struggling the most to find a new *raison d'être*.

Third, Casanova mentions the influential privatization thesis, according to which self-expression and self-realization are now the West's "invisible religion" (Thomas Luckmann's phrase). This represents the last stage of a privatizing turn away from God at the center of public reality. Instead, we have an officially secular public world in which God is unnecessary, or more correctly optional. Some minimum of shared meaning and values is demanded by

---

15. Casanova, "Secularization, Enlightenment and Modern Religion."

social integration but, beyond that, the meaning of life has become an entirely private matter.

Charles Taylor gives us a fourth aspect of secularization from the perspective of sociology.[16] Like Casanova, he points to the structural emancipation of various spheres of life from religion, adding the educational, political, and recreational realms to those Casanova identifies. He mentions also the falling-off of religious belief and practice that makes many feel nostalgic for a bygone religious age. Taylor's distinctive perspective, however, which he devotes his book to exploring, is secularization understood as the imaginative shift that makes faith a *choice*, an option—even for the staunchest believer—where once it was virtually impossible not to believe in God, or at least to be affected profoundly by the Church's influence in every sphere of life. This fourth aspect of secularization is the emergence of choice as a key social determinant and expectation—as a new human right, in fact. I will have more to say about choice in the discussion of consumer culture two sections hence, and the identification of some standard current options for faith following on from that.

Another perspective on secularization can be obtained if we move on from what sociology can reveal to the history of ideas. Once again, Charles Taylor proves a reliable guide. He identifies two linked perspectives on the historical trajectory of the Western mind towards modernity and secularization.[17] First of all, he acknowledges an influential thesis looking chiefly to the late Middle Ages and its nexus of changing ideas about God, philosophy, the human person and society, from which modern atheism and nihilism are understood to emerge as consequences. He calls this perspective, associated most recently with the brilliant younger minds of the Radical Orthodoxy push in theology, the "Intellectual Deviation" story, and he likes it. I will be discussing this account early in my next chapter, because it brings into clear relief a number of important things about modernity as an imaginative system. Taylor, however, prefers a different, though partly overlapping account.

He attends to the same broad imaginative transformations in the modern West—the disembedding from religious patterns of life, also from the kind of tacit assumptions that underpin a society's view of the world and itself—with reference to what he sees as modernity's key organizing idea: that of *reform*. Taylor's preferred story of secularization, which he calls "The Reform Master Narrative," can be seen to interweave with and complement

16. Taylor, *A Secular Age*.
17. Ibid., 773–76.

the "Intellectual Deviation" approach. But it views reform as the main driver, turbo-charging the West's turn toward more individually shaped religious belonging and believing. Of course, it is not that change is a new thing. The study of history cures that misapprehension. But the modern world elevates change to the status of a moral imperative and virtually deifies progress. Only more recently, among the many wrecks of twentieth-century history, has this modern dogma been assailed by doubt—though in the forward march of our technology and consumption habits, modern Western faith in change remains undiminished.

A further perspective on the phenomenon of secularization can be found if we shift attention to anthropology, attending to the way human experience is shaped by the social matrix embedding it, and how changes in the latter affect the former. Mary Douglas provides significant theoretical insight about this. I refer to her classic discussion of worldviews according to standard types of family system, considered against the extent of self-expression typical of the surrounding society in which these family types are located. This simple comparison throws up a comprehensive range of recognizable human life patterns based on a grid typology.[18]

So, for instance, a family system that bases personal identity on one's position in the family, with a socially restricted approach to self-expression in speech, would go with a conservative traditional society of reticent, role-defined individuals, who probably feel secure and settled in their tacit belonging. Douglas talks about "the bog Irish" in this regard. On the other hand, a family system placing a premium on the personal and the individual in its approach to members, and accustomed to elaborated speech patterns, would reflect a more progressive and liberated arrangement attuned to individual success and self-realization, though perhaps at the expense of some performance anxiety and some uncertainty in the face of too many life-options. This recalls the significant transition of Western society in the 1960s, as social roles loosened up, recalling also the difference between working class and middle class aspiration—for instance, the reliable, traditional worker and "good provider" with his wife at home versus today's go-ahead young couple who see themselves as having "a relationship." In the latter case we have a reliable recipe for the homeless heart.

Douglas hones this typology into her influential account of "Group and Grid." The type of cosmology we inhabit—our basic orientation toward life

---

18. Douglas, *Natural Symbols*. The two typologies referred to are represented graphically on 50 and 84 respectively.

and the world, if you like—can be predicted. This prediction is based on the extent to which a shared classification scheme governs individual options in our social milieu—that is, a strong or else weak "Grid"—cross-referenced with the extent to which this scheme is enforced—that is, a strong or weak "Group." So, for instance, "strong Group and Grid" reflects a highly controlled society with communities embedded in a largely cohesive worldview, while "weak Group and Grid" brings to mind a plural, unregulated society of individuals guided by private beliefs. *In terms of social structure, viewed anthropologically, this is the shift that sociology of religion traces in its theory of secularization.*

We have been considering the individualizing, isolating, and volatilizing of faith, which has contributed to the widespread reality of homeless hearts. I want to step aside now from faith and its disembedding to look more generally at the modern Western experience. First, I want to consider how our sense of community has drained away, leaving many people isolated and anxious. Second, I will be trying to unpack the highly formative consumer culture that has emerged to imaginatively dominate the modern West, offering to fill the void of meaning, faith, and community that modernity and secularization has opened up.

THE LOSS OF COMMUNITY

The rise of the modern individual is at the expense of belonging to community and to place. I offer a typical example from my own residential locality (I cannot call it a community). The suburb outbound from us had long been served by a Neighborhood Watch Group (i.e., an association of civic-minded residents meeting regularly to keep up with local trends in property crime, and committed to "keeping an eye out" in the interests of protecting the neighborhood from burglary, vandalism, etc.). That group folded after twenty-one years because of "lack of interest from young people," as its former secretary lamented in the local news, hoping that one day the service might revive. The young people in question are the young singles and professional couples who are flocking to the new apartment buildings springing up in Canberra's inner-North, displacing the older homes typical of these former working class areas. These Gen X and Y newcomers have opted to live conveniently near to their city jobs, and in the relative anonymity of apartment life they are free for active social and sexual lives.

To be sure, young urban Westerners seek out ecstatic tribal experiences in the club and rave scenes, and subcultures remain important options for many (from extreme sports to music preference to the celebration of iconic narratives, like the "Trekkies"); but this represents volitional rather than organic belonging on the part of those whose identity is primarily individual. The involvement of my young co-residents with the quotidian actual local community is limited, like my own, to minimal patronage of the corner grocery and the fish-and-chip shop (for those without an identity focused on a glamorous or athletic self-image). Perhaps the alternative café scene nearby promoted some identification with the locality, or the adjacent greenbelt affording an enjoyable walk or cycle ride to and from the city; but if so, that is more about young people choosing to live somewhere in tune with an existing self-image (or one to which they aspire) rather than anything to do with actual geographical belonging.

None of us newcomers, whether baby-boomers, Gen X or Gen Y, could begin to make sense of the "Neighborhood Watch world" of yesterday, involving sustained relationships with others whose long-term identity is invested in the locality, an attitude of vigilance toward other people's collections of old personal property, and attending bring-a-plate suppers, which are more about maintaining social bonds than transacting business. Rarely in today's English-speaking West would you find *urban* dwellers interested in this—apart from short-term activism perhaps—or quite intentional local schemes to rebuild social capital. Consequently, all sorts of civic groups, service clubs, and community-based congregations are going the way of the Dickson Neighborhood Watch. Many of us are reasonably content to dwell in this "zone between loneliness and communication," as Charles Taylor puts it. Regarding the predominately younger crowd from my apartment building, Taylor is dead right that "[n]ew consumer culture, expressivism and spaces of mutual display connect in our world to produce their own kind of synergy."[19] And that is that.

Sociologist Robert D. Putnam explores this phenomenon in the United States, as the great civic generation, the baby boomers' parents, vacate the stage. With them vanishes their energy for joining, volunteering, identifying, and "schmoozing" (i.e., socializing and networking). While the Internet, grassroots religious conservatism, and the rising phenomenon of self-help and personal support groups tell against the trend, a lot of this follows a narrowly personal agenda, while any embrace of causes often means little more than receiving a newsletter and perhaps writing a check. This has an effect on the nature of human experience, as "[t]hin, single-stranded, surf-by interactions are gradually replacing dense, multi-stranded, well-exercised bonds."[20] This

---

19. Taylor, *A Secular Age*, 483.
20. Putnam, *Bowling Alone*, 183–84.

all represents a risk to the American way of life, according to Putnam, who hopes Gen X will turn this around. But it is hard for people to go back to an earlier, less differentiated way of life, as we saw also in our discussion of tribal faith giving way to individualized faith.

Among the causes of this trend, Putnam identifies the time and money pressure on young two-career families, the effect of suburban sprawl (both in terms of commuting time and the separation of work from community), the isolating effect of television and electronic entertainment and, overall, the generational change already mentioned, away from the taken-for-grantedness of civic engagement.[21] Reading carefully, television is the big killer. Putnam notes (striking me with the shock of recognition) that if you say TV is your primary form of entertainment, it marks you as one of the most socially disconnected.[22]

Rowan Williams, the Archbishop of Canterbury, offers a theological account of this turn away from community in tandem with secularization. When identity is what you make for yourself, community is what you establish by contract, and the sacred is a private opinion of little or no public import, then nothing outside yourself has much claim on you or offers any meaning that can embrace you. The "social miracle" as evident in the medieval guilds is ultimately Eucharistic, according to the Archbishop (here following the Church historian John Bossy), while today there is no objective reality external to our own self-creation that can offer us grace or call us into judgment. We have lost "the iconic eye," as he puts it.[23]

I had a sense of this in 1996 when we happened to be in Florence as the seven-hundredth anniversary of the Duomo was being celebrated. Even though Brunelleschi's remarkable fifteenth-century dome powerfully prefigures modern science and engineering, and while Italy is now a highly secularized modern state, nevertheless the whole scene strongly recalled the pre-modern world. In festive mood, the town guilds were all out in force in their various ancient costumes, parading before the Archbishop of Florence on his dais, while the whole city streamed through the cathedral, kept ablaze with candlelight and open all hours. People seemed at least a little nostalgic for the integrally sacred and communal bygone world evoked by this occasion.

---

21. Ibid. See the helpful summary and pie chart on 283–84.
22. Ibid., 231.
23. Williams, *Lost Icons*.

CONSUMER CULTURE AND THE ANXIOUS INDIVIDUAL

The loss of community I have been describing, like the shift from tribal to individualized faith also characteristic of modernity, is widely recognized as anxiety producing. Existentialism registered the extent to which the brave new world of meaning-making individuals was emotionally exposed. Søren Kierkegaard famously concluded that the swoon of possibility confronting Enlightenment moderns, and the sense of powerlessness that this challenge to subdue reality in the making of personal meaning can generate, is at the root of modern anxiety.[24] So-called "freedom" regularly pays the price of a homeless heart.

The post-modern language regularly used of our late-modern, global world refers to the completion of a process that Kierkegaard, Nietzsche, and other nineteenth-century prophets intuited at its advent, according to which all given systems of meaning—from metaphysical systems and cosmologies to cultural totalities and religious faiths—come to be understood chiefly as human creations. It is over the ruins of these former certainties that today's Westerners must pick in order to make what meaning they can. We have all become *bricoleurs*, charged with crafting our own selves by the choices we make, no longer simply falling into a ready-made identity. There is no home for us other than the one we choose, adapt, or create for ourselves from the huge range of options and resources available in the marketplace.

Secularization and the Emergence of Consumer Culture

This cultural and social state of affairs is strongly correlated with the way Western economies changed across the twentieth century. The Fordist economy based on finely-tuned factory production, emerging from the rise of modern capitalism that Weber analyzes, has given way to an economy in which consumption is center stage. Consumption is not just an option—not just the acme of immoral materialist excess that the moral critics of globalization and the green lobby regularly accuse it of being, with vocal support from

---

24. Kierkegaard, *The Concept of Anxiety*. Kierkegaard's account holds up well according to the wide-ranging historical, cultural, and clinical analysis of anxiety offered by Rollo May in *The Meaning of Anxiety*. My conclusions about abiding faith and spiritual maturity, in chapter 6 below, echo May's conviction that integrated, generative, creative, and mature selves only emerge by facing the threat of non-being and otherness, and struggling through the resultant anxieties. Anxious adherents of the false sacred (see chapters 3 and 6 below), on the other hand, typically avoid this challenge and opportunity.

the Churches. It is not commodities that are the key, as if consumer culture is primarily about *stuff*. It is really about the *process* of consumption, the creation and transfer of desire, and the endlessly deferred becoming of individuals who have no other home than the global market and the dreams it peddles. If the global market is God, then the commodity is its sacrament.

Karl Marx noted how workers lost control of the means of production as cottage industry gave way to industrialization, becoming alienated from their labor and their trade skills when they became wage-earners in factories. The new cash economy meant that commodities had to be purchased, with their value related to that of other commodities by a market removed from the originating context of those commodities. Hence the "commodity fetish," referring to the naked quality of these products separated from the conditions of their production. So the evolving capitalist system contributes to the disempowerment, isolation, and hence anxiety of the workers, in a life of consumption alienated from production.

There is more to it than that, of course. Max Weber's account of secularization finds the roots of modern capitalism in Puritanism's turn towards the world. While this accounts for the transfer of religious zeal to the realm of production, however, the shift from production to consumption is harder to source in the stern Puritan vision. Yet consumer culture, too—positively celebrating Marx's commodity fetish—can in fact be seen to draw its energy from the secularizing of Western Christian imagination.

The individualizing turn we have examined also had a pietistic, inward element, and that is the key. It gave birth to modern self-consciousness and favored the cultivation of interior states, where identity came most reliably to reside. With the waning of a Puritanism based on dogma, morality, and judgment, from the Cambridge Platonists of the English Civil War period onward, a more generous assessment of human goodness and divine benevolence emerged, and an emotional ethic of Christian sensibility took shape.

Romanticism came to regard this new sensibility and emotionality as the truest indicator of godliness, just as its liking for gothic horror in fiction nicely transferred the nastier aspects of Puritan doctrine to the secular realm. Romanticism was an enormously self-preoccupied and navel-gazing movement after all, which in the period from the French Revolution through the Napoleonic Wars threw up a range of emotional states, from sweet melancholy through *tedium vitae* to *Weltschmerz*, for the creative but troubled souls of British letters to enjoy.[25] Their needy interiority mined the realms of nature

25. Here I am indebted to Sickels, *The Gloomy Egoist*.

and culture for resources to voice, sooth, and divert their inner burdens, in a way, which with hindsight, looks quite consumerist.

Puritan virtue in an increasingly secular environment evolved into good taste for the middle classes, which like virtue had to be demonstrated. Hence the rise of fashion, on the back of Romantic artistic creativity and an energetic cloth trade, as a major arena of self-creation and self-justification before the newly sacred judgment of taste. This trend was further stiffened by a Wesleyan-inspired need for one's inner truth to be made visible. So the "proper" middle classes, inheriting the Puritan mantle (as we have seen from Weber), demonstrated their assured moral superiority (especially over the decadent aristocracy) through rightly intuiting and virtuously following the path of good taste. Their imaginative focus having been turned inward, however, and now primed by Romantic restlessness and its exaltation of the artistic and the creative, which threw up lots of new things to try, the secular middle classes where set on the path of consumption as on a religious exercise.

Thus, by a roundabout route, we come to what Colin Campbell, whose detailed account I have been seeking to follow here, calls "autonomous, self-illusory hedonism"—a hedonism of the mind, more than an obsession with actual commodities: a culturally-propelled, self-definitional longing to make imagination into reality, hence driving the endless consumption of novelty. Americans like Ralph Waldo Emerson and Henry David Thoreau hated Benjamin Franklin's utilitarianism, which is the path Weber identifies as leading from Puritanism to the spirit of modern capitalism in its productive mode. They do, however, represent this other path, which from Puritan beginnings secularizes remarkably via the inward turn of Romanticism into the spirit of modern consumerism.[26]

In the Grip of Consumer Culture

The result is that consumption becomes a social responsibility with its own logic.[27] Commodities, having lost their context in the means of production, find a new context thanks to advertising, which provides its own system of signification. The reason this has worked so spectacularly has to do with the way things are now marketed. To be sure, new populations are drawn into consumption as globalization takes hold (e.g. motor cars in China, deregu-

---

26. Campbell, *The Romantic Ethic and the Spirit of Modern Consumerism*.
27. See Miller, *Consuming Religion*, 32–72.

lated smoking in the developing world); but in the West it is largely through creating lots of new markets within existing populations.

Think about it. If you can create distinct age groups whose identity, dreams, and hence spending priorities require the production and consumption of whole different product lines for their expression—with three distinct subcultures from the age of ten to the age of sixteen, for instance, each with its own wardrobe, music, magazines, films, and toys planned and marketed to fit each niche—then you can sell a lot more *stuff*. And if households fragment and proliferate then this variety of identities, and the consumption upon which each of these rely, can in turn proliferate. For instance, a whole system of production in the extended-family household ending in the family meal, which was the only possible meal available for everyone in the household, now becomes several meals of different types and sources eaten in one or two-person households. And many of these households will in turn rupture and diversify over time so that more and more goods are needed to create the new lifestyles and support the new relationships that emerge.[28] All this is good news for the economy, with every increase in social instability and isolation paying dividends. Advertising serves this individualizing and destabilizing of bonds by playing on insecurities, annexing—and hence eroding—cultural symbols, and relentlessly commodifying minority cultural perspectives in the interests of niche marketing.

Needless to say, political action that might limit the powers of markets at the government level, or distract individuals from the anxious, self-seeking treadmill of consumption toward community involvement and even political action, is rendered increasingly deviant and unlikely. As the Anglo-Polish sociologist Zygmunt Bauman summarizes it, "There is the nasty fly of impotence in the tasty ointment of freedom cooked in the cauldron of individualization."[29] Bauman refers to our era as "liquid modernity." The image has to do with chronic orchestrated instability, fluidity, and impermanence as today's guiding cultural norms. At the root of it all is the economy and the shift from "heavy modernity" in the Fordist era of production to "liquid modernity" in the new era of fast-moving global capital, purely utilitarian and short-term bonds, and the cultural totality that consumption is becoming.

Bauman employs imagery to evoke the transformation. The era of heavy ships gives way to that of pilotless aircraft,[30] and corpulent capitalists yield

---

28. Bauman, *Consuming Life*, 78.
29. Bauman, *Liquid Modernity*, 35.
30. Ibid., 58, 59, 128, 183–84, 200, 214.

to skinny networkers, while heavy luggage is replaced by cabin baggage only. More concretely, savings books give way to credit cards, faith to chronic mistrust, deviance and rebellion to the seeking of shelter. Likewise, abiding institutions as a focus for life-long attention and commitment are undermined until our own bodies become the most enduring things we know across a lifetime marked by relentless change, and hence today's universal body fixation in the West.

Similarly, common causes give way to spectacles and patriotism to "patriotainment" (we may not be willing to serve in the armed forces of our country, but we will swell with pride at a World Cup victory).[31] Community is romanticized and toyed with, but it cannot be tolerated as a serious option, with today's taste for "carnivals" providing "séances for people to gather together to hold hands and call back the ghost of deceased community from the netherworld . . . safe in their awareness that the guest won't outstay its invitation."[32] Groups with strong connective tissue are now regularly replaced by "swarms," linked only by rapid mimicry of others' desires.

The Sorbonne theorist Michel Maffesoli insists that post-modernity replaces modernity's individualism with a new tribalism;[33] but there is not the structure and shared long-term memory necessary for real tribalism. Bauman's image of swarming is a better way of understanding how individualism remains at the center of post-modern human being in the West, coupled with Maffesoli's own observation that late-modern individualism has become less promethean.[34] Indeed this weakening is essential, so anxious individuals will keep consuming. Identity is what you are condemned to make by negotiating this endless plethora of choices, ensuring what sociologist Ulrick Beck unsparingly calls the "solitary confinement of the ego."[35]

The virtues of endurance are now replaced by those of transience, and the capacity to compose an identity across time is undermined. An example will help make the point. There is an advertisement showing in Australian cinemas at the time of writing, no doubt targeting the younger demographic more reliably than television advertising. It is an advertisement for a mobile- (i.e., cellular-) phone network, produced in realistic animation, and saying

31. Bauman, *Consuming Life*, 75.
32. Ibid., 76.
33. Maffesoli, "The Return of Dionysus."
34. Ibid., 24.
35. Beck, "On the Mortality of Industrial Society"; cited in Bauman, *Liquid Modernity*, 37.

nothing directly about mobile phones at all. Instead, it celebrates the one-day lifespan of the adult stage of the common mayfly, portrayed as emerging from the water, flying about the jungle, sporting with another mayfly, and romancing a mate, at last enjoying the sunset (i.e. of its life). A faintly reverential, youthful voiceover commends the insect's earnest and untroubled inclination and wherewithal to "seize the day." No doubt the carefree, experience-oriented and hedonistic life of the ideal young consumer is being evoked here, of which the mobile phone is an indispensable accessory. I also suspect the invitation is to jettison whichever other mobile-phone plan you might currently be on (never more than two years these days, anyway) for a new carrier whose "product" is not a phone plan but actually a more imaginatively satisfying image of your life. And, of course, brand loyalty does not matter if you are a creature constructed day by day via new desires. Bauman observes that eternity has lost cultural meaning, and that in liquid modernity the tyranny of *carpé diem* replaces the pre-modern tyranny of *memento mori*.[36]

Bauman's disturbing conclusion is that we ourselves have become commodities, investing in our own self-esteem and social membership as the only conceivable vocation in service to the sovereign market. Hence the characteristic post-modern unhappiness whereby old-fashioned Western guilt over the breaking of generally accepted rules now becomes a perpetual sense of inadequacy, because we can never catch up with constantly shifting, market-driven ideals of the perfect self and the perfect life. Confidence and connection are sapped as people learn to negotiate life without the sense of boundaries, reticence, and realism that governed needs and desires in earlier generations, delivering at least a modest satisfaction.[37] This is the disillusioned, depressed mood of today's homeless heart in the grip of a manufactured, marketed, restless anxiety. This commodification of selves is increasingly evident in the worlds of work and relationships.

Gone is "the career" as a long-term adventure of identity formation bound up with a particular local community, a profession or trade, a workforce of long-term colleagues, an enterprise committed to a worthwhile cause or product, and a respected body of skill. Gone too is the type of character and personhood that can only be crafted by such long-term engagements, weaving a narrative of solidarity that is maintained in season and out. Flexible, short-term, and profit-driven enterprises shorn of social context or commitment to the staff are increasingly the norm, creating a great mass of

36. Bauman, *Consuming Life*, 104 ("seize the day" replaces "remember your death").
37. Ibid., 94, 46.

isolated, over-mortgaged, stressed, and anxious Westerners living under threat of redundancy. Fear of being left behind in a world of unrelenting change creates a new priesthood of reckless managerial adventurers whose regular failures are rewarded, because "steady as she goes" is the only unacceptable course. The human ecology of workplaces is destroyed despite regular claims that disembedded workers constantly redeployed in flexible "teams" can do more with less. "Delayering," "vertical disaggregation," and "re-engineering" are among the Gnostic words of power that unlock managerialism's mythical cosmos of success, while in reality good businesses, utilities, and public entities are gutted and reliable workforces are traumatized and decimated.[38] Pliancy and superficiality mark the new starting points of upward mobility on today's "Snakes and Ladders" board, while loyalty and experience mark the way down.

There are counterexamples, of course, as in the extraordinary recent memoir of an American corporate high-flier cast on the scrapheap who at the age of sixty-four finds a new life, community, dignity, purpose, and identity by working at Starbucks, which emerges as a company with a heart for the outsider and the disadvantaged that still seems to do great business. Loyalty might just pay dividends after all. But this is such a striking story precisely because it is so against-the-grain nowadays.[39] At the time of writing, however, even Starbucks has begun large-scale staff layoffs as the discretional expenditure of one-time customers has been trimmed in response to increased fuel prices (though in Australia Starbucks is doing its best for the casualties, offering them compensation, counseling, and help with finding new jobs).

Relationships are also significantly caught up in commodification. What sociologist Anthony Giddens calls "the reflexive project of the self" refers to today's imperative of self creation, and sexuality is now normally understood to serve that end. Giddens talks about "the pure relationship," "plastic sexuality," and "confluent love," all referring to the deregulation of sexuality from wider family and community obligations and its emergence as a kind of free-floating erotic field offering enormous possibilities for constructing a satisfying lifestyle.[40] Giddens rightly welcomes an end to many stifling repressions encoded in bygone sexual roles and identities, and the recovery of the erotic as a new energy in Western culture; but he is not oblivious to the anxiety that today's normative instability and impermanence in sexual relationships has created.

38. See Sennett, *The Corrosion of Character*.
39. Gill, *How Starbucks Saved My Life*.
40. Giddens, *The Transformation of Intimacy*.

Zygmunt Bauman champions traditional marriage as an antidote to today's sexual commodification of persons, and as a reliable basis for the identity-formation that consumer culture programmatically undermines. From shopping for sexual partners on the Internet to breaking up by text message ("easy come, easy go") to wife-swapping as an increasingly popular means of sexual consumption (because it is less risky than free-range adultery), Bauman sees a widespread trend to avoid the risk of commitment and continuity, which alone build skills for relationship, family life, and wider sociality. Partners and now children are reduced to consumer vehicles for individual fulfillment, as part of a lifestyle package commodified in terms of personal satisfaction and well-being. Hence alterity, mystery, and respect are overcome by the logic of commodification, with its attendant redundancy and wastage. The fear of AIDS, according to Bauman, focused a diffuse cultural disquiet over sex losing its former bearings in a larger context of human commitment.[41]

Once again the economy and the cultural logic of late modernity are never far away as the chief rationale for these trends. The commercially profitable sexualization of commodities is the key here, as Bauman points out using the example of selling cars. "After the era in which sexual energy had to be sublimated in order to keep the car assembly line moving came an era when sexual energy needed to be beefed up, given freedom to select any channel of discharge at hand and encouraged to go rampant, so that cars leaving the assembly line might be lusted after as sexual objects."[42]

In the two areas mentioned, of work and relationships, there is a ruthlessness abroad that Bauman identifies as typical of liquid modernity, and a major cause of the homeless heart. It is interesting to see the way bygone social capital is celebrated nostalgically in films and television series today. For example, the 2004 Swedish film *As It Is in Heaven*, about the rediscovery of community through singing together in a church choir, set in the remote wintry north of Sweden in a small town long blighted by loveless religion and dysfunctional relationships, has been the longest-running film in Australian cinema history. At the other end of the scale, however, and more accurately reflecting the liquid modern state of affairs, are the popular "reality television" vehicles such as *Survivor*, *The Weakest Link*, and *Big Brother*. The message in these programs is that social ecology is a thing of the past, and that it is everyone for themselves. These morality tales for our times also teach that virtue is no longer rewarded and that life is about blows falling senselessly

---

41. Bauman's fullest assessment of these issues is in *Liquid Love*.
42. Ibid., 57.

on the undeserving. The life-skills they commend are how to second-guess, blindside, and overcome others in a lifelong struggle for limited resources, and that being "in" is everything—our worth is defined by inclusion, and denied by exclusion. Bauman points out that in George Orwell's original version of Big Brother, in his novel *Nineteen Eighty-Four*, the point of totalitarian control was to keep people in, as was the case throughout the "heavy modern" period. Now television's *Big Brother* and his cognates in the "liquid modern" era concentrate on the othering and exclusion of undesirables—with keeping people out.[43] I will have more to say about modernity and its characteristic exclusions in chapter 3 below.

This serves to introduce some more general fears that typically accompany today's culture of consumerism, according to Bauman.[44] Rather than face the fact that, despite our Enlightenment overconfidence, we cannot fix our world, and as we awaken to terrorism as the downside of globalization, we demonstrate what he calls "the Titanic Syndrome." That 1997 disaster film was popular because it allowed widespread but unspoken fears about the modern West being in immanent danger to find expression. The collapse of social order in New Orleans after Hurricane Katrina in 2005—so quickly that the social order might as well never have existed in the first place—was a sobering, real-world demonstration that these fears are justified. The sense is abroad, though often unacknowledged, that the nation-state—that quintessential Enlightenment creation—cannot help us when the chips are down.

For every individual taking serious issues such as climate change to heart, in a way that might mobilize political will for change, an array of substitute fears are created to obsess and hence distract the homeless hearts of rank and file modern Westerners: the pedophile, the stalker, the serial killer, the illegal immigrant, let alone obesity and other health issues that preoccupy us. The gated community and the tank-like SUV are standard ways that consumer culture ministers to these fears, selling us an illusory invincibility. Ironically, perhaps, though actually inevitably, climate change itself is being exploited to produce a niche market for environmentally friendly and even carbon-neutral products, services, and utilities—in the latter instance selling a scarcely verifiable promise, as is the case with every other commodity nowadays. On sale is not so much a dish detergent that will reduce algal blooms in rivers, or a

---

43. See, e.g., Bauman, *Liquid Fear*, 22–29; Bauman, *Consuming Life*, 145; Bauman, *Liquid Modernity*, 26–30.

44. For this discussion I draw on Bauman, *Liquid Fear*.

ride on the allegedly carbon-neutral bus, but chiefly a self-image that puts you among the righteous, or at least salves your conscience.

Faith is a further casualty of this whole state of affairs. The abiding experience of a lifetime, against which the promises of faith might be confirmed, scarcely seems credible any longer.[45] Faith no longer makes sense as a necessarily long-term undertaking in what is now such a short-term world. It is not allowed to make sense. However, human beings cannot be likened to mayflies at all, as in the advertisement I mentioned earlier. We humans do not live to consume furiously for a day against an absent horizon of meaning. Rather, we are composed in reliance upon past ages across a lifetime normally long enough to build significant relationships and social capital, and for a good number of us to establish an institutional footprint in the ongoing history of our kind. In other words, to make a difference. The culture of consumerism is the sworn enemy of any such humane and humanizing vision. What are some of the key ways that faith plays out today?

CONSUMER CULTURE, CERTAINTY, AND FAITH FOR THE HOMELESS HEART

In a pre-modern culture there would have been little religious choice, apart from the allowed range of expressions within a religion itself. So one might (though not always) have the choice of whether to marry or seek the cloister, and if the cloister then as a monk or a friar, perhaps, or if as a monk then in a stricter or laxer religious order. And people certainly made religious choices and struggled with religious doubts throughout the biblical period and Church history. In our own time, however, the choices are more fundamental, concerning one's bedrock religious identity.

To reiterate aspects of our earlier discussion, secularization announces the end of religious belonging as a given of one's time and place, and its disembedding from the communally-shared structures of everyday life, so that religious involvement becomes a choice. Further, today's religious pluralism means that our choice at some level has to take other options into account. Even cradle church members normally have to make choices on their way to becoming active adult participants in their formative traditions. Religious individualism and merely associational religious bodies are the unavoidable norm today, with expressive individualism undergirding every religious identity—even for those who are culturally or philosophically drawn to a

---

45. Bauman, "Faith and Instant Gratification," in *The Individualized Society*, 153–60.

more organic understanding of faith. The American sociologist Peter Berger famously announced this state of affairs three decades ago, pointing out that the root meaning of "heresy" is "choice," so that today all religious believers have become "heretics."[46]

Since then the unquestioned allegiance given to any type of objective authority has declined even further, as the sociologist Steve Bruce points out.

> Once culture was defined by experts. Now we accept the freedom of personal taste: I may not know much about art but I know what I like. In the late 1960s claims for personal autonomy moved to a second stage of matters of personal behavior: I may not know much about ethics and morals but I know what I like to do and claim my right to do it. In the third stage the same attitude is applied to areas of expert knowledge: I may not know much about the nervous system but I know what I like to believe in and I believe in chakras and Shiatsu massage and acupuncture.[47]

This deepening "heretical imperative" plays out against the background of consumer culture that I have been setting out, with its characteristic obsessions and anxieties. The result is clearly a riot of religious diversity, but I want to mention three characteristic types of religious response today. They represent diversity in terms of beliefs—ranging from certainty to skepticism, and from involvement to detachment—but at another level they have a lot in common. All of them manifest expressive individualism at work creating meaning, with a greater or lesser drive to comprehensiveness, and an eye to their utility in fostering the successful living of life. I refer to *conservative Christianity*, *consumer spirituality*, and *atheism*. The latter comes in two forms that I am calling "atheist chic" and "atheism-lite," both of which are consumer options not much different from consumer spirituality—apart from their content.

Conservative Christianity

The rise of fundamentalism and Pentecostalism is a sign of the times. Conservative Christianity is a powerful option for the homeless heart, offering community and certainty where these have been eroded, and an institutional authoritarianism that protects and re-assures many—though at the expense of many others who are ill-treated and excluded by it. Fundamentalism is a kind of nouveau-tribalism that defines insiders at the expense of outsiders,

---

46. Berger, *The Heretical Imperative*, 1–31.
47. Bruce, *God is Dead*, 86.

and around the world it provides a rallying cry for those who are bypassed in the global economy, ghettoized, and devalued, and who are seeking identity and empowerment.

Muslim youth in the West, for instance, who feel isolated and adrift between the old world and the new, are drawn to fundamentalism for identity and empowerment, even if involvement with jihadism could well cost their lives. The collapse of communism also generates fundamentalism when the old order seeks to revive tribal enmity in the hope it might cling to power, as in Karadzic's demonizing of Muslims in the former Yugoslavia.[48] Being hated strengthens the fundamentalist group. Class resentment is a factor in both these cases, as it was when militant English Puritans smashed tombs of the ruling classes under cover of clearing churches of religious symbols.[49]

The emergence of American fundamentalism as a major religious option, nowadays defining itself against liberal secular elites through the so-called "culture wars," reflects the collapse of a reassuring form of life and the search for a new religious expression retaining the key "old-time values." Lynchburg in Virginia, for instance, home of the Jerry Falwell phenomenon, has been described as the sort of "new South" community where those who have lost their connection to the land and to traditional community life seek to recreate it through fundamentalist Church involvement. Fundamentalist Church life there is described in one anthropological study as communitarian rather than ideological, in the sense of putting people over principle, family-oriented, patriotic, and socially conservative—though one-time taboos like divorce are more acceptable, showing that this is a significantly contemporary phenomenon.[50] The embrace of creationism by this religious demographic does not necessarily reflect a studied commitment to scriptural inerrancy after weighing up all the evidence (just as atheism is not necessarily thought through, of which more shortly). Rather, cultural isolation and a sense of dissatisfaction with the modern world, the government, education, liberal elites, and other obvious targets of frustration come out indirectly through the invincible stubbornness of creation science. This ideology is a pawn in a larger game rather than an end in itself.

---

48. See Morton, "Manufacturing Ancient Hatreds."

49. See Wilding, "Something Better," 215.

50. Ault, *Spirit and Flesh*. See a similar point, about the role of conservative religion maintaining identity for displaced Southerners elsewhere in the United States, in Wuthnow, *Christianity in the Twenty-First Century*, 23–24.

Fundamentalist community meets a sociological need, with fundamentalist believing following fundamentalist belonging. Indeed, in America the political culture is such that religious sub-groups can create worlds of their own, sharing a religious vision that is rarely challenged. For example, in Lynchburg fundamentalist church life, as studied by the religiously skeptical sociologist Steve Bruce, an entire subculture has been created. One's social life is confined entirely to the church, one's television watching is limited to the fundamentalist Christian network, one's holiday is spent at the Christian theme park, and the education of one's children is through fundamentalist schools and universities, all contributing to maintaining a coherent subworld more like a medieval community in its totality than anything you could find in Britain or continental Europe today.[51] While it may appear that such continuing religious vigor is a powerful counterexample to the secularization thesis, it is more correct to see American fundamentalism as a response to secularization and proof positive that it is *working*.

There is also a rising fundamentalist mood in the Catholic Church where "new ecclesial movements" such as Opus Dei, the Neo-Catechumenal Way, and Legionaries for Christ, along with unofficial apocalyptic, sectarian conventicles, such as Australia's "Little Pebble" and "Magnificat Meal" movements, represent highly disciplined enclaves offering more intensive belonging and believing than normal church membership allows, and often at the expense of almost total separation from the wider Church. The endorsement by Pope Benedict of the Latin mass is exciting many conservatives in Catholic blogdom, and the disdain of these enthusiasts for "normal Catholics" is often plain—as it must surely be, for instance, to readers of Christopher Pearson's regular diatribes on this issue in his column for *The Weekend Australian* newspaper. These movements and trends reflect the dualism and authoritarianism of a more recent official Catholic Church profile, as the liberalizing trends of Vatican II strike many Catholics and their leaders as inadequate means for maintaining a powerful, distinctive Catholic culture.[52] Vatican support for Catholic conservatism, however, has not been matched by Vatican leadership in the clergy child abuse crisis, which in America and throughout the world has revealed a psychological immaturity and abusive edge to much Catholic Church life.[53] Dissident Catholics, such as Hans Küng and Jacques Pohier—

---

51. Bruce, *God is Dead*, 225–27.

52. See Collins, "Catholicism and Fundamentalism."

53. See the devastating critical analysis by a retired Australian Bishop, in Robinson, *Confronting Power and Sex in the Catholic Church*. For the American situation see Cozzens, *Sacred Silence*.

the latter having left the Dominicans because he felt he could not "grow up" emotionally in the conservative Church and the conforming, disempowering totality of clerical culture—point to the costs of religious conservatism and its stifling obsession with psychological security and certainty.[54]

David Jenkins, a controversial Bishop of Durham in Margaret Thatcher's England, who suffered much at the hands of Anglican fundamentalists—those he called "certainty wallahs"—describes fundamentalism as a psychological problem, neurotic in nature, turning men "whom I thought of as some of my most decent and efficient priests into angry, disagreeable and hostile *little* men."[55] Zygmunt Bauman believes that the agony of choice in a liquid modern, consumer age makes fundamentalist groups attractive: "Their allure is the promise to put paid to the agony of individual choice by abolishing the choice itself; to heal the pain of individual uncertainty and hesitation by finishing off the cacophony of voices which makes one unsure of the wisdom of one's decisions. Their bait is that of . . . a world unambiguous again, sending unequivocal signals; that is, of an identity no longer multi-layered, multi dimensional and 'until-further-notice.'"[56]

Many isolated young people in the West experience a need for religious certainty and psychic security, which is ministered to by fundamentalist churches full of like-minded young people whose worship is often cast in the form of entertainment events.[57] The connection with today's spirit of consumerism is strong here, as I will be suggesting in the next section. For now I mention a striking cover image on one edition of the themed Australian journal of social criticism *Griffith Review*, titled "The Lure of Fundamentalism," featuring a good-looking young woman worshipping at Sydney's bigger-than-big Hillsong Church, with head thrown back and hands on heart, lost in isolated ecstasy.[58] The young man next to her is miles away, locked into his own expressive individualist moment. This image of a young woman in religious rapture is plainly sexual, too, like Bernini's seventeenth-century *Ecstasy*

---

54. See two moving and informative memoirs: Küng, *My Struggle for Freedom*; and Pohier, *God—In Fragments*.

55. Jenkins, *The Calling of a Cuckoo*, 152.

56. Bauman, "Modernity and Clarity," in *The Individualized Society*, 57–70, 70.

57. Porter, "Beyond the Cathedral Doors," 183. Porter's critical analysis of the uniquely conservative and powerful Anglican Diocese of Sydney is continued in *The New Puritans*.

58. This cover picture can be viewed on the journal's Web site. Online: http://www3.griffith.edu.au/01/griffithreview/past_editions.php?id=83.

of St. Teresa sculpture, in Rome's Church of Santa Maria della Vittoria. Both women are clearly following the religious road to a very nice place of their own private enjoyment. But there is a further dimension in the Hillsong picture, evident if you look inside the journal at an advertisement for Griffith University facing page 7 and make comparison with a very similar picture you will find there. Here we see another handsome young woman gazing out at us from a Griffith University classroom—looking very pleased with herself, we are told, because she has opted for a university that has attracted some national teaching awards. Both girls have chosen environments where their needs are clearly being met. One of these environments is religious while the other is educational, but both of them are consumer-inspired vehicles for expressive individualism.

It is interesting, too, that Hillsong offers a "prosperity Gospel" promising that worldly and spiritual success go together. This is more generally true of the Pentecostal movement, especially where it serves as a modernizing agent in the developing world. It fosters disciplined communities of hard-working, domestically-engaged men and hence builds the kind of virtues Weber associated with modern capitalism. Similarities with the role of American fundamentalism in creating alternative social capital are clear. Women in particular benefit from Pentecostalism in the developing world, as a movement that delivers them from the worst excesses of patriarchal culture. It also serves formerly tribal cultures, as in Africa, with a social space to negotiate their transition to the more individually-oriented, self-reliant, post-tribal world of modernity. Thus Pentecostalism emerges as one of the key modernizing movements of our times,[59] and hence as a dimension of secularization.

Consumer Spirituality

To summarize, consumer culture "constructs every person as the author of his or her own identity, expressed aesthetically through the consumption and display of commodities."[60] This culture is more powerful than traditional cultures in its agile appropriation of cultural fragments. Our eclectic dress, home furnishing, and decoration, and the international scope of our diets, music, and holidays in today's West amply demonstrate this appropriation, as every culture is mined for saleable symbols, tastes, images, artifacts, and experiences that can be consumed apart from any profound encounter with the

---

59. See Martin, "Evangelical Expansion in Global Society," and "Pentecostalism: A Major Narrative of Modernity," in *On Secularization*, 26–43, and 141–54.

60. Miller, *Consuming Religion*, 30.

host culture. Religions are a type of culture, made up of symbols, languages, practices, and stories, and these too are mined for what Western consumers can make of them. This annexation of religion by Western consumer culture is ultimately an economically-driven process which unseats authoritative traditions and beliefs that were once inhabited by communities, and makes them into resources for personal spiritual consumption. This is now a universal Western phenomenon, both inside and outside the Churches. The New Age movement is quite explicit in drawing resources for personal wellbeing from many religious traditions, without regard for their strict logical compatibility. Religious symbols are also widely decontextualized apart from any obvious spiritual motive—from the classics of sacred music used as soundtracks for action films to crucifixes worn as bling, following the lead of Madonna ("I like the crucifix because it has a naked man on it").

A 2007 film, *The Darjeeling Limited*, provides an amusingly perceptive illumination of this phenomenon. Three rich, Gen X brothers from America travel across India by train on "a spiritual journey" of family reconciliation, spending big and sampling a range of Indian spiritual practices to aid them in their goal. But when it comes to the real thing, as in the Hindu funeral of a drowned boy they are invited to attend in a traditional village, having tried but failed to save the boy's life, they are shown to be what they in fact are: outsiders to a coherent but essentially impenetrable religious world (though they try to look the part by dressing in their first-class sleeper pajamas). Eventually the brothers find their widowed mother, who has become a Catholic nun high in the mountains; but despite her faith language and apparent embrace of the convent's local mission, she decamps and leaves her sons when they need her, just as she always has in the past, proving that she too is not actually being transformed by the spirituality she has chosen. Vincent Miller is unerring in his analysis of this whole trend.

> In its desire for self-fulfillment and freedom of choice to meet its own needs, the therapeutic self is precisely the consumer self. Its engagement with the world is one of choosing the goods most consonant with its own particular *lifestyle*. In this culture, religion, like other commodities, serves to fill-in the identity of the consumer. It can do this only insofar as it confirms the fundamental form of the self as consumer. Thus, the form of religion we have been discussing—abstracted sentiment divorced from practice— is ideally suited to this world. It supplies the veneer of meaning and conviction of which modern existence so often deprives us,

without disrupting the underlying forms of our lives—our obligation to consume.[61]

The fundamentalism discussed in the last section would represent a choice by someone whose need for meaning and a unified experience of life was great, reflecting a higher level of anxiety perhaps, so a whole religious identity is chosen "off the rack." Many others are less anxious, and these are the ones who are more likely to pic-n-mix religious elements. Australians, for instance, are not noted for being an angst-ridden people, and their typical religious reticence is culturally conditioned. Recent literature on spirituality in Australia suggests that a search for meaning is too cerebral a concept to capture the reality, though a hopeful attitude and good inner feelings—the sort of things noted in the earlier discussion of secularization, Romanticism, and the roots of consumerism—prove to be important for those Australians who look to religion and spirituality. Australian priest and sociologist Gary Bouma discerns a preference for "celebration, not cerebration" and a shift "from an emphasis on orthodoxy—correct belief—to orthopassy—correct feelings."[62] Younger Australians are likewise found to be in the typical modern Western business of crafting an identity from the commodities on offer, feeling free to draw widely on religious resources without acknowledging any religious authority beyond their own personal choice. But while the homeless heart is present among Generation Y in Australia, there is not a strong sense of loneliness or melancholy reflected in the statistics. Spiritual resources are sought by some, but many seem to manage their anxiety and stave off questions of meaning "perhaps indefinitely, by short-term, low-level meanings, by a lifestyle filled with 'distractions' and 'noise'."[63]

So we discern a range of consumer responses, from those who desire a whole religious identity to give them meaning and identity, through to those content with what we might call "meaning-lite," such as many young Australians who might pick at disconnected religious beliefs (such as reincarnation, which appears to represent an unexamined folk belief rather than a reflectively settled conviction) but do not seek more actively to cobble together a spirituality or embrace a religion.

Nothing in this discussion is meant to deny the reality of encounter with God through consumer spirituality, however. There are surely many for whom

---

61. Miller, *Consuming Religion*, 88.
62. Bouma, *Australian Soul*, 92, 93.
63. Mason, *The Spirit of Generation Y*, 335.

a strictly incoherent and inconsistently inhabited spiritual universe nevertheless mediates a real sense of identity, compassion, and useful purpose—a quality of life that any catholic-minded theologian or pastor would identify with the presence of God. Indeed, in what we might regard as the limiting case of consumer religion, an American nurse called Sheila Larsen famously informed sociologist Robert Bellah and his colleagues that she had made up her own spiritual perspective and practice that she called "Sheilaism." Nonetheless, Sheila testified to the personal healing she received through her DIY faith, also believing that her work as a nurse was used by God to help others.[64] Even if this is possible, however, there are other things that consumer spirituality makes much more difficult. I mention four of them.

The burden of Robert Bellah's classic study of this whole phenomenon is that today's Americans who cobble together spiritual and religious elements may be genuinely plumbing significant spiritual depths, *but they will not normally have the language to articulate those depths*. A whole life-giving, community-sustaining web of traditional meaning, linking the divine with the historical, also the community and the nation with individual thriving, is being lost to America. In this new context, therapeutically-and-technically-minded individuals, who are "trained" to think about life in terms of what they can get for themselves, "cannot think about themselves or others except as arbitrary centers of volition. They cannot express the fullness of being that is actually theirs."[65] Vincent Miller insists, however, that we must not accuse all who approach religion and spirituality this way of selfish narcissism. It is difficult, even for the well-intentioned, to let religion be more than "a decorative veneer of meaning over the vacuousness of everyday life in advanced capitalist societies."[66]

A second consequence of consumer spirituality is that by separating religious beliefs not only from the fuller canons of sacred narrative and doctrine that make them coherent, but also from the context of community belonging, support, and practice apart from which no genuine religious believer would recognize their religion, the chances of being transformed by those beliefs in any significant way is effectively removed. This is a religious or spiritual life answering to no authority but that of desire constructed by market forces that determine our sense of who we are or wish to be, with no objective claim available to challenge, surprise or transform us. Vincent Miller concludes

64. Bellah, *Habits of the Heart*, 221, 235.
65. Ibid., 81.
66. Miller, *Consuming Religion*, 225.

that "spiritually we are trained to seek, search and choose but not to follow-through and commit."[67]

Third, it is unlikely that the spiritual consumer will see herself or himself as contributing to their own religious tradition, taking responsibility for its life, or consciously participating in its mission.[68] The consumer-minded Church is not going to be fixed by superficial managerial solutions about the recovery of its relevance to life today when the very spirit of life today prevents Christianity from being taken really seriously, whole, and entire by the great majority of its own adherents. Their spiritual imaginations are more likely to reflect consumer culture than something more comprehensive—something that might make life into a calling, and overcome the power of the commodity form.

And here is my fourth point. It is not likely that anyone formed by consumer culture, and who approaches spirituality and religion in its spirit, will be willing or able to mount any significant challenge to consumer culture. This is the particular burden of theologian Jeremy Carette and religious studies scholar Richard King in a powerful polemic against the annexation of spirituality by consumer culture. They refer to "capitalist spirituality" as the "spiritual" vision, the guiding imaginative worldview, of today's global market and its ruling ideology of neo-liberalism—which allows some wealthy individuals and less than a thousand large corporations to shape the present and the future in their interests. Carrette and King identify the eight aspects of this "capitalist spirituality" as atomization, self-interest, corporatism, utilitarianism, consumerism, quietism, political myopia, and thought control (referring in particular to the way individuals' private thoughts are accommodated to this system).[69]

Consumer spirituality is thus the new opium of the people or, to update Marx, it is today's "Cultural Prozac."[70] Individuals more or less lost in life are quieted and turned inward, learning to cope with alienating features of today's bottom-line culture rather than rising up against that culture. So the typical approach to systemic problems in our therapeutic age, which is learning to cope with them rather than to step out of our powerless interiority and confront them, co-opts the elements of religion. And this co-opting is what spirituality amounts to today—to therapeutically packaged body

67. Ibid., 142.
68. Ibid., 212.
69. Carrette and King, *Selling Spirituality*, 21–22.
70. Ibid., 138, 77.

parts scavenged from the corpse of religion. "Spirituality becomes," according to Carrette's and King's confronting assessment, "a GMR—a Genetically Modified Religion—the tasty food additive that makes neo-liberalism more palatable."[71] Their call is for genuine religious traditions genuinely inhabited, that will galvanize people to take back meaning-control from the markets—for "new 'atheisms' that reject the God of money."[72] And now, what about the older, more familiar atheisms?

Atheism(s)

There is far too much involved in this topic to do other than make a few remarks at this point. I will be looking in more detail at the imaginative roots of unbelief in the next chapter and posing some of its questions to my own emerging perspective on faith in chapter 5. For now I simply want to link atheism with the immediately prior discussions of conservative religion and consumer spirituality—highlighting the continuities and suggesting that atheism in two main forms emerges as a product of late-modern, global culture in tandem with that culture's characteristic forms of religion and spirituality.

The first type or mood of atheism I am calling *atheist chic*. It has found a great champion in Richard Dawkins, who I choose from a vocal group of writers reacting against the worldwide resurgence of conservative religion after 9/11. Much is wrong with Dawkins' militant diatribe, *The God Delusion*,[73] in which this leading evolutionary biologist turned popular-science writer makes his case for science against conservative religion by venturing well outside his area of expertise. He writes in an insufferably bullish and superior tone, declaring all religious people to be deluded fools. He hints regularly at a certain grudging fondness for reasonable Anglicanism (we "reasonable Anglicans" know how to deal with his type, however, so he cannot afford take us too seriously). He also affirms the literary merit of the King James Bible. But otherwise he is angry and dismissive. And having closed the front door to conservative religion, he closes the back door to the French deconstructionists and anyone else who, with a modicum of epistemological subtlety, presumes to question a rigid distinction between science and religion, referring to them as "franconphonies."

---

71. Ibid.,132.

72. Ibid., 178.

73. Dawkins, *The God Delusion*. See, e.g., the frank and helpful critique by Lash, "Where Does *The God Delusion* Come From?"

This is an exercise in what Peter Sloterdijk calls "pugnacious reason," which is anything but dispassionate and scientific. Rather, it "is from the start an activist and untranquil reason that at no price lets itself be made fluid and *never* subjects itself to the precedence of what is common, universal and encompassing."[74] Interestingly, however, its contempt for widespread religious sentiment does in fact reveal religious roots, which Charles Taylor identifies in the spurned Evangelicalism of emergent mid-Victorian skepticism. Self-responsible rational freedom was an Enlightenment obligation, which under Romantic influence acquired "a kind of heroism of unbelief" that dared to face the bitter, unconsoling truth, to which specifically Victorian priorities added a high and ultimately compassion-driven view of science and technology in the service of human betterment. "Thus," as Taylor concludes, "the turn from religion to science not only betokened a greater purity of spirit and greater manliness but also aligned [the Victorians] with the demands of human progress and welfare."[75] And the roots of this purity and honesty, though now turned skeptical, were Evangelical. It was an alternative ethical vision, an "imperious moral demand not to believe," that turned these Victorians away from the faith of their fathers.[76]

Today this sort of reaction still seems right to many in the West—this sense that science and religion are at loggerheads and that decent, thoughtful, liberal-minded people ought to think as Dawkins does. In other words, they want to look the part, and Dawkins' book is the necessary accessory. I suspect that a great many people who either did not or could not read Stephen Hawking's 1988 bestseller *A Brief History of Time*, but who bought it so they could demonstrate their openness to the latest ideas and their favored rational persona more generally, are like those who eagerly bought *The God Delusion*—or *The Da Vinci Code* for that matter. It is about self-creation via commodity acquisition, in this case the book staking a claim that the one who buys it belongs among the "cool kids." Hence my category of atheist chic.

As conservative religion serves some in their search for a confident identity, so its mirror image packages others in the posture of "ethical unbelief."

---

74. Sloterdijk, *Critique of Cynical Reason*, 545.

75. Taylor, *Sources of the Self*, 405.

76. Ibid., 406. Darwin's theory put the skeptical cat among the religious pigeons in England, because the argument from design had loomed so large in the English religious imagination, supporting the connection between God and the world's underlying order that had been re-minted at the Enlightenment. See Cupitt, "Darwinism and English Religious Thought."

Referring to the growing popularity of Dawkins's militant atheist crusade in America, English religious journalist Andrew Brown makes an astute assessment along these lines. "Dawkins-type atheism has a distinct social role over there," he writes. "It is fundamentalism for the college-educated, offering the same kind of certainties, and a similar range of enemies, in a world that has grown threatening, impersonal, and insecure for everyone."[77] This continues a trend identified by Steve Bruce, who argues that Darwinism was not widely popular in nineteenth-century America because people had examined the case carefully but, rather, because "the very idea of evolution resonated with the self-confidence and growing prosperity of the era."[78]

This skeptical mirroring of conservative religion, which Dawkins uncritically recycles in our day, was not lost on prominent nineteenth-century critics who saw this reaction as offering little advance on the religion it despised. Kierkegaard accuses both the rigidly orthodox believer insisting on historically certain religious origins and the freethinker who denies them of both fearing what he calls "inwardness"—both having sacrificed a genuine faith that can cope with uncertainty in favor of a brittle and superficial one that is prey to anxiety.[79] Nietzsche's critical interpreter and inheritor Max Scheler, in his classic discussion of the bad faith and turbo-charged *Schadenfreude* called *Ressentiment*, is convinced that the skeptical mood remains locked into revenge against its own religiously-believing past, so that claims to the metaphysical truth of a mechanistic worldview (such as we find in Dawkins) are "only the immense intellectual *symbol* of the slave revolt in morality."[80] Nietzsche himself is at his most savage on this point, lambasting skeptics for their failure to be free of the spirit they despise.

> These deniers and outsiders of today, these absolutists in a single respect—in their claim to intellectual hygiene—these hard, severe, abstemious, heroic spirits, who constitute the pride of our age, all these pale atheists, anti-Christians, immoralists, nihilists, these spiritual sceptics, . . . these last idealists of knowledge, these men in whom the intellectual conscience is alone embodied and dwells today—they believe themselves to be as free as possible from the

---

77. Brown, "Review of 2007: Press."
78. Bruce, *God is Dead*, 107.
79. Kierkegaard, *The Concept of Anxiety*, 142–43.
80. Scheler, *Ressentiment*, 124.

ascetic ideal, . . . and yet, . . . this self-same ideal is *their* ideal too, . . . they themselves are its most spiritualized product . . .[81]

Nietzsche's point here is that the alleged free thinkers, like Dawkins, remain idealists, committed to the objectivity of truth, and in that sense they perpetuate what he saw to be a key religious delusion. Others today of atheist leanings are less stubborn on this point, however, and their tone is not the rigid certainty of old-fashioned skeptics. Rather than the hardness—perhaps more correctly the *faux* hardness—of atheist chic, there is a lighter, less aggressive, less certainty-obsessed version.

What I am calling *atheism-lite* is more or less convinced in its perspective, but its tone and approach are different. Taylor identifies an atheistic trend of this sort in the nineteenth-century Romantic mood of expressive integrity found in the poets Goethe and Matthew Arnold—of self-completion through the pursuit of art and culture, perceived to be a more reliable path than traditional religion, but also less rationalistic than scientific atheism.[82] Taylor acknowledges that the rationalistic and Romantic forms of atheism blended in Marxism, which found extraordinary power in combining "scientistic materialism with the aspiration to expressive wholeness."[83] But Marxism is not a live option in today's liquid modern West, so I will not pursue this merging as a serious possibility.

An example of atheism-lite is the counter-movement of young American Hemant Mehta, the self-styled "friendly atheist," who is troubled that the hostility of today's militantly rationalistic "new atheist" writers risks spoiling the message. His popular blog and speaking program follows the success of a widely reported stunt. Mehta "sold his soul" on eBay, with the successful bidder being given the opportunity to try and convert him.[84] This is a playful, ironic, and, in that sense, post-modern version of atheism which is convinced but not dogmatic. Mehta is successful at attracting a sympathetic hearing from religious conservatives (even getting published by them) because they do not experience in him the hostility of their "evil twin," channeled for them by Richard Dawkins.

My favorite writer of this stamp is England's "atheist priest" Don Cupitt, whose post-Christian philosophy and spirituality has evolved over the quarter-

---

81. Nietzsche, *On the Genealogy of Morals*, 126.
82. Taylor, *Sources of the Self*, 408–9.
83. Ibid., 409–10.
84. Mehta, *I Sold My Soul on eBay*.

century since his infamous "taking-leave of God."[85] He has heeded Kierkegaard and Nietzsche, abandoning philosophical idealism and embracing those who Dawkins calls "franconphonies." The post-modern philosophies of "outside-lessness," which understand all meaning and truth as human constructions entirely within the bounds of our languages and forms of life, with no wider objective truth deemed necessary, yield a spirituality aiming at a non-anxious, joyful, and expressive life, content with finiteness and ordinariness. Cupitt calls this "solar living," understanding today's spiritual and ethical imperative to be simply the pouring out of our life in creativity and compassion. It is a very chilled, Buddhist vision, metaphysically gossamer thin.[86]

Cupitt was trained in the natural sciences, but his formative studies in the philosophy of science taught him that science too is full of myths and orthodoxies, with its authority confined to its method. He extends the later Wittgenstein's commitment to ordinary, everyday language as the key to philosophy in a fascinating original project, uncovering what he believes to be a coherent but entirely non-foundational philosophy of life and plain man's religion in the range of speech idioms that have grown up around the word "life." It is stoic but also joyful, and neither conventionally religious nor militantly atheistic.[87] Cupitt has great regard for ordinary people who just get on with it[88]—the sort of people who provide the main funeral trade for English and Australian clergy, for instance, who come to the Church for traditional rites of passage but are really looking for resources to "celebrate the life" of their deceased loved one. The Church and its faith provide software on these occasions, for a spiritual vision that requires no hardware—no infallible creed, Pope or Bible, though no infallible Richard Dawkins either. The emphasis is on living and loving and getting on with it, and not on intellectual closure—whether orthodox or atheistic. I will have more to say about this approach in chapter 5.

The bricolage typical of consumer spirituality is also very much at work in atheism-lite, with many people happy to be more or less atheistic or unbelieving while still hedging their bets. So atheism-lite can also refer to

---

85. I wrote the first critical study of Cupitt. See Cowdell, *Atheist Priest?* I have followed Cupitt's extensive publishing program subsequently, which has led far from the ground covered in that early study.

86. See, e.g., Cupitt, *The Way to Happiness*; and Cupitt, *The Great Questions of Life*.

87. For a good overview of this program, with a list of over two hundred and fifty of today's "life idioms," see Cupitt, *Life, Life*; see 143–47 for the list.

88. See, e.g., Cupitt, *The Meaning of It All in Everyday Speech*.

those who might express an opinion suggesting religious or spiritual beliefs when approached for a survey, while in reality this opinion is not held at all deeply—like the third of young Australians who claim to believe in reincarnation,[89] which may simply reflect a reluctance to entirely let go of personal immortality while, otherwise, orthodox Christianity has been entirely abandoned. The religiously skeptical sociologist Steve Bruce makes much of the way surveys into religious or spiritual belief and practice regularly overstate the case. People may simply choose the least specific response available, or affirm some religious belief or other so as not to seem impolite or crass. He is also concerned when surveys incorrectly assume that if "respondents show evidence of considering anything more precious or abstract than the dishwasher they are being religious."[90]

Bruce believes the typical posture today to be just plain indifference, rather than much actual rejection of belief. Atheism lite is effectively what these people embrace, though "embrace" is perhaps too active a word. Secular modernity in the West simply does not require religion or spirituality to be comprehensive categories. If people believe or disbelieve this or that relic of orthodox faith, it does not necessarily imply firm belief, or else firm atheism. What I am calling atheism lite is a way to conceive the broad range of non-Dawkins-style options, from convinced and articulate though not ideological or hostile atheism (e.g., Don Cupitt), to the relatively untroubled, post-religious habits of many ordinary secular people in today's West. Some of these tend to the "meaning lite" that "sort of believes" in "something or other," while others lean more to the unbelieving end of atheism-lite, though they are not dogmatic about it. Consumer spirituality is well represented at both ends of this spectrum, with Christians as well as atheists doing their own pic'n and mix—the beliefs may vary, but the consumer dynamic is the same.

TO CONCLUDE

The flight from the monastery, more generally from the religiously embedded world of pre-modern times, has led to the brave new world of individualistic Western modernity. But freedom and autonomy nurse many fears, and the homeless heart is a regular consequence. Faith remains in various forms under the anxious aegis of consumer culture, mirrored by parallel types of atheism. On the way to part 2 of this book, and my case for the recovery of faith in

---

89. Mason, *The Spirit of Generation Y*, 149.
90. Bruce, *God is Dead*, 191.

strong and abiding form, I want to look in more detail at some aspects of faith in the modern world. Modernity with its emphasis on certainty, closure, and control has itself set the agenda of faith, in particular influencing faith's perceived content. The modern impact on our sense of God and the sacred will be the subject of chapter 2, while chapter 3 will go more deeply into the motives and consequences of our hitching the sacred to modernity's star.

Looking ahead to part 2 of the book, my aim there will not be the recovery of tribal faith, as if that were seriously possible, nor the uncritical championing of individualized faith, though that probably has to be the starting point of an abiding faith for the future that I will be commending. Rather, the post-tribal but also post-individual faith of the Carthusian monks we met through *Into Great Silence*, and other examples, point to a new synthesis. Such abiding faith is a profoundly contemporary option, whether or not it appears in old-fashioned dress. But it also reveals an ancient pedigree and an unbroken tradition through the period of modernity—albeit an underground one. More of this in due course; for now, the fate of God under modernity.

2

Faith in "the System"
The Modern Captivity of God

In this first part of the book I am considering different aspects of faith under the conditions of modernity. Our main objective in the previous chapter was to understand secularization and the modern Western individual's disembedding from a collective religious vision. Under pressure from a modern economy geared to the production and consumption of commodities, a consumer culture has grown up to dominate the Western imagination and to set the agenda for faith. In these conditions a range of linked spiritual reactions provide "the soul of soulless conditions" for modernity's homeless hearts, among which I included full-strength and lite atheisms as well. That discussion was focused on the religious individual and their options.

I now want to take a rather different tack and look at how God has fared over the some period. Though, of course, as we consider how God and the sacred have been annexed to the modern project, we are at the same time reflecting on how modern Westerners have experienced and reacted to this God. Suffice it to say that false sacred conceptions have intruded on the scene, and God has been subordinated to the anxious modern passion for closure, certainty, and control. Chapter 3, to follow, will be my beginning attempt at a theoretical account of this process, as an aid to understanding the great harm this false sacred reality has done by producing a whole world of victims. For now I want to introduce this misapprehension, misrepresentation, and misuse of God from its late-medieval origins, thence to its emergence as a whole system of meaning and purpose from the seventeenth-century beginnings of Europe's Enlightenment. Guiding me in this discussion of the Enlightenment will be a striking thesis in the history of ideas offered by Stephen Toulmin in his book *Cosmopolis*.

Stephen Toulmin offers a reading of modernity, from the start of the seventeenth century, as an overarching worldview—as a system of meaning, constructed to calm the anxious nerves of traumatized Europeans at a time of major political and social upheaval. He calls this construction a Cosmopolis: a mixture of *cosmos* and *polis*, of cosmology and politics. In its various manifestations, the Cosmopolis of modernity provides certainty for the individual, working God into a larger vision of reality that emphasizes reassuring clarity and control. Toulmin is not alone in seeing all such modern certainty as beginning to collapse from the First World War, though his assessment of the subsequent post modern period is upbeat and hopeful. He believes that nowadays we are much closer again to humane and likeable figures of the late Renaissance like Montaigne and Shakespeare, who showed it was possible to live at peace amid the complexity of unexplained events without the intellectual closure that modernity sought to provide. Of course the devils of nihilism and violence have also been released now that the house of Western imagination has been swept clean of its modern certainties, so Toulmin's assessment of post-modernity bears examination. Indeed, my conclusions in the previous chapter lead me to doubt seriously that a new Cosmopolis fit to shelter homeless hearts is emerging in the West.

But, first, there is an earlier stage that Toulmin does not consider. Since the appearance of the Western individual, from its first stirrings in the Christianity of the late Roman Empire, the homeless heart was kept at bay thanks to a powerful spiritual synthesis in which, despite the many rigors of pre-modern life, individuals nevertheless knew themselves to be occupying a place of belonging in God's world. The intellectual triumph of this vision came in the work of Thomas Aquinas, who Christianized the whole testimony of classical antiquity to a world that reveals God.[1] But it was not to last, and with the convulsions of late-medieval Europe in the fourteenth century this unified world order gave way before a range of pre-modern currents. These bear closer examination, as they set Toulmin's discussion in a broader context. Indeed, it is to this earlier period that revisionist historians have been drawn, with the Radical Orthodoxy school in theology identifying this period as *the*

---

1. Von Balthasar, *The Glory of The Lord*, vol. 5, 2.

wrong turn in Christian intellectual history, from which many modern problems with faith originate.

In chapter 1, I mentioned the advantages of such an exploration—of what Charles Taylor calls the "Intellectual Deviation" story of secularization—because of the light it casts on how God was made ready for annexation by modernity. I warn the reader, however, that the next section, and especially the one after that on *nominalism*, in which I try to set out the major features and implications of the "Intellectual Deviation" account, are the most technical passages in the book (had I been more expert, no doubt I could have made them more straightforward). If in these sections I am responsible for you experiencing unhelpfully heavy weather, I encourage you to skip forward and pick up the main thread when I introduce Toulmin's account in a section headed "Birth Pangs of the Modern Order."

APPROACHING THE MODERN DETOUR

The Western individual is regularly credited as the discovery of Augustine of Hippo (354–430) in the *Confessions*, who shifts attention inward where he believed the God of antiquity's rationally-ordered cosmos could best be known. This surety that comes with self-presence is a major signpost of the coming modern Western synthesis—a kind of proto-cogito, twelve hundred years before Descartes, in which God is known by inner contemplation. The knower seeks withdrawal from the outer world, such that "the route to the higher passes within."[2] This Western Christian individual remained secure in the embrace of contemplative inwardness right up to the time of Thomas Aquinas (ca 1225–1274), however, while the cultural scope of individualism grew.

The rising tide of individualism had both sacred and profane elements. From the twelfth century, "spirituality" ceased referring to the whole of embodied Christian life and began to find its now-familiar focus in the realm of the soul and the inner life.[3] This followed the beginnings of the de-corporatizing of Eucharistic piety and the rise of private devotions from the late eleventh century, along with the confessor's growing concern for inner attitudes and intentions. The passion of Christ and the fellowship of his sufferings emerged as a major cultural theme beyond the earlier, more objective celebration of Christ's victory over sin and evil. These new spiritual trends were matched by

---

2. Taylor, *Sources of the Self*, 139 (here following Etienne Gilson).

3. McIntosh, *Mystical Theology*, 7. The more holistic vision of Christian antiquity came apart from this time, so that theology, spirituality and Christian practice have been struggling to stay in touch ever since. More of this in chapter 4.

a growing fascination with inner attitudes, and motivations, and emerging autobiography of a nascent psychological sort. This was also the age in which friendship and romantic love were celebrated in verse and song. It witnessed the beginnings of companionate marriage, early portraiture and anti-social satire, in all of which the individual emerged more clearly from the nexus of wider obligation.[4]

Yet this individual remained well short of the homeless heart that arose in more recent Western experience, remaining integrated in a life-giving, theological-spiritual vision. In the synthesis of Thomas Aquinas the individual abides in contemplative union with the transcendent God, really joined to God, but without the philosophical purchase on God that modernity has claimed. Contrary to the standard later interpretation of Aquinas, God is not rationally accessible to the human intellect via "proofs." Aquinas did not offer a metaphysical system propped up by God, so much as "metalinguistic rules"[5] that clarified the extent to which God could and could not be humanly understood.

God was neither accessible to the human mind via a kind of philosophical theism, nor hidden entirely behind revelation so that a Bible-only fideism was required. Rather, Aquinas allows us to speak of God by analogy. We can use the same words about God that we use about our own attributes, such as wisdom and goodness, but this does not give us purchase on God's own being. This analogical approach seeks to reassure us that our talk about God is not *equivocal*, such that we can have no reliable access to God at all, while warning us that it is not *univocal*, either, whereby God is understood to share the same level of being with us. Rather, while God remains beyond the realm of being that we creatures occupy, nevertheless we are really joined to God in the life of faith—though joined as to one unknown.[6] Here is a God who transcends creaturely existence, yet whose gift of being holds the world in God's loving embrace and makes us what we are, subsisting in a marvelous created dignity yet not self-subsisting—always dependent on God sustaining our being, possessing from God what John Milbank strikingly calls an "alien actuality."[7]

It is important to realize that the distance of God from creatures, according to this view, is not the abyss that it becomes in the next stage of the

---

4. Morris, *The Discovery of the Individual*.
5. Placher, *The Domestication of Transcendence*, 31.
6. Kerr, "Thomas Aquinas," 213–14.
7. Milbank, "Only Theology Overcomes Metaphysics," 44.

account. As Hans Urs von Balthasar puts it, seeking to clarify this paradoxical farness yet nearness of God, "it is precisely when the creature feels itself to be separate in being from God that it knows itself to be the most immediate object of God's love and concern; and it is precisely when its essential finitude shows it to be something quite different from God that it knows that, as a real being, it has had bestowed upon it that most extravagant gift—participation in the real being of God."[8] None of this fits readily with a more typically modern account, this medieval picture in which we humans are nothing and all our good depends on the creation and preservation of God. Yet in this participatory vision we are also able to abide in God and know our identity—contingently, yes, yet surely and joyfully thanks to the love and mercy of God. This decidedly non-modern, God-centered vision has us humans existing really yet derivatively, individually yet by no means as the centre and circumference of meaning, to which dubious centrality modernity has brought us. This participatory understanding of Christian existence is fully continuous with the Bible and the Fathers, and it survived underground in mystical literature, to resurface variously in post-modern theology. This alternative tradition will be traced in chapter 4.

Here with Aquinas we are still in the thought-world of feudal relationships—a world of strict hierarchy yet mutual belonging—whereby the feudal king, and the lord, and the serf, though by no means sharing the same level of "social being," were nevertheless truly bonded together, with the serf enjoying the protection and loyalty of the king. In the rapid demise of this system, however, the more autonomous rule of later kingship replaced the almost organic belonging-together of feudalism. And this new understanding—the association of individuals by covenant across a vast abyss of power—influenced how human beings and God were thought to be related. This nascent modern vision emerged as Aquinas' vision gave way, and the Dominican synthesis was defeated by a Franciscan one that would have had the *poverello* of Assisi turning in his grave.

LATE-MEDIEVAL NOMINALISM AND ITS IMPACT

The trend discussed in this section has been traced back to the colorful Peter Abelard and his onetime teacher, the controversialist Roscelin, for undermining the so-called *realism* of Plato's metaphysics, which had strongly influenced theological imagination from the age of the Creeds onwards. Behind every

---

8. Von Balthasar, *The Glory of The Lord*, vol. 4, 404.

actual thing, according to Plato, was its "form"—its more real (or, as we would say, its "ideal") version. Under Plato's influence, faith looked away from things in themselves, and beyond the world, to the higher world of "forms." Breaking with this powerful tradition, Abelard (1079–1142) declared that Plato's universals were merely names (*nomina*)—mental concepts, that is. They were not "more real" at all, and in fact had no actual existence. This shift heralded a conception of creaturely existence in which individuals emerged more distinctively in their own right, out of the "sea of being."[9] Then there was Averroism, the Muslim school of thought that claimed the definitive reading of Aristotle—Christianity's other great philosophical patron of antiquity. Averroism made its impact in Europe from the mid-thirteenth century, influencing the repositioning of God-talk under philosophical control. But it was the Franciscans who carry the story forward.

God Becomes a "Thing"—Like Other "Things"

In the writings of Bonaventure (ca 1217–1274), the Franciscan General and a contemporary of Thomas Aquinas, human minds and wills began the first stirrings of independence from God. Where God was the first cause of everything acting through secondary causes, according to Aquinas, Bonaventure (following his Franciscan teacher Alexander of Hales) saw our minds enlightened by God and our actions guided by God. But not like before. Rather, he imagined it in less integral terms[10]—more conjointly, as it were; more side-by-side than "in, with, and under"; more the stuff of our own, active concurrence. Humans are able to know and act independently of God to some extent, and this free space for independent human action expanded subsequently into the realm of pure nature in seventeenth-century science—it is the root of today's widespread separation of science from religion, and nature from God. And of course this notion of an entirely independent realm of matter was swooped-upon by Enlightenment skepticism.

After the watershed in medieval thought that came with the Bishop of Paris's condemnation in 1277 of theology too much in debt to Averroes and Aristotle, power in the university shifted to those with a more traditionally Augustinian approach, less caught up with the Aristotelianism of Thomas Aquinas and his Dominicans. Yet with these Franciscans, glad no doubt to have gained the upper hand over their mendicant competitors, an apparent

9. Gillespie, *Nihilism Before Nietzsche*, 13.
10. Milbank, *The Suspended Middle*, 96–97 (here following Jacob Schmutz).

triumph of theology and spirituality over philosophy and rationality yielded unexpected results. The Franciscan spiritual tradition was one in which love and obedience mattered more than knowledge. This inspired them to cut through philosophical complications toward a clearer view of God's knowability. So Henry of Ghent, for instance, had emphasized that God's being was knowable,[11] along with ramping up divine freedom and declaring an autonomous will for humans.[12] But it was the famous Franciscan theologians Duns Scotus and William of Ockham who really got the nominalist revolution going.

This is territory made familiar by Umberto Eco in his historical novel *The Name of the Rose*, in which a Franciscan sleuth, William of Baskerville—played by Sean Connery in the movie version—employs novel scientific methods based on nominalism. He uses these near-modern detective skills to solve a series of murders in a great Benedictine Abbey. Eco's novel introduces us to a number of key themes. There is the era's concern about the influence of Aristotle, which precipitates the story's climax. There is the powerful new empiricism opened up by nominalism. There is the Franciscan poverty crisis that forms a backdrop to the theology of Ockham. And there is the despairing mood of Europe in a time of crisis, with apocalyptic jitters aplenty among the monks. Some of this bears mention here. But first the theology.

Duns Scotus (ca 1266–1308), the "Subtle Doctor," sought to rescue theology and the revelation of God from philosophical control. How? By ceding to philosophy its own language of being for discussing God and creation, allowing theology to get on with resourcing the practical business of human wills obeying the divine will. So Scotus cut through the knots of previous philosophical speculation concerning being. Being, for Aquinas, had been God's multi-layered gift in which all creatures abided. Being linked creatures to God via a web of causal dependency. Whereas in Scotus's metaphysically leaner, nominalist view, being was denied any reality apart from that of a mental concept. And this mental concept was handed over to the philosophers. Being now served for philosophy as the essence grounding all things, divine as well as created. But philosophy, and the category of being, could not yield any knowledge of God nor any purchase on God. It was because God was knowable by means of God's own, freely-willed self-revelation alone that philosophy could be allowed its own limited realm of God talk. So philosophy was permitted to go only so far, leaving what mattered most to Franciscans secure

11. Milbank, "Only Theology Overcomes Metaphysics," 44.
12. Gillespie, *Nihilism before Nietzsche*, 14.

in the realm of faith. But in this new approach, despite its anti-philosophical motives, God's attributes lost the mystery they had retained under Aquinas. Hence a problem arose; a crack appeared in a proper Christian sense of God. And the problem was this: God's attributes became, simply, far greater expressions of our human attributes—God became wise and good like we are, for instance, but to a greater extent.

In other words, the language of being had become *univocal*, and this is the crucial point. The removal of Aquinas's account of being, which had sought to highlight the participation of God throughout God's world, had yielded to a new version of transcendence for God. This led in turn to a transformed sense of human dependence on God on a level playing field now freely yielded by theology to reason. The Augustinian tradition and its distinction between the God of the philosophers and the God of the Bible thereby reached a new height, and one that will be familiar from today's neo-orthodox and other fideistic theologies, also from Bible-only Protestant fundamentalism. Thus the philosopher was set on a path towards secularization. At the same time the theologian lost the imaginative resources for communicating the faith that Aquinas offered with his doctrine of analogy, which had provided real access to the mystery of God through the symbolically charged medieval imagination, though without for a moment yielding God to philosophy. So a sense of "abiding knowing" gave way to naked faith in what God revealed across a yawning void.[13] As Rowan Williams puts it, "knowledge of God [became] essentially the willed human response to God's willed self-disclosure: will rather than understanding . . . determines faith."[14]

Already the attempt to secure faith, by shifting it from the public world of the philosophers into a more private realm of Christian will and obedience, has begun to change the nature of faith. And this is where the tragedy of this whole turn begins to reveal itself. If being is yielded to philosophy, but as a concept it is now used *univocally* of God and human beings, then the nature of God's transcendence changes. No longer is God quite different from us, though a knowable mystery thanks to the mediation of being. Rather, God moves to the same level of being as us. And so God's transcendence can only be imagined by other means. Hence God is understood to possess being more intensely—God's is infinite being while ours is finite being. Thus the transcendent God, who was intimate with every part of creation through the mediation of being, is now well on the way to becoming the big, remote

13. Von Balthasar, *The Glory of the Lord*, vol. 5, 18–19.
14. Williams, *The Wound of Knowledge*, 139.

individual God of a lot of separate human individuals that appears in William of Ockham. This yields a poignant outcome which Catherine Pickstock calls "the Scotist paradox, whereby a univocally proximal God is also the most distant God."[15]

William of Ockham (c. 1285–1349) bequeathed to later science his famous philosophical tool, "Ockham's Razor," which represents a further step in this radical Franciscan turn away from metaphysical generalities such as categories and species towards individual entities in their particularity—in their specific "thisness." Like being itself, according to Ockham the nominalist, all such categories are just mental concepts that we apply. Here empiricism emerges, with its powerful attention to what we see rather than what we predetermine to be the case.

Empiricism is also fostered by the demise of Aristotle's understanding of causality that Ockham ushers in. In Aquinas the four causes of Aristotle remain, whereby an event is caused by a combination of four factors all operating at once. There is the familiar, *efficient* cause (hitting a golf ball), but the outcome also calls for a *material* cause (based on the ball's material nature—what golf balls are like), a *formal* cause (based on its participation in an ideal platonic *form*—what would an ideal golf ball do when hit?), and a *teleological* cause (based on the proper end, or *telos*, of the action—what are golf balls hit for?). But with Ockham we move to more familiar modern turf, with only material and efficient causes remaining (i.e. to achieve the outcome, you need a standard golf ball and you need to hit it, but you no longer need to involve any realm of forms or assume that some non-physical tendency will somehow assert itself).

This undeniably valuable gain in the power of scientific explanation came at the expense of Western spiritual imagination. The good news theologically in Aquinas' view of causation was that God's action in the world could be imagined holistically, with God acting through natural events by providing the *telos*, the end, of the action, as well as maintaining the material integrity of everything involved and also holding it in being, ensuring its continued participation in the realm of forms. Thus God is at work as the primary cause through secondary causes, in a way that honors the nature of each individual entity but without fundamentally isolating it from every other entity in its own "thisness." God's action, according to this so-called "double-agency" view, is lure, influence, and support, insinuating our own good into each outcome. But with Ockham, the admittedly wonderful scientific method, that makes our

15. Pickstock, *After Writing*, 150.

modern world, nevertheless leaves us fundamentally cut off from everything else in that world, subject to the power of a remote, disconnected God.

Humans in their distinctive "thisness" are now metaphysically isolated individuals like never before, and free from an imposed teleology—from a predetermined end. But they are not free in the modern liberal sense to make whatever world they like for themselves, because the God of power looms over them and, basically, competes with them for power. And with this power came arbitrariness. Demonstrating a relish that with hindsight is rather worrying, Ockham and like-minded others emphasized God's pure freedom to create whatever God wills, bound by no rationality shared with human beings. Hans Urs von Balthasar sets out the consequences.

> And [so] the Franciscan image of God—love beyond the limits of knowledge—must therefore degenerate into an image of fear (which is no longer even that of the Old Testament), since this God of pure freedom might always posit and demand what is contrary; for instance, that man should hate him (Robert Holkot), that the innocent should be damned and the guilty saved (Ockham), and why should he not be able to destroy the world in such a way that it would never have existed (Jean de Mirecourt)? And, of course, the late Augustinianism of double predestination makes its appearance here with renewed virulence (Gregory of Rimini); from here, it will be bequeathed to the Reformers.[16]

This is the omnipotent and distant God that Luther and Calvin knew, and their struggle was to re-inject some Gospel. Only in that way could the terrible incomprehensibility of this God be able to reveal a different face through Jesus Christ. As Michael Gillespie concludes, "the Reformation thus accepts and proclaims the nominalist doctrine of divine omnipotence but seeks to reduce the terror that this induces by opening up a new way of understanding divine will."[17]

That, in overview, is the theology. It arose at a time of strain for the Franciscan order, for the mendicant movements more generally, and throughout the Church, not to mention difficult times for Europe as a whole. The nominalist God of power found echoes in these various political contexts, but also no doubt provided imaginative resources as power relations were transformed in Church and society. Ironically, the Franciscan poverty crisis—brought on by a desire to renounce power via the renunciation of property, and hence to

---

16. Von Balthasar, *The Glory of The Lord*, vol. 5, 20.
17. Gillespie, *Nihilism before Nietzsche*, 26.

become more Christlike—provided the catalyst for new notions of power and individuality to emerge under theological influence. Thus began the concrete recasting of how power in Church and Western society was understood.

A God of Absolute Power and a New Social Order

The Franciscan poverty crisis is an unlikely candidate for recasting the imaginative future of Western culture, but so it was.[18] The poverty issue is only really the supporting act, however. The real action is in the area of power, both papal and divine. Peter John Olivi, the head of the Franciscan Spirituals, insisted on the *usus pauper*—a poverty not only of ownership but of use, so that Franciscans were not able to live in fine style in well-appointed Friaries provided there was no private ownership of the property. Mother Teresa applied a similar rule to her Missionaries of Charity houses throughout the world. When an earlier Pope's support for the Spiritual Franciscans' case was withdrawn by a later Pope, however, there were unexpected consequences. On the one hand, individual conscience based on one's own sense of Catholic truth was championed in the face of unacceptable papal teaching (which represents a stage in the emergence of what I am calling individualized faith, most immediately giving rise to Counter Reformation debates on the place of conscience in moral theology, which still divides Roman Catholics over official teachings on birth control). On the other hand, the infallibility of the Pope emerges at this time from a more general confidence in the Church's "indefectibility" (the term Hans Küng prefers). Why? So that no subsequent Pope could change the ruling of an earlier one, and in particular to preserve the official status of the *usus pauper* for Spiritual Franciscans. As Eco illustrates in *The Name of the Rose*, the antimaterialistic enthusiasm of some Spiritual Franciscans inclined them to the heretical, Gnostic movements of medieval Europe, and eventually their continued existence could no longer be tolerated. But the implications for thinking about power that emerged from the Franciscan poverty crisis remain.

Papal power was also needed to protect the mendicant movements from resentful claims by the established secular (i.e., parish) clergy, who insisted that the authority of the local parish priest was needed before a friar could hear a confession. But the effect of giving friars the independent authority they needed was to increase the power attributed to priestly individuals apart from the network of ecclesial accountability in which they abided, and also to

---

18. See, e.g., Shogimen, "Academic Controversies."

increase papal power since, once again, the mendicants needed a papal champion. So as God's *potentia absoluta* (power to do whatever God wanted) overtook the earlier notion of *potentia ordinata* (the more circumspect expectation that God's power would be exercised within the weave of natural constraint, respecting bounds both rational and revealed), so this newly, entirely unconstrained scope of divine power resonated with the newly infallible, far more highly empowered papacy. "Power itself acquires an independent reality," as Catherine Pickstock observes, "which corresponds to the arbitrary Scotist will detached from teleological determination."[19]

Of course papal power does not necessarily unify the Church, and from the Great Schism in 1378 and the nearly forty years of Avignon papacy that followed there were two then eventually three Popes in competition, along with pre-Reformation currents in John Wycliff, (who mercifully died in time to avoid censure) and Jan Hus of Prague (who did not). In addition to the Church beginning its long and as yet unresolved break up, the Black Death roamed Europe, with the terror and incomprehensibility of God's newly deregulated power reckoned to be fully on display. Apocalyptic sects flourished, testifying to people's inability to find rational purpose in the way of things any more. A traumatized Europe invented dances of death, and books of consolation, with the stage then set for the revival of antiquity's tragic vision, emerging eventually in Shakespeare.[20] Here was an imaginative crisis to match the one focused upon by Toulmin at the end of the sixteenth century, which led to the modern synthesis (of which more shortly).

Catherine Pickstock approaches this whole late-medieval nominalist episode as *the* great transition of Western Christian civilization. Gone was a networked world of imaginative belonging and in its place "[a] fusion of social atomism and unbridled authoritarianism."[21] Out went the liturgical logic of participation in a highly networked, meaningful social whole and in came a raft of new social arrangements, all with their imaginative outworking in the way God's relationship with humanity was conceived: contractual relations replace participation in being; the emerging nation state and what became the divine right of kings end the feudal vision of interdependence; beyond feudalism, and the more integral style of kinship it entailed, individual choice and rights arise, with *de jure* power replacing a network of custom. Here we

19. Pickstock, *After Writing*, 138.
20. Von Balthasar, *The Glory of The Lord*, vol. 5, 12.
21. Pickstock, *After Writing*, 137 n51.

have an increasingly active state and its increasingly passive subjects, with social peace secured by law.

The spiritual correlate was the policing of interior states by penitential discipline and enhanced, increasingly independent pastoral authority. Social sins affecting the collective gave way to control of the passions, as the focus of Christianity retreated inward—the Church went for the soul, as the state now had control of the body. Here we see the differentiation of religion from the rest of life, first named by the Renaissance thinker Marsilius of Ficino (1433–1499), which inadvertently helped clear the way to unbelieving post-Enlightenment secularization. The Church, with its passive laity at their Eucharistic devotions, was no longer the body of Christ so much as the arena in which the body of Christ was displayed in Eucharistic form, literally making a spectacle of the new power relations.[22] The Eucharistic cult served the same purpose for God and the Church as the spectacle of public executions later served for displaying royal power, as established by Michel Foucault.[23]

Faith Becomes a System

Two more names[24] carry this account of origins through to where Descartes picks it up and the modern Cosmopolis begins. The Dominican General, Cardinal Cajetan (1469–1534), who as papal legate in Germany was a dialog partner with Luther, was the first to *systematize* Aquinas's very-nearly equivocating use of analogical language into something new: a full-blown "theory of analogy." This happened from 1498 when Cajetan, as he became, was the young teacher Thomas de Vio, keen to clarify just how philosophical and theological uses of language could be reconciled in the face of Renaissance humanists who were separating them. Cajetan favored "analogy of proportion" from among the options for God-talk that he clarified. For example, visual "seeing" and "seeing" as insight involve different uses of the same term, though these different uses are "proportional" to the object referred to. Indeed, Cajetan's use of "proper proportionality" favored univocity, cementing what Scotus (the opponent of Aquinas) had begun. Accordingly, you could now

---

22. Ibid., 140–64. On what he interprets as the curse of legalism in Western Catholicism, inherited from Roman law, and its implications for the body of Christ, see also Ramsey, *The Gospel and the Catholic Church*, 165–70.

23. Foucault, *Discipline and Punish*, 3–31.

24. On Cajetan and Suarez I am indebted to Placher, *The Domestication of Transcendence*, 71–76.

say that God was wise and good in the same way that we are, just more so. Size does matter.

Francisco Suarez (1548–1617) was a Spanish Jesuit concerned for the Jesuit missions and how his brothers were to communicate Christian faith to those of other cultures. There was also the growing pressure to find common ground for debate with Protestants (and to tighten Roman Catholic discipline after the Council of Trent). However, Suarez's synthesis outlived this purpose and, being better known than the work of Cajetan, provided the standard reading of Aquinas until mid-twentieth century *nouvelle theologie* began to recover the actually-far-less-systematic voice of "the Angelic Doctor." Indeed, the Baroque neo-Scholasticism of Spain persevered well into the seventeenth century, while "the Spanish Jesuits" remained standard fare in Roman Catholic seminary education right up to the 1950s. Hans Urs von Balthasar laments the spiritually deadening effect of so rationalistic and cerebral a tradition on Church life and preaching, with the wellsprings of spiritual life (in Suarez's own case, that of the Ignatian Exercises) kept so far from the controlling, clarifying mood of his theology.[25]

Suarez took up a version of analogy that Cajetan had dismissed, the "analogy of attribution." Cajetan had thought this version of analogy too metaphorical for his purposes (e.g., causes of health are different from signs of health, the term "health" being "attributed" differently). But Suarez found a tighter version of it to be acceptable, called "internal attribution," with nothing metaphorical about it. So, for instance, if the pan is hot one can non-metaphorically, by analogy, draw conclusions about the heat of the fire. Similarly, while Suarez sought to limit the univocity into which Scotus and Cajetan before him were drawn, there was little difference between Suarez and these predecessors: God shared goodness, wisdom, substance, and so forth with creatures, though to a greater extent. This is what subsequent centuries thought Aquinas meant by analogy.

From this point the late-medieval, nominalist tradition handed on its vision to Descartes and to modern philosophy and theology. The roots of modern skepticism and the homeless heart are all here. First, there is the God of arbitrary power, who a subsequent era subjected to moral judgment. Second, there is the intriguing consequence of thinking univocally about God's being and ours, with God no longer causally active "in, with and under" the working of the whole world. Instead, God becomes another agent, alongside

---

25. Von Balthasar, *The Glory of The Lord*, vol. 5, 23–26.

creatures; God is at work on our level, in our territory,[26] with atheism eventually concluding that God was our competitor and that we would be better off without God. Third, there was the spiritual, symbolic evacuation of the material world in favor of a remote God and an increasingly, scientifically self-sufficient realm of nature ripe for the claims of secular, materialist theories (e.g., Marxism). All this—with clear, concise, propositional beliefs becoming the stuff of Christian orthodoxy, independent of Christian narrative, practice and liturgical participation—left the Church in a situation where, in Rowan Williams's lament, "the equivalence of faith, knowledge and will serves to render belief invulnerable at the cost of making it finally incommunicable."[27] And all for such good reasons at the time. Thus to the heart of this account, and to the brink of modernity.

BIRTH PANGS OF THE MODERN ORDER

Here is a lament by John Donne (ca 1571–1631) for a vanishing order of things, from his poem "An Anatomy of the World."

> The Sun is lost, and th'earth, and no mans wit
> Can well direct him, where to looke for it.
> And freely men confesse that this world's spent . . .
> 'Tis all in peeces, all cohaerance gone;
> All just supply, and all Relation . . .
> For every man alone thinkes . . . that there can bee
> None of that kinde, of which he is, but hee.

It is 1611, the year of the King James Bible, which represented an authoritative attempt to bring religious unity on the part of a king unsympathetic to Puritans, whose successor Charles I proved in suffering regicide just how little compromise with the Catholic spirit remained possible in seventeenth-century England. King Henry IV of France, Henry of Navarre, had been assassinated the year before, and with him the possibility of religious tolerance in continental Europe. The Edict of Nantes, whereby in 1598 Henry had sought to establish peaceful coexistence between Catholic and (Protestant) Huguenot in France, was progressively dismantled, with the Thirty Years' War (1618–1648) looming. England and France, the two great and stable countries of Europe, were soon to convulse in an extraordinary period of upheaval. Gone was the contextual wisdom of the Renaissance, the nondogmatic psychological

---

26. Milbank, *The Suspended Middle*, 91.
27. Williams, *The Wound of Knowledge*, 142.

curiosity of Shakespeare, the loose-limbed skepticism of Montaigne, the earthy humanism of Rabelais, and the generous Christian spirit of Erasmus, all of which Henry of Navarre represented—a Protestant convert to Rome for the sake of peace in his nation, famously believing that "Paris was worth a mass."

Donne was a convert to Anglicanism from Rome, a conservative dismayed by the rising tide of disunity and dogmatism in Europe. The heavens, too, were ceasing to declare the glory of God, and while Europe was half a century short of Newton's celestial clockwork and the beginning of God's evacuation from a closed world of scientific law, nevertheless it was in the grip of the Copernican revolution. Galileo had discovered the first three moons of Jupiter, and the stately completeness of the Elizabethan cosmos was slipping. Even the weather was closing in. The so-called "Little Ice Age" in Europe, ranging from the thirteenth well into the nineteenth century, was making its presence felt in London, with the first Frost Fair on a frozen Thames in 1608—the year Pocahontas saved Captain John Smith during a similarly bitter winter for Puritans in search of freedom abroad. Donne senses the socio-political resonances of all this, with natural convulsions signaling social disorder, chiefly the rampant growth of individualism. His mood is clearly Hobbesian, as coherence of the state gives way before the clash of religions and the press of individual wills—Thomas Hobbes' war "of every man against every man."

This is the beginning of modernity according to Stephen Toulmin. He rejects the good-news story of modern origins that prevailed between the world wars, when a new rational attempt was being made—from philosophy to economics to incipient management theory—to restore order to the European imagination after the chaos of World War I (more of this two sections hence). While the prosperity of seventeenth-century Europe, the sidelining of Church and tradition, the emergence of vernacular secular life, the rise of the nation state and the wholesale embrace of rational principles in science and philosophy were the standard markers of modernity, according to this good-news version, Toulmin's reading is rather less upbeat.[28]

He laments the decline of robust Renaissance reasonableness and "contextual wisdom," which was practical and rational without being obsessed by theoretical closure and controlling dogmatism as the European mind soon became. Gone, for instance, was the ease with which Michel de Montaigne (1533–1592) addressed the plurality and complexity of experience. Listen

28. Toulmin, *Cosmopolis*, 169.

as Montaigne demonstrates a dash of the Gallic insouciance found later in Foucault, writing "Of Presumption":

> Those men who bestraddle the epicycle of Mercury and see so far into the heavens get on my nerves. For when in my studies, whose subject is Man, I find so great a variety of opinions, so inextricable a maze of obscurities one on top of the other, so great variance and uncertainty in the school of Wisdom, you may judge (since those men have been unable to agree in their knowledge of themselves and their own condition, which is ever present to their eyes, which is within them; since they do not know how those things move which they themselves set in motion, nor how to describe and explain the springs of action which they themselves hold and manage), you may imagine, I say, how far I can believe them when they explain the causes of the flow and ebb of the river Nile. The curiosity to know things has been given to man for a scourge, says Holy Scripture.[29]

Here, only a generation earlier than Donne, Montaigne demonstrates a mood of untroubled skepticism about the stirrings of a new science, almost cheerfully circumspect in light of his regularly unresolved humanistic studies. This is the last hurrah for what Toulmin calls a Cosmopolis.

The beginnings of its collapse were identified in late-medieval crises discussed in the last sections, which were not resolved by the Reformation. But sixteenth-century Europe was prosperous enough, newly globally expansive enough and, despite its religious ferment, generally peaceful enough that the late-medieval sense of crisis passed off. Montaigne had plainly lost the sense of a divinely-ordered cosmos that had persevered from antiquity up to the late Middle Ages, and in recognizably nominalist mood he contented himself with analyzing the specifics of human nature. His method was a skeptical introspection—a sort of empirically-minded retreat from generalities. And in this version of the rising tide of individualism, he sets an introspective course that became typical of modernity.[30] But while Montaigne could live with a good measure of skepticism, this proved no longer possible as the new crises of early seventeenth-century Europe supervened. Hence the other dimension of modernity—not the skeptical, introspective one but the anxious, controlling one—emerged as the loss of Cosmopolis became more keenly felt.

---

29. Montaigne, "Of Presumption," 83–84.
30. Taylor, *Sources of the Self*, 182.

This term "Cosmopolis" refers to the widespread appetite in antiquity (chiefly in Stoicism) for a unified vision of *cosmos* and *polis*, of nature and society, that the Renaissance had recovered with Dante,[31] and which Donne lamented at its demise. Ahead of Donne, the apocalypse of England's Commonwealth and continental Europe's Thirty Years' War; around him, the wintry uncertainties of religious conflict in a mood of growing intolerance and collapsing social cohesion; above him, the unraveling of a previously ordered cosmos. A new authoritative synthesis was needed to reunify nature and society, to re-establish social and imaginative order, and to quell anxiety. Out with Montaigne and the easy skepticism that seemed no longer sustainable; in with René Descartes (1596–1650) and his new philosophy of near-geometric certainty.

Here then is Toulmin's revisionist account of modern origins. It is a bad-news story, whereby traumatized Europe sought a new surety of faith, a firmer sacred reality, restoring the imaginative and political certainty that by 1611 was ebbing away—a year, by the way, when young Descartes was pupil in a Jesuit school officially mourning Henry of Navarre, on the cusp of an adult life that was to be lived entirely under the shadow of the Thirty-Years War.

THE MODERN COSMOPOLIS: FAITH IN "THE SYSTEM"

René Descartes was a scientific genius who set the future pattern of scientific theorizing, even if the likes of Isaac Newton quickly outstripped Descartes' own solutions for scientific problems such as planetary motion. So the drive to certainty came not so much in unique, unsurpassable answers for this or that natural question. Rather, we see it in the method, such as coming up with a way of using algebra to plot geometric figures on a graph (the Cartesian plane), also giving visual expression to the behavior of algebraic functions. Many will recall the wonder of first encountering this synthesis of algebra, geometry, trigonometry, and mechanics in high school mathematics, and in later years seeing the power of this formalism flourish in the singular discovery of Descartes' successors: Newton and Leibniz. The infinitesimal calculus followed naturally from Descartes' achievement and allowed a range of physical phenomena to be mapped and predicted in their changing fluidity.

Studying all of this in undergraduate physics, and the sense of control over complex phenomena one discovers, surely numbers among the great intellectual joys of youth. Of course, physics sets itself soluble problems, so that the complexity of real-world phenomena is regularly trimmed to fit the

---

31. Toulmin, *Cosmopolis*, 67–69.

behavior of equations used to model them. Descartes the scientist knew about this complexity, claiming none of the certainty in his physics that he did in his philosophy.[32] Still, the search for clear and distinct ideas that brought such a powerful, simplifying, and, yes, controlling method to the physical sciences, despite no grand unified theory ever emerging for Descartes (or any subsequent physicist, for that matter), did nevertheless yield the certainty his era craved in Descartes' philosophical work on epistemology and metaphysics. The famous *cogito*, "I think therefore I am," cements the great Western turn inwards for certain, indisputable knowledge. First radical doubt, acknowledging the unreliability of what we experience through the senses then, second, a retreat to the edifice of inner certainty in the clarity and undeniability of mental experiences.

Hence rhetoric yields to analysis and logic, with a mood of impartial rational certainty beckoning a troubled culture. Analysis, logic, and a timeless, universal theory displaced "the oral, the particular, the local, the timely and the concrete,"[33] capturing the ground where Montaigne—with a less-certain, Renaissance brand of rationality—had made his more modest stand.

Yet this is not only powerful science and a new beginning for philosophy. The cosmopolitical function of this new mindset emerged in a theological and political role for this sort of scientific and philosophical thinking. Toulmin mentions another traumatized seventeenth-century European in this connection. Gottfried Wilhelm Leibniz (1646–1716) grew up in Germany, which had borne the brunt of the Thirty Years' War not long ended, in which 35 percent of the population had perished. His too were the dreams of a certainty-craving rationalism—a rational method, a unified science and an exact language—and he devoted his life to building communication and understanding in Europe on this basis. But it was thanks to that surpassing genius Isaac Newton (1642–1727), who had discovered calculus in his early twenties, and who was by the time of the Glorious Revolution presenting his theory of universal gravitation to a ready public, that the Cartesian project became a Cosmopolis.

The scaffolding of the modern mindset rests on the basic Cartesian division of mind from matter (thus Descartes, who divided the world between *res cogitans* and *res extensa*). Hence similar divisions take hold, separating inner certainty from outer confusion, and the human from the natural. Toulmin further unpacks this duality as follows: the realm of nature entails

32. Ibid., 72–75.
33. Ibid., 75.

- fixed natural laws, set up at creation (which was fairly recent);
- matter as inert and certainly unthinking;
- a divine order in nature extending from higher to lower; and
- motion in nature flowing downward.

The human realm, on the other hand, is distinguished by

- rational thought and action as its essence;
- human thought and action not susceptible to the natural rules of causality, so no causal science can explain the human (psychology was a long way off);
- humanly established stable systems in society, like those of nature;
- humans living mixed lives, involving reason, intellect, and spirit, but also emotion and the carnality that goes with our embodied state; and
- reason frustrated by emotion.[34]

In Restoration England this "set of provisional and speculative half-truths"[35] caught on, forming a kind of Newtonian oral tradition, "conferring Divine legitimacy on the political order of the sovereign nation-state."[36] This comprehensive worldview based on law-governed stability was popular not because of widespread public engagement with Newton's highly technical mathematical theories but because, after the trauma of the Commonwealth, it provided such a powerful allegory of safe and certain national life—especially as "the Stuart Catastrophe" gave way in a rational transition of power to a constitutional monarchy under William and Mary then, after the triumphs of Queen Anne, to the conservative stability of the Hanoverian era and the new British Empire. Here was the promise of rational control coming top-down in society, offering reassurance that the lower orders, like inert matter, were not going to be the source of political disruption. Here was a planetary model of society, with the king at the centre and the newly emerging social classes (and colonies) ranged outward in orbit around the centre. In France, too, these views were popular, but initially it was not the newer English-style constitutional monarchy they supported, but the absolute monarchy of the

---

34. Ibid., 109.
35. Ibid., 117.
36. Ibid., 128.

Sun King, Louis XIV, living in his model cosmos at Versailles, on continuous display at the centre of social and national life.

In England, it was the religious non-conformists who dissented from the Anglican-establishment-friendly vision, and "dissenting science" advanced the view that atoms were independent centers of action, just as radical political voices challenged the constitutional monarchy from below, seeking political tolerance for their independent religion and thought. Joseph Priestley, the Unitarian, who was effectively exiled to the United States for supporting the French Revolution, summed up in his own person both the scientific and political dissent that highlights the cosmopolitical force of Newton's synthesis. He denied that Newton's physics demanded the inertness of matter, likewise denying the proper quiescence of society's lower orders. In pre-Revolutionary France, similar dissent nevertheless began to make more intentional use of the Cosmopolis, so that it found a second lease of life as the rational basis for emancipation.

Scientists like Julien La Mettrie also questioned the dogma of inert matter, while Voltaire introduced Newton to France. The Encyclopaedists (Diderot, D'Alembert, Voltaire, Rousseau, Montesquieu), who led the Enlightenment onslaught in France with the thirty-five volumes of their great work, from 1751 to 1780, took up the rationality and systematic comprehensiveness of Newton's system but edged God out of it—to its origin and its edges, as the English Deists had also done, but in some cases edged out altogether.

> Facing an alliance of Bourbon autocrats and the Gallican Church, the Encyclopaedists were less concerned than Newton about the theological respectability of the new Cosmopolis. In giving the established French political system an intellectual shakeup, they did not mind shocking the religious authorities, too. The audacious Paul Henri, Baron d'Holbach, transformed Newton's account of Nature: instead of remaining the prop of a vaguely respectable theism, Newtonianism now became the conscious vehicle of atheism and materialism. Holbach, that is, secularized the Newtonian philosophy and made it into a weapon against Catholic believers in the Divine Right of the Bourbon Monarchy.[37]

And so the Cosmopolis that settled conservatively in England as the prop of a respectable Anglican theism switched allegiance, becoming a radical tool in France for overthrowing the *ancien regime*, as a constitutional, rational,

---

37. Ibid., 141.

ordered, and class-based national life became the common denominator on both sides of the Channel.

As for the atheism, it is not just skepticism and the mood of self-sufficient materialism that makes the atheist, then as now. There is also a cosmopolitical element. God is a prop in modernity's Cosmopolis; faith in God is, to some extent at least, faith in the system. And transforming the system brings redundancies—absolute monarchs for instance, even God. The all-powerful God, who emerged under nominalist patronage in late-medieval Europe, now falls before the rival claim of all-powerful modern individuals claiming their own turf in the shared arena of being—the theistic tree planted in the late Middle Ages, half a millennium on, has borne atheistic fruit. The response from theology at the time was problematic. The surprising recourse of seventeenth-century theology to largely philosophical argument in the face of this atheistic challenge contributed further to the separation of theology in the modern period from the living, spiritual source of actual lived faith.[38]

Concerning new theological trends, Toulmin also points to the new preference for authorized manuals, replacing the free-ranging world of *Summas* more familiar from less-regulated medieval times.[39] In ethics the gentler, more prudent mood of Renaissance ethical casuistry, attuned to the complexity, plurality, and context-dependence of human moral experience, gave way to the systematized, rule-governed approach to morality characteristic of the Counter Reformation. And this too had a Cosmopolitical function. "The scaffolding of modernity was used to rationalize respectable moral and social doctrines that had hitherto been merely the 'rigorist' extreme of an acceptable spectrum," as Toulmin points out, adding that "in this way, the educated oligarchy used its social power to reinforce its position in a self-serving way."[40] Hence the command and control mood of modernity influenced Counter-Reformation Roman Catholicism, at the same time that Protestant Scholasticism was codifying and systematizing doctrine in the interests of its own self-definitional imperative. John Ralston Saul, for instance, describes Ignatius Loyola as the first modern systems man.[41] So, as the theological response to atheism separated theological conviction from the wellsprings of Christian experience, the systematizing, clarifying trends of official theology and Christian ethics at this time placed a premium on rationality, certainty and control. Both aspects

38. Cowdell, *A God for This World*, 26–28.
39. Toulmin, *Cosmopolis*, 78.
40. Ibid., 136.
41. Saul, *Voltaire's Bastards*, 43–47.

of seventeenth-century theology clearly warranted Pascal's famous rejoinder: "The heart has its reasons of which reason knows nothing—It is the heart which perceives God and not the reason."[42]

In the hands of the extraordinarily influential English Puritan philosopher and radical political thinker John Locke (1632–1704), a way of being emerged under these signs of rational modernity that is still going strong. The self having been radically set apart in the world, and the institutional mediation of God by the Church having been set aside, a new form of being human that Charles Taylor calls "the punctual self" emerged in the West.[43] With none of the bohemianism that this independent self later acquired in an environment of Romantic expressivism, this remains a recognizably English, North American, and Australian personality. It is world-and-work focused, dutifully and properly engaged in the sober pursuits of family, householding, and building wealth, expecting "life, liberty and the pursuit of happiness" as God's will for individuals whose lot is cast vocationally in the realm of affairs. It is a self that makes itself, and which can conceive social mobility. The increasingly popular literature of the novel from the late-eighteenth century focused on the trials of individuals venturing to find their dream in this new environment, from Samuel Richardson's *Clarissa* and *Pamela* to Jane Austen's *Pride and Prejudice* to *Bridget Jones' Diary* today. Gone is the mystery and the priestcraft, then, with otherworldly asceticism replaced by a this-worldly asceticism of disciplined habits favoring the task of self-creation, which at the same time serves the demands of commerce and social order. This is territory I visited in the previous chapter.

There is a radical, post-modern reading of these modern trends offered by Michel Foucault, who identifies what he calls this "carceral self" emerging as the product of heightened state power—the spectacle of public executions which established the power of an absolute monarch later became the proliferation of controlling, ordering, and monitoring technologies and bureaucracies serving to normalize everyone's life, creating the modern individual as a reliably uniform product.[44] Both communism (think Stalin) and capitalism (think Henry Ford) reaped the benefits of such a disciplined, relatively quiescent, secular populace—a willing workforce with modest, manageable, this-worldly ambitions. This willing worker has become also the obsessive and endlessly manipulable consumer, as we saw in the previous chapter, with

42. Pascal, *Pensees*, #423 and #424.
43. See Taylor, *Sources of the Self*, 159–76.
44. See Foucault, *Discipline and Punish*.

the secular sublimation of religious impulses that began in the seventeenth century continuing to veil the Western imagination, insuring that its heart remains homeless.

THE COLLAPSE OF "THE SYSTEM"

The end of the modern Cosmopolis came with a new worldwide crisis early in the twentieth century. It had been long prefigured, of course—with the rise of atheism; also with the shift of Locke's choosing self into Søren Kierkegaard's realm of existentialism, where all the objective certainty vanished. There was also the constructivist view of reality that followed Immanuel Kant in the extreme idealism of Johann Gottlieb Fichte (1762–1814). He radicalized the Cartesian project to the extent that the external world lost its objectivity altogether and became a construction of the human mind. We have seen how the controlling God of late-medieval nominalism gave way before human selves attempting to create a sense of control in the newly uncertain world of the seventeenth century. In the radical idealism of Fichte—whose achievement was to cut the nerve of having to deal with "the system's" anxiety-producing, ill-fitting "other" by dismissing that other altogether—God's role in "the system" was usurped by the modern meaning-making individual. This, in turn, fed the Dionysian mood of Friedrich Nietzsche (1844–1900).[45] In *Thus Spake Zarathustra* (1891) it is clear that there is a battle of wills going on, and God loses this competition with the *Übermensch*—the God who was reduced to our level of being by theologians in the late-Middle Ages, having become the god of our own system of meaning, was meant to order and confirm our world. But the newly independent modern individual could not help but become God's competitor, with atheism and the eventual collapse of that system becoming inevitable.

This inexorable trend is politicized in the promethean mood of Russian nihilism. Despite warnings from the likes of Ivan Turgenev, whose nihilistic protagonist Bazarov in *Fathers and Sons* (1861) is controversially portrayed as humanly out-of-touch and self-destructively wrongheaded, the "coming men" at last won the day. Under Bolshevism, Lenin (the convert to nihilism) and Trotsky (who believed in permanent revolution) opened the door to Stalin's nightmare purifying vision of liberation as relentless murderous purgation. So "[a]t the end of modernity," as Michael Gillespie concludes, "the dark God of

---

45. On Fichte as a stepping-stone to Nietzsche I am grateful here to the discussion in Gillespie, *Nihilism before Nietzsche*, 64–100. The point about Fichte's cutting the nerve of otherness is on 85.

nominalism appears enthroned within the bastion of reason as the grim lord of Stalin's universal terror."[46]

It was World War I that provided a most obvious end-point for the modern Cosmopolis. One could also mention the final surpassing of Newton's physics in the great 1905 papers on Special and General Relativity by Albert Einstein, along with the epochal loss of the *Titanic* in 1912, as highly-suggestive precursors to this collapse of meaning—Descartes's unsinkable modern certainty was sinking fast. William Butler Yeats in 1921, like John Donne reading the mood of crisis in 1611, picked all this up on the poetic antenna:

> Turning and turning in the widening gyre
> The falcon cannot hear the falconer;
> Things fall apart; the centre cannot hold;
> Mere anarchy is loosed upon the world,
> The blood-dimmed tide is loosed, and everywhere
> The ceremony of innocence is drowned.
> The best lack all conviction, while the worst
> Are full of passionate intensity.[47]

The apocalyptic imagery of Yeats's poem "The Second Coming," like all apocalyptic, bespeaks the end of an order of things, the collapse of a system of meaning, in which God's presence and purpose, and the psychically habitable human world it underpins, is thrown into crisis.

By the time the Great Depression (1929–1939) had delivered a further blow to the already staggering figure of modern certainty, new formalistic attempts were being made in Western arts and letters to restore that certainty —from the unyielding rigor of Bauhaus architecture, to serial composition in the musical *avant garde,* to the linguistic philosophy of the early Ludwig Wittgenstein and the logical positivism of the Vienna Circle. One can, however, identify veiled eruptions of a repressed irrationality among these currents. Think of Alban Berg's opera *Lulu,* or the architectural scorched-earth vision of Walter Gropius.[48] This was an era when Sigmund Freud (1856–1939) was revealing the fact of repression—offering the first causal theory of human irrationality, and thus reconnecting the scientific and the human that modernity had put asunder. This new spirit of formalism was also evident in various

---

46. Ibid., 173.

47. Yeats, "The Second Coming."

48. See two highly stimulating discussions by the conservative Roman Catholic critic E. Michael Jones: *Dionysos Rising*; and *Living Machines.*

forms of fascism that grew up in the wake of World War I to re-establish the nation state. Nazism was scarcely rational in its Dionysian motivations, though it was superlatively (and, of course, evilly) rational in its propaganda methods and its cold-blooded execution of the final solution. One can also point to early post-modern currents committed to the deconstruction of rational certainty, but nevertheless implicated in the pseudo-rationality of fascism. Friedrich Nietzsche, Martin Heidegger, and Carl Jung have all been linked with Nazi Aryanism, while in France the transgressive anti-reason of that Sadean degenerate Georges Bataille found common cause with the spirit of World War II, while Maurice Blanchot fell in with Vichy anti-Semitism.[49] Yeats ceremony of (modern rational) innocence was indeed drowned.

It is also worth remembering the apocalyptic mood that has grown in America through the Cold War, and especially since 9/11, into the vision of a rational (and hence, *surely*, a universally acceptable) *Pax Americana*, identifying government policy with God's will. Reinhold Niebuhr, however, in *The Irony of American History* (1952), had prophetically named the hysterical edge to such controlling, Enlightenment-based, modern American faith in "the system," warning that a nuclear-armed America might be tempted to bring history to an end rather than have to live with history's unresolved perplexities.[50]

A more upbeat assessment of present circumstances is Stephen Toulmin's parting gift in *Cosmopolis*, reporting a return in the West to something like the intellectual modesty and gracious humanism of sixteenth-century figures such as Montaigne since the 1960s, with New Social Movements redefining politics as an ad hoc business best pursued from the ground up—no longer a grand, modern-style, controlling, rational imposition on the flux of existence. Toulmin predicts the emergence of a new, post-modern Cosmopolis that will be rational but not rationalistic, recovering the holism that both nature and humanity need. It will be closer to the pre-modern than the modern, he thinks, without losing the many undeniable advantages of modernity.[51] One hopes that Toulmin is right. But one does well to remember Yeats's warning, in "The Second Coming," that irrationality is the harbinger of apocalyptic:

> what rough beast, its hour come round at last,
> Slouches towards Bethlehem to be born.

49. See Wolin, *The Seduction of Unreason*.
50. See Niebuhr, *The Irony of American History*, 146; cited in Keller, "Preemption and Omnipotence: A Niebuhrian Prophecy," in *God and Power*, 17–31, 28–29.
51. Toulmin, *Cosmopolis*, 160–67, 185–201.

There has been, and there remains, plenty of this to worry about since the end of World War I, with fear and anxiety driving the West's search for a system of control, as was also the case early in the seventeenth century when modern faith in "the system" began. The discussion in the previous chapter might suggest that the global market and consumer culture have annexed the modern individual and are holding the Cosmopolitical impulse at bay, maintaining productive instability. Or, viewed from another perspective, perhaps they themselves represent the new Cosmopolis.

TO CONCLUDE

Rather than an all-powerful god, however (the dubious, theistic fruit of late-medieval nominalism)—the god against whom the modern individual, made in this god's image, is bound to struggle in an inevitable theistic-atheistic rivalry—there is another story of God that has nothing to do with the system. This God is not the all-powerful albeit ultimately unbearable projection of human anxiety. I refer to none other than the God of Jesus Christ, who is anything but the idol of control the West has preferred, in whom faith can only mean certainty. Rather, Jesus is the icon of God in whom faith is more like a life lived courageously in the face of uncertainty. This is not theism, as American feminist theologian Catherine Keller points out, which from late-medieval nominalism and its all-powerful god was handed on via Calvin to the Puritan founders of American nationhood as a shock and awe vision of divine omnipotence. Instead, Keller calls American culture (and the West more generally) back to a kinder, gentler vision of God. "Let the hierarchical universe of unilateral and omnipotent sovereignty fade into a more wildly democratic cosmos of unpredictable and uncontrollable—but never unordered—interrelations. God is called upon not as a unilateral superpower but as a relational force, not an omnipotent creator from nothing, imposing order upon chaos, but the lure to a self-organizing complexity, creating out of the chaos."[52] This is the sort of God Toulmin ought to allow, to underpin his putative, newly-emerging, post-modern Cosmopolis of peace and holism, beyond the failed god (the idol, that is) of modernity's system. It is to a more thorough exploration of such gods of "the system" that the discussion now turns, and to the naming of their victims.

---

52. Keller, *God and Power*, 31.

The False Sacred
Modernity and Its Victims

As our exploration of faith in the crucible of modernity continues, my aim in this chapter is to explore the deeper motivation and the controlling, ultimately violent logic of cultural and religious system-building. This will help to better understand the edifices of meaning built up in the West from the late-Middle Ages, eventually becoming a Cosmopolis, as traced in the last chapter. I begin with some insights from anthropology, but while these are helpfully descriptive and classificatory they are not explanatory. In search of that explanation, and disregarding typical post-modern concerns about too-ambitious theorizing, I look to the leading French American theorist René Girard. He offers the best way I know to account for all of this, doing so both comprehensively and compellingly.

In the light of these beginnings, the downside of modern system-building will then be explored. In dialogue with Girard, I suggest that the Cosmopolis is a false sacred reality and, as with all such false sacred realities, there are sacrificial victims. I attempt a conversation between Girard, the left-wing French theorist Michel Foucault, and post-colonial theory, striving to identify these victims and gain a better understanding of modernity's "other." In this I am also helped by feminism, animal liberation, queer theory, and other voices from the margins of "normality." I hope to show that faith in the false sacred is an excluding, violent, scapegoating faith. After this discussion, we will move on to the fully Christian alternative that I will be setting out, defending and, hopefully, commending in part 2 of the book

BUILDING "THE SYSTEM" AS A UNIVERSAL ANTHROPOLOGICAL TREND

How are we to understand this phenomenon of God being co-opted in the cause of cultural construction and reinforcement? Surely it comes as no surprise in the light of all that structural anthropology has brought to light. Human cultures typically create an intricately elaborated worldview against which all the business of life can be transacted. Such worldviews account for and regulate the dynamics of life together: in relationships, marriage and kinship; in the way animals are classified and treated; and in the various ways our human body, with its functions, drives, and boundaries, is linked symbolically to the world as a whole. Accordingly, the sacred and the practical dynamics of tribal life are typically woven fine. Religion is best understood collectively and totemistically rather than privately and psychologically, as Emile Durkheim demonstrated classically in *The Elementary Forms of Religious Life* (1912). That "God" came to be understood as the projection of tribal culture was a proper skeptical conclusion, just as "God" revealed to be a projection in socio-economic history (Marx) and of personal psychology (Freud) also contributed to the death of God—by which of course I refer to the "God" of the modern Cosmopolis.

Claude Lévi-Strauss is pre-eminent in the philosophical development of this tradition—he, for instance, of *Totemism* and *The Savage Mind* (both 1962). Particularly helpful, however, is Mary Douglas, who accounts for the homeless heart characteristic of today's West in structural terms, with this loss of belonging in a ritually-structured world of clear values and priorities understood as a casualty of transformed relationship patterns and communication styles. A more personally elaborated style of communication, accompanying a more personally liberated style of life, has left late-modern Western individuals prone to dwell adrift, in a transition that began with Protestant shifts from a Catholic worldview that was ritual and collective to a more ethical and personal reality under the shadow of emerging Western modernity. Here is perhaps the clearest reason why many young people seem no longer able to connect imaginatively with the sort of ritually elaborated world still celebrated with stubborn conviction in the liturgical Churches. But none of this is novel, as Douglas also identifies premodern tribal versions of the same transition—wherever the conditions are the same, the felt reality is also similar.[1] Here Douglas provides a clear pointer to the cosmopolitical imperative as typical of human meaning making, with the beginnings of an account of how all this is unraveling in the post-modern West and so giving rise to the homeless heart. I touched on this in chapter 1, in a discussion of secularization from an anthropological perspective.

Douglas is particularly helpful on another inevitable dimension of the cosmopolitical process: the way all cultures have their characteristic structural revulsions and exclusions. That is, they cohere around a vision of what is proper and acceptable in terms of contact with substances, types of behavior, and concerning categories of persons. The fact of exclusion is culturally universal, then, though manifested differently depending on each culture's structural characteristics. In other words, the need to divide and categorize is culturally and linguistically universal, with notions of defilement and danger inevitably emerging in response to threats of un-control and disorder. So, plainly, Western modernity is not alone in worrying about control. All cultures identify the distasteful, the ill-fitting, and the dangerous based on cosmological rather than just plainly practical considerations. So, for instance, there is more to our distaste for pollution at bodily orifices than a sober concern about germs can account for, since notions of hygiene are always cosmologically charged. Douglas recognizes of course that ambiguity is not always allowed to cause a panic—that poetry, art, and humor help us deal positively with the ambiguous, before a threshold is reached when pollution becomes dangerous and requires exclusion. "Dirt is matter out of place," as she famously asserts, adding that "Where there is dirt, there is system."[2]

Douglas's insights on the cosmological function of typical modern Western attitudes to food and cleaning point to the tidying aspects of Western modernity, demonstrating our version of universal ordering phenomena as revealed by anthropology. And our tidying away the wrong sort of people represents their natural extension. One example is the cross-cultural phenomenon of witchcraft, which for the early modern West was a symptom of panic in situations of cultural unease and destabilized group cohesion. "Witchcraft . . . is found in the non-structure," Douglas concludes. "Witches are social equivalents of beetles and spiders who live in the cracks of the walls and

---

1. Douglas, *Natural Symbols*, especially the typology on 50 and the discussions on 55–56 and 190–91.
2. Douglas, *Purity and Danger*, 43–50, 44.

wainscoting. They attract the fears and dislikes which other ambiguities and contradictions attract in other thought structures."[3]

To understand this universal structural dynamic, however, we must go beyond the naming of it that has characterized structural anthropology from Lévi-Strauss onward. René Girard reinterprets this intellectual tradition at a deeper level by accounting for the exclusions and kinship prohibitions of "primitive" totemism in terms of his own mimetic theory. Beyond what even Freud concluded concerning sexual prohibitions, for instance, there is a simpler and more basic explanation to be found in each culture's repressed memory of how it avoided the escalation of conflicted desire and envy into violence.[4] In the same way, the anthropologist's identification of what is sacred to a particular culture is accounted for by deconstructing its sacred myths to reveal the actual sacrificial murders postulated to lie at that culture's origin, in turn giving rise to these myths. Further, the collapse of Toulmin's modern Cosmopolis into nihilism and violence is readily accounted for in Girard's account of how the sacrificial mechanism is breaking down.

RENÉ GIRARD, THE FALSE SACRED, AND THE SYSTEM

Like structural anthropology—but unlike Sigmund Freud, whose analysis of human behavior is focused on individual psychology—René Girard looks to the collective reality of human life for understanding. The prime site at which the defining human realities are disclosed is not individual, then, but *interdividual*, as he terms it, whereby individuals mutually constitute one another. To understand the psychological dynamics affecting a person or a group, then, systemic concerns come first—this is the insight that gives family systems theory its advantage over attending to the personal psychology of individual participants in explicating the conflicted dynamics of groups. Girard certainly has a simple mechanism for understanding personal psychological motivation, and it is in the play of desire between persons that this deep clue to human behavior reveals itself. Girard's is a theory of desire based on imitation, or *mimesis* as he calls it, borrowing a classical term.

---

3. Ibid., 127. See also her discussion of witchcraft as the characteristic means of accounting for the problem of evil in sectarian conventicles and other clearly bounded but internally unstructured situations of "small group," in *Natural Symbols*, 88, 136–52.

4. See, e.g., Girard, *Things Hidden since the Foundation of the World*, 73–79; see also Fleming, "Short Excursus on Lévi-Strauss and Structuralism," in his helpful overview of Girard's project and its impact: *René Girard*, 84–89.

Girard insists that this understanding of *mimesis* is not his discovery, however, but that he unearthed it in the best and most insightful Western literature. In his first major study, *Deceit, Desire and the Novel* (1961), Girard offers a close reading of five major novelists: Cervantes, Stendhal, Flaubert, Proust, and Dostoyevsky.[5] He discerns in various forms the triangular nature of desire, as he calls it, illuminated by various characters in their novels. As his great theological interpreter James Alison aptly summarizes Girard's insight, "human beings desire not lineally, as most thought presupposes (i.e., a subject desires an object—Tarzan, he love Jane), nor even . . . by desiring the desire *of* another (i.e., what I really want is that you should want me—Tarzan, he want Jane to love Tarzan). Rather we desire *according* to the desire of the other (Visiting Hollywood Director fancies Jane, and Tarzan, suddenly, he find Jane fascinating). All desire is triangular, and is suggested by a mediator or model."[6] This nature of desire is still not widely recognized, as Girard laments, though it was unearthed as early as the late Renaissance by Cervantes. Later, in a most comprehensive treatment, Girard reveals this account of the nature of desire in Cervantes's contemporary, William Shakespeare. Rather than rub the audience's nose in it, however, Shakespeare is often subtle in his presentation of desire. One of several examples that Girard elaborates exhaustively is the endlessly shifting desire of the four young lovers in *A Midsummer Night's Dream*—all victims of Puck, the fairy, and his love juice. For Girard, however, such supernatural agencies are really Shakespeare's literary devices for the reality of desire mediated mimetically. Love is not a force of attachment to an object so much as the unstable product of another's desire, and hence its chronically feckless nature according to this great work that Girard ascribes to Shakespeare's early maturity.[7]

This imitative and indeterminate nature of desire is hardwired into human beings as the essential principle whereby we copy others in learning to speak, to name, and to negotiate reality—to grow as nascent humans.[8] Who we are is constituted by the desires of others, who are our models. *Interdividuality* involves not just the non-controversial acknowledgement that we are *influenced* by others, then, but the more radical claim that who we are

5. Girard, *Deceit, Desire and the Novel.*
6. Alison, *The Joy of Being Wrong*, 9.
7. Girard, *A Theater of Envy*, 29–79, 234–42.
8. See two books about latest brain science, on mirror neurons and the scientific basis they provide for Girard's mimetic theory: Rizzolatti and Sinigaglia, *Mirrors in the Brain*; and (especially helpful) Iacoboni, *Mirroring People.*

is *constituted* by the other. Mimesis has various manifestations according to Girard. There is envy, or conflictual mimesis, wherein the mediator or model of desire becomes a rival claimant for the object. And at its heart there is metaphysical desire, in which we desire the being of the one we envy—our competitor for the object must have something we lack, with envy for the being of the mediating other leading to rivalry. Thus the contagious nature of mimesis emerges, in which the desire of the subject ramps up based on the escalating desire of the model. Conflictual mimesis can lead to frenzy as more and more people are drawn into this doubling of desire. Mimetic doubles, according to Girard, are individuals whose desires become undifferentiated. They leave the original object behind and, locked together as mirror images, their indistinguishable, rivalrous obsessions—each with the other—rush them towards violence.[9]

This leads to the other major dimension of Girard's theory of mimesis, which has to do with violence as the likely outcome of desire, also the way desire acts to expel violence. Violent contagion grips a community and an undifferentiated mass of envious persons emerges, no longer desiring whatever the original object was but now desiring victory over each other. Here is an escalating crisis that will lead to explosive levels of conflict unless something is done, and so the characteristic Girardian safety valve for violence reveals itself. It is the victim or scapegoat mechanism, whereby some luckless, hapless individual or class of individuals is summarily set upon by the mob as the handy catalyst and focus of a collective murderous desire. Suddenly all are of one mind and the peace of the community is secured by its new, violent unanimity. Paradoxically, this collective exclusion or murder makes peace—Satan has cast out Satan; all become convinced that the trouble has been expelled, and harmony reigns.

Girard gives example after example of this from the Western literature he examines, going on to canvas classical tragedy and mythology, structural anthropology and the history of religions to illustrate what he concludes is the universal mechanism of cultural creation. This is the false sacred—the universal role of exclusion and violence in establishing any human structure of harmony and order. This is the idol, the beast, Satan, "the system." This is what makes the world go round, according to René Girard.

---

9. Girard goes on in *Things Hidden since the Foundation of the World* to give an competitive account of his theory against that of Freud in simplifying issues of sexuality, sado-masochism, hypnosis and possession, psychosis, and the Oedipus complex.

In a succession of studies incorporated in his best-known work, *Violence and the Sacred* (1972), then in *Things Hidden since the Foundation of the World* (1978), *The Scapegoat* (1982), more recently in *I See Satan Fall Like Lightning* (1999), and *Evolution and Conversion* (2007), Girard elaborates the breadth and depth of his theory. The usually socially ill-fitting, somehow-marred transgressor[10] is the one a group lights upon—like Oedipus,[11] or the scarcely human victim of a collective murder that brings peace to Ephesus in the myth of healing associated with Appolonius of Tyana.[12] The wrongdoer is murdered, leaving a heap of stones over the body perhaps, which survives in repressed memory under the forms of sacred mounds and pyramids. Such victims are remembered in the founding myth of the community as gods or heroes, just as pending sacrificial victims were made kings for a time in various African and South American cultures.

Rituals and community festivals recall the mimetic crisis and the founding murder in ways that spare us the truth, hence tricking the violent mimetic impulse into not reasserting itself. Hence a Dionysian blurring of social and animal-human distinctions (e.g. use of masks) is common in ritual and festival, reflecting the crisis of a community's descent into mimetic doubling and violence, before resolution comes and order is re-established as the hero or god (code for the victim of the founding murder) is exalted.[13] Thus the repetition of ritual as the basis of social order is seen not as charming and folkloric so much as practical and necessary.[14]

Religion, then, like culture and indeed human consciousness itself, emerges for Girard from the founding murder that establishes for the first time the unanimity of a community, and is recapitulated thereafter as the falsely sacralized structures of that community. The truth of culture is of human origin, violent, and hard to face, hence universally hidden in myth, ritual, and religious practice. The sacred is about ensuring that the mimetic crisis is kept at bay—the great flood that God promises Noah will not return, for instance—and hence a new depth is added to the insight of structural

---

10. See, e.g., Girard, "Stereotypes of Persecution," in *The Scapegoat*, 12–23.

11. See e.g., Girard, "Oedipus and the Surrogate Victim," in *Violence and the Sacred*, 68–88.

12. See e.g., Girard, "The Horrible Miracle of Appolonius of Tyana," in *I See Satan Fall Like Lightning*, 49–61.

13. Girard's most sustained discussion of all this is in "Book I: Fundamental Anthropology," in *Things Hidden since the Foundation of the World*, 3–138.

14. See, e.g., Girard, "The Unity of All Rites," in *Violence and the Sacred*, 274–308.

anthropology that religion is essentially social cohesion writ large. Hence the sort of exclusions and taboos to do with sexual relations that are identified in various tribal cultures, touching also on animals that can be eaten or sacrificed ritually (which Girard believes re-enacts the founding murder with a symbolic substitute), and various other rules, are each accounted for by Girard in terms of the mimetic crisis they recall and hence symbolically bypass.[15] All this demonstrates Girard's claim to account for what structural anthropology can only name.

A number of fruitful insights into the modern Cosmopolis are found in Girard's vision. First, there is his emphasis on envious competition at the heart of things. God comes to share the same realm of being as human beings, though to a greater extent, as identified in the trajectory beginning with late-medieval nominalism. Hence God looms over mere mortals and competes with them for control. God is eventually overcome in this rivalry, though the Promethean spirit of modern atheism is rather like the all-powerful God it replaces, in a plain instance of mimetic doubling.

Second, where the modern Cosmopolis begins to collapse since the First World War and new excesses of violence are released in the uniquely blood-soaked twentieth century, Girard's proposal is that scapegoating mechanisms of the false sacred have ceased working; consequently mimetic contagion spins more readily out of control. No scapegoat emerged to ease the tension between Germany and its allied opponents in World War II, for instance, and so violence escalated indefinitely, until Germany was bludgeoned at last into final submission. One might speculate, however, that the sacrifice of Hiroshima and Nagasaki provided the scapegoat that falsely sacred Japanese militarism needed, before it could acknowledge the absolute warrior superiority of its enemy and so make peace with honor. Without that scapegoat, however, we would most likely have witnessed a bloodbath unimaginably worse than Japan's defense of Guadalcanal, for instance, with its maniacal fight to the death.

The relatively peaceful end to the Cold War demonstrates a further nuance to this perspective. The Cold War's gridlock of opposed doubles, with the nuclear threat of mutually assured destruction, represented as good a picture of a mimetic crisis threatening to engulf the world as anything from pre-

---

15. See e.g., Girard, "*Totem and Taboo* and the Incest Prohibition"; and Girard, "Lévi-Strauss, Structuralism and Marriage Laws," in *Violence and the Sacred*, 193–249; see also Girard, "The Development of Culture and Institutions," in *Things Hidden since the Foundation of the World*, 48–83.

history or antiquity that Girard has identified. But, like the seemingly intractable troubles in Northern Ireland, the Cold War ended once an expanding global economy extended the possibility of economic prosperity to the formerly aggrieved party, so that rivalry largely evaporated. Thus an enormous carnage was averted, though perhaps at the expense of the natural environment as scapegoat, struggling as it is under the waste output of former communist and developing countries now aspiring to Western levels of affluence. We could draw similar conclusions about the present War on Terror. Girard himself analyses 9/11 and its aftermath in mimetic terms, with American prosperity as the model of desire for frustrated hordes who would once have united under the banner of communism, but now rally to militant Islam as America's mimetic double.[16] As with the Cold War and Northern Ireland, however, so too with the War on Terror—the only thing that will bring about a climb-down from the brink is an end to mimetic rivalry as some of America's prosperity, educational opportunities, etc. become available in impoverished Islamic countries like Pakistan. Otherwise mimetic contagion can be expected to grow—unless, of course, some as yet unanticipated scapegoat can be found to reconcile the putative "clash of civilizations."

The third and major way Girard helps to interpret the Cosmopolis as an instance of the false sacred is by pointing to the inevitability of victims that are the concomitant of cool, rational modernity in the West. This is the theme I will be exploring in the remainder of this chapter.

VICTIMS OF MODERNITY: DEVIANCE AND FOREIGNNESS

The objective in this section is to reveal the victims of our modern Cosmopolis, around whose exclusion and suffering the stable structure of modernity's system found its identity and confidence. This means recognizing various faces of modernity's "other," against which the modern West has defined itself. The controlling rationality of modernity has feared and despised the irrational, the chaotic and the ungovernable, the weak, the hybrid, and the errant, so that by identifying, containing, repressing, and regularly murdering people like this, "the system" secures and maintains itself. A range of examples informs this discussion and they can be gathered fruitfully under two headings. These "zones of otherness" are classified here as *deviance* and *foreignness*.

---

16. I refer here to an interview with Girard from *Le Monde*; see Tincq, "'What Is Occurring Today Is Mimetic Rivalry on a Planetary Scale.'"

First, with regard to *deviance*, Michel Foucault is a most alert guide, and here one cannot overlook his treatment of the origins of prisons and asylums. His insights are just as apposite to today's widespread criminalizing of the underclass and other nonperforming casualties of the global economy. But to introduce this discussion of deviance, there is a fine example right at the start of Europe's period of crisis, when the Cosmopolis first emerged. It involves a supposed demonic possession in a French Convent on the disputed boundary between Catholic and Protestant worlds. Second, with regard to *foreignness*, there is the overwhelming fact of "the colonial" as Western modernity's other, and therewith the brittle unanimity forced on the West by delineating and controlling such foreignness. A current echo of this posture is found throughout today's West in our harsh treatment of asylum seekers. All this is deeply linked to the repression of the feminine and the natural that are also typical of modernity. George Orwell and Oscar Wilde are two literary figures who felt, named, and hence began the unraveling of this characteristic self-defining aspect of modern exclusion.

Deviance

An early suppression of modernity's despised other in the realm of deviance involved the convent of Ursuline nuns at Loudun, France, in the years 1632 to 1640. The possession and eventual exorcism of these Ursulines, the textbook scapegoat execution of the *Curé*, Father Urbain Grandier (helping resolve an extraordinary mimetic crisis), and the location of all this on a fault line of extraordinary spiritual crisis in early-modern Europe makes Loudun a powerful example knitting together the various aspects of the argument here emerging.

Loudun bore all the pains of early seventeenth-century Europe. It had received two doses of the plague and had felt the Thirty Years War with a vengeance. What is more, this Catholic town had a sizeable Protestant population and was located right on the border with Huguenot territory. This was the decade of Descartes's epistemological revolution, and skeptical scientific observers were present throughout the whole extended spectacle, with the first appearance of atheism as a mainstream cultural possibility providing a backdrop to the drama. Hence the theatrical goings on of Mother Jeanne des Anges and her nuns: contorting, acting and speaking with crowd-pleasing profanity, and hence voicing the dangerous otherness that so threatened their secure Catholic world—a world that was fast slipping away. All this served as a theatre of reassurance for a Church that needed to shore up its claims with proof of spiritual power over the encroaching other. Mother Jeanne became a national heroine for her trouble, commended by Cardinal Richelieu, having provided a reassuringly cathartic psychodrama at a time of crisis (a role for possession and exorcism still valued in Pentecostalism today).

Aldous Huxley's popular treatment of the possession at Loudun brings out the extraordinarily bitchy and internecine rivalry of this provincial town,[17] with all the marks of mimetic contagion evident in a mass of intrigues and counter intrigues. To this contagion was added the rapidly escalating imitation of Jeanne des Anges's supposed possession behavior by the other nuns, fuelled in turn by the standard literature of demonic possession as well as the desires both of the crowds and the official exorcists. Significantly, a similar contagion touched other border locations during this period. Elsewhere, however, these phenomena were firmly suppressed, while at Loudun they were officially encouraged. Mother Jeanne seems to have been an intensely suggestive person driven by frustrated personal neediness, a compulsive liar, and hence a ready antenna for receiving and broadcasting mimetic contagion.

Eventually the parish priest, Urbain Grandier, emerged as a ready scapegoat. He was a worldly cleric, a womanizer who took a pro-Protestant position on clerical celibacy and hence blurred the key distinctions between lay and clerical, Protestant and Catholic that helped define the ordered Catholic worldview of the day. And he also drew attention to himself by being an outsider, an impudent seducer, and altogether too-clever-by-half. A classic Girardian victim-in-waiting, he was accused of sorcery for having caused the nuns' possession and burned at the stake. So Grandier was the scapegoat who helped restore social calm—indeed, he bore his suffering so well that the scapegoat quickly attracted a reputation for heroism and sainthood, as Girard's theory would predict for one who was sacrificed to keep the peace. Daily public rituals of exorcism provided a further cathartic avenue for keeping the crisis at bay, as the nuns played the role set out for them in possession literature—inflamed in their own desire for this excess by the equally excessive desire of Father Surin and the other official exorcists. Hence in scapegoating the *Curé* and maintaining a range of "licensed insanities" for dealing with the threatening other, this other was contained so that reassuring order and control in Loudun was eventually restored.[18]

17. Huxley, *The Devils of Loudun*.

18. Although he does not invoke Girard, nevertheless the most astute treatment of the possession as a theatrical re-establishment of threatened order at a time of acute imaginative crisis in Europe is that of the late French Jesuit historian, Michel de Certeau, in *The Possession at Loudun*.

As the modern Cosmopolis took hold in Europe subsequently, the deviant other became more clearly defined as the necessary by-product and regular sparring partner of modernity's order and rationality. Michel Foucault traces the emergence of criminality and madness as categories of unacceptable otherness that modernity punished and ostracized in the unlucky persons of those who manifested these characteristics. From the socially reassuring spectacle of publicly executing the instability-causing other in pre-revolutionary France, Foucault traces the emergence of what he calls the "carceral texture of society."[19] This is the world we inhabit, where individuals emerge as products of social disciplines for observing, monitoring, recording, statistically measuring, ranking, scientifically normalizing, regularizing, disciplining, and ordering that constitute the bureaucratic flip-side of Western Enlightenment. And of all such power technologies intended to identify, manage, or else root-out deviance as the unacceptable face of modernity's system, the modern prison holds pride of place.

But for Foucault it is not best understood as an altruistic reformatory, far in advance of dungeons from yesteryear. Rather, he sees the prison's chief purpose as helping to define modernity's other in "the maintenance of delinquency, the encouragement of recidivism, the transformation of the occasional offender into a habitual delinquent, the organization of a closed milieu of delinquency."[20] And in this creation and maintenance of a class of delinquents, Western modernity is well served. It is reassured that its "other" has been expelled—made the offending scapegoat whose punishment brings reassurance to a society nervous about law and order. Further, this mechanism serves by seldom reforming anyone and hence adding to society's reassurance the comforting sense that evil and the threat of disorder are not a society-wide reality but, rather, the stain marking a particular category of persons. This spirit is alive and well wherever deviance, class, and race remain tightly bound, as in the American justice system—where poor black men are regularly executed as the ill-fitting scapegoats needed for placating a mimetically charged, violent, gun-crazy society.

Zygmunt Bauman explores this downside of modernity at length. He extends his reflection on discarded lovers and retrenched workers among the characteristic offscourings of consumer culture, and of modernity's controlling obsession with change and reform, by pointing to a new criminal and deviant class. These are the losers in today's global economy. "Consumers are

---

19. Foucault, *Discipline and Punish*, 304.
20. Ibid., 272.

the prime assets of the consumer society," he concludes, therefore "flawed consumers are its most irksome and costly liabilities."[21]

At the same time as the developments Foucault traces in France, Britain was exporting its delinquent class to the colonies—to that further realm of otherness linked here to *foreignness*. But before moving on to that, there is another face of deviance that Foucault identifies, found not in the prison but in its sister institution: the asylum.

In a classic discussion of the history of insanity since medieval times, Foucault hints at a sovereign realm of unreason that modernity has sought to control as its other.[22] In the Renaissance, which was less obsessed with rational control than the modern Cosmopolis became, madness still attracted a measure of respect. The mad were embarked in "ships of fools," on journeys pointing to the transcendent that madness was understood to evoke. In the grip of the Cosmopolis, however, madness was confined not embarked. A stage of this transformation of perspective emerges in the sixteenth-century art of Pieter Brueghel, where images of madness became images of apocalypse, symbolic of the edge and the end.

In the era of confinement, madness was not at first separated from every other form of social uselessness but locked up with it, while also put on display before an eager public as a reassuring glimpse of what the safely-sequestered other looked like. With the humane end to harsh confinement, however, came the internalizing of responsibility for dealing with madness under the professional control of medicine in the asylum, which also represented a reassertion of patriarchal and familial authority in the person of the medical overseer and his staff (Ian Holm played such a role in a 1994 film, *The Madness of King George*). Unreason thus loses its onetime independent glory as the mad are disciplined into giving madness up. Sigmund Freud with his "talking cure" completes this imposition of the authority of the doctor as the modern champion of rational authority—unreason is allowed to speak, because it has become so controlled by this stage that it no longer requires silencing and confinement.

The emergence of a normalized, treatable version of insanity in the West represents the triumph of reason over a potentially terrifying other, at the cost of particular individuals being branded as bearers of the disorder. And creating this scapegoat class of the mad has regularly involved repressive violence—until unreason reclaimed a place for itself with Nietzsche, also in

21. Bauman, *Wasted Lives*, 39.
22. Foucault, *Madness and Civilization*.

the art of Goya and van Gogh, opening again an abyss before the world of reason. This collapse of the Cosmopolis into violent disorder in the West is what Foucault has in mind. Nowadays, however, all such suspicion of the ill-fitting in the service of normalizing the mainstream is being subverted in the growing celebration of unreason that emerges with post-modern culture, just as the demimonde has burst its socially-sanctioned banks since the 1960s, swamping the cultural mainstream with a once-concealed deviance.

Christianity at its best has resisted the offloading of sin onto the other and maintained a penitential self-awareness, just as Christian unreason has kept alive a sense of the not-entirely-rational as a pointer to the transcendent. John Schad, among others, mentions Oscar Wilde in this connection, who commended a decadent Catholic and homosexual subversion of proper Protestant social order.[23] More will be said about Wilde as the discussion moves on to foreignness as yet one more realm of otherness in modernity.

Foreignness

In the same way that the purportedly demonic, the delinquent, and the insane were all removed from within to without according to this account—in the same way that identifying, projecting and hence excluding the other has been a self-definitional constant of modernity in the realm of *deviance*—so this has also been true in regard to *foreignness*, with strong links to the realms of femininity and nature where the suppressive control characteristic of modernity has also been deployed. Of course, foreignness is still feared, even in our global age. Indeed, expressly so. Zygmunt Bauman points to the way refugees, asylum seekers, and "guest workers" are a feared and hated class throughout the West, reminding anxious moderns at some unspoken level that they too are at risk in a global economy that is no respecter of persons. If for no other reason, these outsiders bring the stench and fear of war and "remind the settled how easily the cocoon of their safe and familiar . . . routine may be pierced or crushed."[24] But this problematizing of foreignness is nothing new. It has a long history in the Western imagination generally and the colonial enterprise in particular.

Edward Said has controversially but powerfully traced the emergence of the Orient as "other" to the Occident, in his classic work of late twentieth-century humanities scholarship, *Orientalism*. This vaguely threatening realm

---

23. Schad, *Queer Fish*, 94–115.
24. Bauman, *Wasted Lives*, 67.

of otherness is constructed through a range of binary oppositions: the mysterious orient versus the rational West, static versus historically developing, classical versus contemporary, emotional versus soberly rational, and debauched versus restrained—indeed, the East is often portrayed in such discourse as the realm of sexual deregulation. Said sees this constructed Orient as fully continuous with other "elements in Western society (delinquents, the insane, women, the poor) having in common an identity best described as lamentable alien."[25] In his "Afterword" to the 1994 edition, Said is explicit about the necessary, defining role of the other, which must be constructed if a society is to define itself.[26]

Here the other has been cast out of the Western self and positioned abroad. The colonial who is put-upon economically and militarily for the sake of the mother country is certainly scapegoated, providing a safe outlet for a lot of violence brewing at home, also by being excluded and programmed for failure as a self-definitional imperative of the successful and superior colonial master. But the colonial subject is also a suffering victim in a deeper and more insidious way, thanks to the psychological damage that imbibing this dualistic identity causes, issuing as it does from the master hating and excluding a part of his self and setting it up in the colony. As the great but bitterly angry "psychoanalyst of colonialism," Frantz Fanon, put it, referring to an ancient brand of dualism, "the Manichaeism of the settler produces a Manichaeism of the native."[27] And so the colonial subject comes to ingest the psychic violence that has led the colonial master to reject part of himself in the first place, coming to believe that "I am the failed other."

Part of this dualism is projected self-hatred on the part of the master, but another part arises from the simple contradiction that the colonizer's mindset demands. On the one hand there is the civilizing myth that claims an interest in improving the colonies, but in reality their status as the subordinate other requires that they be denied any chance of success on par with that of the mother country, either economically or in terms of the personal success of more than a token few individual colonials. So for Fanon, as Homi Bhabha puts it, the colonizer's psychology is (also) chronically divided by "collaborations of political and psychic violence *within* civic virtue, alienation within identity." There is a further instance, then, of "post-Enlightenment

25. Said, *Orientalism*, 207.
26. Ibid., 332.
27. Fanon, *The Wretched of the Earth*, 93; see also the section on "Colonial War and Mental Disorders," 249–310, especially 250–51.

man tethered to, *not* confronted by, his dark reflection, the shadow of colonized man."[28]

There is a truly *interdividual* relation at work here, as each party lives in the desires of the other. The colonizer desires to see in the colony the idealized order and civilization that is mediated to him by every memory and representative of home, and of course achieving that involves creating in the colony the same suppression of otherness that exists at home in other forms. So the characteristically violent victim mechanism of modernity now oppresses the colonial, who must live in the colonizer's imagination as a delinquent failure in perpetual need of being "whipped into shape." But as a consequence of this conditioning, to which the native is subjected, desire for what the master has—power and self-determination, in effect for superior being—requires the violent rejection of everything the master is. This is how violently resolute colonial revolutionaries emerge "from below," transposing the desire of those dominating them "from above."

A Girardian reading of this would lead us to identify all the unacknowledged and shameful aspects of Western colonial self-definition as yet another culture-defining myth that has at its heart a founding murder. Girard also helps us understand the particular virulence of the colonial revolutionary, whose desire to succeed has been primed in line with the colonizer's myth of superior being yet who is doomed to fail by obstacles that the colonizer places in the way. As Girard reminds us, "Only someone who prevents us from satisfying a desire which he himself has inspired in us is truly an object of hatred. The person who hates first hates himself for the secret admiration concealed by his hatred. In an effort to hide this desperate admiration from others, and from himself, he no longer wants to see in his mediator anything but an obstacle."[29]

In what I take to be an example of this spirit of hatred, Frantz Fanon champions violent colonial revolution as a necessary cathartic step for the violently colonized—psychically colonized, that is, as well as geographically, economically, and culturally. The native must assert his own being at the expense of the being of his rival, the master. Consequently, the revolution involves violent rejection of the bourgeois values, lifestyle, and ultimately bogus humanitarian agenda of the Western colonizer, to match the colonizer's unacknowledged but nonetheless programmatic keeping down and keeping other of the colonized. Here the appearance of mimetic doubles seems especially

28. Bhabha, *The Location of Culture*, 62.
29. Girard, *Deceit, Desire and the Novel*, 9–10.

obvious, as the colonial revolution witnesses a spiral of violence with indistinguishable atrocities on both sides. And here the Christian alternative cannot be clearer. Liberation theology, which swims in the same postcolonial waters, condemns violent mimetic doubling. Instead the "pacific mimesis" of which Girard speaks emerges in the mirroring not of hatred but of liberation borne of Christlike compassion. As Gustavo Gutierrez put it, "Universal love is that which in solidarity with the oppressed seeks also to liberate the oppressors from their own power, from their ambition, and from their selfishness."[30]

There is one further dimension to be taken into account, however. The native, in order to be able to wage violent revolution, has to reject in himself all the softness and lack of resolve that the master has himself disavowed and projected onto the native as the master's own antitype. Conversely, the native expects the master to be as resolute, disciplined, and powerful as the master's own self-proclaimed confident modern Western identity demands of him. Consequently, fuelled by this expectation of his subordinates, the colonial master has to ramp up his own controlling masculinity in response to the desire of those being dominated.

The Indian social theorist Ashis Nandy fascinatingly explores this particular manifestation of colonial psychology, comparing three British products of the colonial mindset in Rudyard Kipling, George Orwell, and Oscar Wilde. At one extreme we have the driven, hyper-masculine sycophant, at the other the homosexual subverter of a culture of aggressive masculinity and, in between, the cooler Orwell. Orwell's deeply-affecting essay about his "Shooting an Elephant" (1936)[31] provides a window on how Girard's theory illuminates the cost to modernity of excluding its own other, as well as showing Orwell's struggle to understand and be free of the *interdividual* bind that all this represents.

Orwell was the product of a colonial family and in younger days served as a policeman in Burma. Confronted by the carnage a rogue elephant had caused in the village, Orwell was caught up in another of those cathartic bits of theatre that are played out when modernity confronts its dangerous other (such as the possession at Loudun). The account is set against the backdrop of Orwell's own despair at the role he plays, overseeing a sullen and hostile native populace and conflicted internally between sympathy and contempt for the locals who hate him. The tale itself is a simple one: he sends for a rifle, goes out to where the elephant (now docile) is feeding in a field and, under

30. Gutierrez, *A Theology of Liberation*, 275.
31. Orwell, *Shooting an Elephant and Other Essays*, 31–40.

the irresistible pressure of eager expectation from a crowd of two thousand natives that has followed him, he shoots the elephant. What else could he do "to avoid looking a fool?" Despite Orwell's compassion for the magnificent animal, also the mahout who would lose his livelihood, and loathing himself, nevertheless the resolute hardness of the colonial master was demanded of him and all compromise, all softness, had to be set aside. The actual killing is of course anything but clean, and the whole thing descends into gruesome farce, with the Western master putting round after round into the fallen animal that will not stop its agonized, gargling death rattle. In the end Orwell slips away having failed to finish the elephant off, while the eager crowd descends with buckets to quickly strip the carcass of meat. Ashis Nandy helps us appreciate the highly compressed relevance of this account to the case being made here. Orwell's essay captures a whole range of colonial themes: there is

> the reification of social bonds through formal, stereotyped, part-object relationships; an instrumental view of nature; created loneliness of the colonizers in the colony through a theory of cultural stratification and exclusivism; an unending search for masculinity and status before the colonized; the perception of the colonized as gullible children who must be impressed with conspicuous machismo (with resultant audience demands binding the colonizer to a given format of "play'); and the suppression of one's self for the sake of an imposed imperial identity—inauthentic and killing in its grandiosity.[32]

As well as illustrating the resolute "othering" that modernity demands when it seeks to dominate and colonize the realm of foreignness, Orwell's account offers some plainly Girardian insights. There is the hunger for being that the natives bring to the colonizer, which they themselves have been stripped of in the colonial process. So while they hate the master they nevertheless need the "fix" of being that his killing the elephant provides. And neither can the master resist the desire of the crowd. Both parties live in the desire of the other. The elephant's death is the object of desire for both parties to this interdividual transaction, but of course the energy comes from the desires of the parties, and has nothing significant to do with the elephant. But the elephant is an obvious scapegoat, right to the point of being eaten like a native tribe's totem animal—killed to restore the order of shared expectations between masters and slaves, so that everything is once again as it should be in the kingdom of the false sacred.

32. Nandy, *The Intimate Enemy*, 40.

This killing of an elephant symbolizes the power of hyper-masculinist modernity, in its colonial incarnation, over the threatening other (though the crisis and decline of modernity, which we have discussed, is also present, symbolized significantly in Orwell's botching of this set-piece execution). In particular, however, an extension from the racial and gender superiority characteristic of the colonial mindset to the domination of animals and nature is easy to draw. Peter Singer begins his controversial but nevertheless groundbreaking critique of "speciesism" with this very connection—that today's new respect for blacks and women ought to entail a new respect for animal life as well.[33]

It has become increasingly clear that ill-treatment of animals is woven into the fabric of modern life. Beauty products meant to keep the "natural ravages" of aging at bay are themselves tested on the skins and eyeballs of animals that live and die under such torment. Similarly, our mental and physical health in modernity is dependent on the suffering of laboratory animals—and not always in procedures that offer reassurance about their rationally objective necessity. It is ironic, for example, that in order to establish a "properly scientific" basis for the role of maternal affect in successfully raising human babies—a connection that John Bowlby had already quite convincingly established by other means—decades of appalling animal experimentation was deemed necessary in classic studies carried out at the University of Wisconsin. Infant rhesus monkeys were encouraged in bonding with "cloth mothers" or else they failed to bond with "wire mothers." They were also permanently traumatized by periods of confinement to isolation chambers, thus "scientifically" demonstrating their need for mothering. Was such experimentation necessary, or does it represent another instance of what Orwell felt when confronted by the crowd's desire for proof of masculine domination in the brutal slaughter of a now-harmless elephant? Reading Deborah Blum's biography of Harry Harlow—the plainly emotionally-damaged chief scientist responsible for this primate experimentation—one is struck not only by the fundamental mistrust rational modernity directs at all notions of affect, so that America required this much convincing of something that was already patently obvious to every parent, but also by the quite unscientific personal pathology that seems to have motivated Harlow's experimentation.[34] One cannot help thinking that the worst the Nazi experimenters did to their "despised other" in medical experiments on Jews at Dachau finds echoes in the tormented

33. Singer, *Animal Liberation*.
34. Blum, *Love at Goon Park*.

monkeys, shampoo-tortured rabbits, crash-tested beagles, electrocuted cats, and other animal sacrifices to American science during the same period.

It is not just animals, however, but nature as a whole. Frantz Fanon has no doubt about the connection between colonizing humans and colonizing nature in modernity's anxious relation to foreignness. "Hostile nature, obstinate and fundamentally rebellious, is in fact represented in the colonies by the bush, by mosquitoes, natives, and fever, and colonization is a success when all this indocile nature has been finally tamed. Railways cross the bush, the draining of swamps and a native population which is non-existent politically and economically are in fact one and the same thing."[35] This is an insight well supported in the critical analysis that today's environmental movement brings to bear. There is contempt for nature evident in exploitative Western corporate and governmental practice that can no longer be sustained, mixed with an exaltation of nature that represents the romantic reaction within modernity without reliably delivering practical environmental outcomes. Environmentalism today seeks to strain a helpful holism from the latter to confront the unhelpful instrumental rationality of the former.

This problem arose with the modern scientific mind as part of the seventeenth-century Cosmopolis, as René Descartes subordinated the realm of matter (*res extensa*) to the realm of mind (*res cogitans*). The father of modern scientific method was the English philosopher (and Lord Chancellor) Francis Bacon (1561–1626) who, in writings such as *New Atlantis* (1624), prefigured the modern research institute. He imagines a scientific priesthood probing, interrogating, dissecting, and subduing nature in terms that feminists have unerringly identified with the language of sexual violence, recalling in particular the witch trials of Bacon's era.[36]

The furthest and most dangerous extent of nature's "othering" emerged at the end of modernity in the Cold War with the threat of mutually assured destruction in a nuclear holocaust. Here the deepest secrets of nature were laid bare by the priesthood of physicists and turned into a weapon for the destruction of everything in the name of modern individual self-determination. Brian Easlea makes this obvious in his illuminating reflection on the Manhattan Project, which built the first atomic bombs.[37] All this represents the opposite of contemplation in the realm of knowing, desiring rather the violent control

---

35. Fanon, *The Wretched of the Earth*, 250.

36. I am indebted here to the discussion by Sheldrake, *The Rebirth of Nature*, 29–32. I subsequently appreciated a more extensive discussion in Merchant, *The Death of Nature*.

37. Easlea, *Fathering the Unthinkable*.

of nature in this ultimate suppression of modernity's threatening other. All such compulsive masculinity and its desire to dominate nature is what Mary Shelley sought to warn about in *Frankenstein* (1818), which was subtitled *The Modern Prometheus*.

One further connection can be made here—from the realm of the foreign, of the colonized, and of excluded nature on to the realm of the feminine. Here is another comprehensive bit of foreignness that has to be excluded and controlled by modernity, again in hyper-masculinist mode. The feminist assessment of patriarchy is well known, with its notion of the feminine as threatening other. But the full extent of this connection, linking all these dimensions of foreignness together, is helpfully focused in a compelling study of pornography by Susan Griffin. She is not a feminist writer like Australia's Catharine Lumby, for instance, who enjoys and champions the use of pornography.[38] Griffin's is a far more sophisticated analysis, identifying Western modernity's cultural sickness as the disavowal of the natural and the carnal within the human self, favoring its pornographic projection in keeping with an anxious agenda of domination. Griffin identifies pornography as a key cultural marker, in which male fantasy projects a despised creatureliness, carnality, and Eros away from itself and onto women, who willingly play the role of wanton, out-of-control "other" to the dominating, in-control male.[39]

Of course, the more or less anxious control of women's sexuality and the securing of paternity are anthropological constants of many tribal cultures. In the same way, male anxiety about sexuality is projected onto women and variously manifested in Muslim culture, where a thriving underground pornographic literature is paralleled in public by the veiling of women. The Algerian feminist Fatna Sabbah argues that both cases represent fear of the feminine, and hence its othering and domination.[40] So it is not just Western modernity that has an issue with the feminine, or indeed that gives rise to pornography. But, in the West, the inclusion of the feminine with other feared manifestations of foreignness that have been identified displays a consistent spiritual pathology.

According to Griffin, the pornographer is a censor. He does away with the highly personal, often tender and playful, frequently matter-of-fact busi-

38. Lumby, "Why Feminists Need Porn."

39. Griffin, *Pornography and Silence*. I have written more about this in a discussion of "vocational sexuality" for Christians as sexuality that is not controlling, in *God's Next Big Thing*, 169–87.

40. Sabbah, *Woman in the Muslim Unconscious*.

ness of human sexuality that ought rightly to be acknowledged and honored as a key part of the way men and women just *are*. Instead, on offer is a censored version of human sexual expression in which easy embodiment, mutual belonging, and a comfortably inhabited sexual nature are never acknowledged or celebrated. Rather, a circus performance is provided, which is strangely disembodied despite all the exposed flesh. Pornography, then, is a dualistic realm in which matter grinds away in perpetual alienation from spirit—ironically, in that sense, manifesting its own version of repression. Hence pornography provides a focal example of what Western modernity thinks about women, and what it fears about itself, in the dark recesses of its anxiety.

Back to colonialism. Ashis Nandy sees George Orwell's essay "Shooting an Elephant" as powerfully insightful into the psychopathology of colonialism. He mentions Rudyard Kipling, by contrast, as someone grown from colonial roots and never able to reconcile his somewhat awed respect for the otherness of India with his own macho programming, so that he vented this unresolved tension through a writing life spent extolling extraverted violence.[41] Thankfully one can now laugh at the legacy of this hyper-masculinity, as Michael Palin did with his 1977 television series *Ripping Yarns*, satirizing the boys'-own version of this mindset in its various manifestations.

At least some of this post-modern ability to laugh at these now-deconstructed colonial orthodoxies is owed to a third British writer that Nandy mentions: Oscar Wilde. Here is the opposite solution to that of Kipling. Wilde is not only homosexual in terms of some sort of natural inclination. Here is something more ideological—something self-consciously politicized and "Queer," as the new branch of theory names itself. As an extension of the protest decadence of the Bloomsbury set came tentative same-sex experimentation in Virginia Woolf and a fully embraced "higher sodomy" in Wilde, playing out in his public conflict with the Marquess of Queensbury. This champion of rule-bound violence under the rubric of "sportsmanship" was of course the father of Bosie, Lord Alfred Douglas, who was Wilde's young lover. Suing the Marquess for libel proved Wilde's undoing. He was sent to Reading Gaol, ultimately, for scandalously flaunting the conventions. According to Nandy,

> Victorian England was willing to tolerate Wilde's sexual identity as long as it was accepted as a part of the lifestyle of a marginal sect and not openly flaunted.

41. Nandy, *The Intimate Enemy*, 64–73.

> But by demonstratively using his homosexuality as a cultural ideology, Wilde threatened to sabotage his community's dominant self-image as a community of well-defined men, with clear-cut man-woman relationships. What the elite culture of England could not tolerate was his blatant deviation from rigidly defined sexual roles in a society which, unknown to the hyper-aesthete Wilde, was working out the political meanings of these definitions in a colony thousands of miles away.[42]

This suggests an extension from the anxious othering of the feminine to the widespread homophobia of modernity. Such concerns are well-represented in the Anglican Communion at the time of writing. But while homosexuality is the new article by which the Anglican Communion stands or falls according to prominent Western conservatives,[43] it is the conservative Central and West African Anglicans who are most viscerally opposed to homosexuality as a taint that must be expunged.

This fact prompts me to Girardian reflections on a reaction that may well have more to do with colonial psychology than with sexual preference. The native desires the hard masculine being of the colonial master and so comes to share his contemptuous expulsion of homosexuality. But now the former master (who is still secretly admired and emulated—look at the traditional way these African bishops dress up in their purple) places an obstacle in the way of this homophobic desire by changing his mind and embracing homosexuality. This is the Girardian recipe for hatred. One might speculate that native respect for the master was structurally if not actually homoerotic, such that the revolutionary impulse named by Fanon, which requires all softness to be expelled in necessary imitation of the master's hardness, ironically but necessarily calls forth in turn a particular hardness toward any hint of homosexuality. So are these formerly colonial Churches still prisoners of a colonial psychodrama in their stance on homosexuality—and this despite the freedom of the Gospel they claim to champion?

One movement in Anglicanism that challenges the rational Protestant mood and the hyper-masculinity of Empire bears mention, and that is Anglo-Catholicism. Its associations with homosexuality were and are significant, as a subterranean zone of tolerance for the aesthetic and the championing of a more embodied, sensual, nonpropositional approach to Christian faith. The ritualist wave of Anglo-Catholicism led to riots in London churches and prosecutions

---

42. Nandy, *The Intimate Enemy*, 44–45.
43. See my essay, "Homosexuality and the Clarity of Scripture."

of ritualist clergy in the nineteenth century, so that Anglo-Catholicism and homosexuality plainly shared an antiestablishment ethos.[44] This was all too foreign for those whom the poet John Betjeman—an inveterate and perhaps bisexual Anglo-Catholic aesthete—dismissed (in a cricketing metaphor) as the "hearty middle-stumpers"[45] of characteristic English divinity.

Interestingly, by becoming part of the religion of England's colonial empire, and in the hands of giants (albeit troubled giants) like Father Trevor Huddleston in apartheid-era South Africa, Anglo-Catholicism found a maturity and a "manliness" abroad that its anti-establishment profile at home could not always rescue reliably from a posture of adolescent rebellion—and this despite much evidence of the movement's evangelistic and pastoral zeal in the slums and docklands of newly-industrialized England.[46] So perhaps the masculinizing pressures of the colonial mindset also worked on Anglo-Catholicism in the colonies, transforming a protest movement into a viable religious life form within the acceptable breadth of Anglican diversity.

As for homosexuality, the Queer challenge remains for the Church as a perpetual disruption of every too-neat, colonial-style, modern exclusion, provoking those who seek complete closure, the so-called "clarity of Scripture," and a worldview constructed of modern binary oppositions. Hence homosexuality serves as a perpetual irritant in the Gospel's challenge to the spirit of Cosmopolis. John Schad, in his discussion of Oscar Wilde and "Christian unreason," refers to it as "the love that dare not speak its *Christian* name."[47] More of this epistemological critique of the modern mindset will come in subsequent chapters.

TO CONCLUDE

For so many of modernity's victims identified here, it is *weakness* that stands at the heart of all that the modern Cosmopolis could not accept in itself and hence sought to expel, project, and dominate in them. One might also have mentioned harsh treatment of the poor by an economic system stacked in favor of capital over labor, and the rise of industrial mass production spawn-

---

44. Hilliard, "Unenglish and Unmanly: Anglo-Catholicism and Homosexuality."

45. Betjeman, *Summoned by Bells*, 84. This is a metaphor for the nature of middle-of-the-road Anglicanism: neither Evangelical nor Catholic in its spiritual mood and liturgical manifestation.

46. For a comprehensive and critically affectionate account, see Pickering, *Anglo-Catholicism*.

47. Schad, *Queer Fish*, 94–115 (italics mine).

ing a working class chained to the machine. A late echo of the Cosmopolis appears in the disciplined, frugal workforce of Henry Ford's production line, all driving their cars to and from the manicured suburbs where a disciplined populace of producers and consumers was warehoused. This capitalist ordering of the modern West had its colonial victims, as has been discussed. It also emotionally deformed generations of children by the harsh pedagogical practices this culture demanded for producing the well-disciplined future adults it needed. There were notable pathological casualties, among whom Alice Miller—a leading analyst and critic of this approach—convincingly identifies Adolf Hitler.[48] Such stern repression of weakness and a strict, controlling parental style remains at the root of political imagination among the American right-wing, as George Lakoff persuasively argues.[49] These examples, and no doubt many more besides, further reveal the down-side of that expansive and impressive edifice, the modern Cosmopolis—constructed on anxiety, committed to certainty, and maintained by violence.

Here is the false sacred that René Girard powerfully identifies at the heart of history, of which Stephen Toulmin provides an account with his *Cosmopolis*. The version of God that emerged in the late Middle Ages with nominalism evolved into the controlling spirit of modernity—a false sacred reality that came to despise weakness and unresolvedness in everything deviant and foreign. This was a god off-loaded quick smart in the Enlightenment as a threat to human autonomy. God was re-made in the image of human desire, and that god became a rival who had to be overcome. Here, as elsewhere, the theory of desire unveiled by René Girard illuminates modernity and its false sacred, as his analysis of sacred violence and scapegoating explicates modernity's penchant for making victims.

As this discussion develops through further stages in the following chapters, it will become clearer just what it is that Jesus Christ brings to this state of affairs. "The Gospel is the only 'twilight of the gods,'" as Henri de Lubac proclaimed.[50] God is not a projection of our need to control and build a sacred reality offering reassurance in the face of anxiety, and ersatz belonging for the homeless heart. Rather, in Jesus Christ, God is revealed in the Spirit as utterly vivacious and life-giving, beyond any taint of the false sacred and its death-dealing exclusions—a God enabling persons of faith to live quietly in

---

48. Miller, *For Your Own Good*.
49. Lakoff, *Moral Politics*.
50. De Lubac, *The Discovery of God*, 180.

their own skins, finding their way through to a tolerable peace amid the anxiety and violence that everywhere constitute the destructive fruit of desire.

Let me be very clear. The tribal faith from which Western individuals became disembedded through the processes of secularization, as discussed in chapter 1, is not what I am wanting to extol, let alone recover. It too could be understood in terms of a false sacred, as the Reformation proclaimed. I do not turn a wistful eye back on the Middle Ages, despite the Gothic Revival and pre-Raphaelite currents beloved of my own Anglo-Catholic tradition. But, then, neither do I advocate an uncritical capitulation to the new false sacred realities of the global market and consumer culture, as I have made even plainer. The abiding faith that I will be defining, defending, and commending in the three chapters of part 2, to follow, is not only a step beyond individualized faith, but also a step beyond the earlier tribal faith as well. As I said in chapter 1, it would be very difficult for our differentiated, modern Western society to reverse the secularizing trend. We must go forward, neither nostalgic about an embedded religious past nor jealous for an autonomous, disembedded religious present, because both are threatened by the false sacred. Instead, what we need is *abiding faith*.

PART II

Belonging, Believing, and Behaving

At Home in Jesus Christ
Abiding Faith

O taste and see that the LORD is good;
happy are those who take refuge in him.
Psalm 34:8 (NRSV)

The word *mysticism* conjures up images of religious esoterica and spiritual athleticism. That is how we have come to understand the word in our modern Western world—to denote practices and experiences that elevate the mystic above everyday Christian belief, worship, and practice. In this chapter I want to reclaim mysticism as a way of talking about what everyday Christian faith was classically understood to be according to pre-modern theology, and can be again in our post-modern world.

In this way I want to commend an understanding of faith taking us beyond the homeless heart of our modern West, with the consumer culture holding it in thrall and setting its spiritual agenda, also taking us beyond the god of modernity's system—beyond the false sacred reality that sustains our anxious modern West at the expense of many excluded and scapegoated victims among the deviant and the foreign. This is a kinder, gentler but also more robust version of faith, with an understanding of God conformed to the Gospel rather than to modern Western culture, and a healing of desire fit to renew the Church for its liberating mission in the world. More on this last point in chapter 6, after weighing all this up against canons of modern and post-modern meaningfulness in chapter 5, to follow. For now, let me set out what I mean by abiding faith.

ABIDING FAITH

This is a term of art that I am introducing, referring to the baptized, Eucharistic life of abiding in the encompassing, liberating, vivifying, and transforming reality that is Jesus Christ, his Spirit, and his Church. The accent is on belonging and participating, experienced more as a gift and a discovery than a moral project or a programmatic spiritual undertaking. Likewise, the posture of belief according to abiding faith is self-involved, hermeneutical, and contemplative, rather than objective, rationalistic, and controlling. It is about rationality fulfilled by intuition and perfected by love. It should not be confused with the uncritical assertions of fideism, which provide so many believers today with their only apparent alternative to relativistic opinion in judgments of faith. This represents a sterile polarity. Clearly, there is a Christian fish here that is very difficult to catch in the net of modern Western imagination.

The abiding faith to which I refer is predicated on coming to experience one's whole life in terms of conversion. It entails the regularly uncomfortable and often disorienting emergence over time of a transformed self. The modern Western self is de-centered by a different reality—not by the epistemological silver bullet of a so-called mystical experience, of the sort that might persuade an uncommitted, sovereign modern individual, but by a whole new sense of self and world in which individualized faith is both fulfilled and transcended.

This unhinging becomes clearer if we turn a Girardian eye on the mechanism of desire, as discussed in the previous chapter. While the center of meaning and value in the modern West is clearly with the sovereign individual, Girard reveals the *interdividual* nature of desire. The individual comes to inhabit the desire of other individuals, so the focus for desire is *really* outside rather than within the individual self. Where do modern Western individuals most truly abide? In the desires of others. Hence the power of consumer culture to colonize our supposedly sovereign interiority so that we consume as others consume. The transformation of the self wrought by what I am calling abiding faith means that Jesus Christ becomes the model of our desire, so that our interiority is shaped by his desire. This is the way, psychologically speaking, that "we may dwell in him, and he in us," as *The Book of Common Prayer* Eucharistic rite puts it. And Jesus's desire is none other than the peaceful desire for God the Father and for our good which, when we take it on, cannot become rivalrous desire of the widespread sort that escalates towards violence.

Consequently, the characteristic therapeutic agenda of modern selves is circumvented by the paradox of finding oneself dwelling secure in the life and purposes of Christ even when the darkness explored by apophatic (imageless) mystical traditions has one in its grip—a darkness which, for the Spanish reformer and spiritual teacher John of the Cross (1542–1591), is like depression, as viewed from a theological perspective.[1] This darkness of faith can be none other than experiencing the homeless heart—feeling the collapse of meaning, purpose, and a sufficient sense of the self—which is at the same time an invitation to find faith on an alternative footing. Put differently, this darkness of faith is the twentieth-century's much vaunted death of God, which I interpret as an instance of the Spirit's perennial overcoming of bad Christian theology and practice. Chief among the idols thus dispatched is our false sacred modern Cosmopolis, which has kept itself going (like all false sacred realities) on the blood of many victims. The abandonment of such bad faith, and the depression that regularly accompanies the collapse of meaning and identity for an inadequately formed self, also accompanies the birth of real faith—abiding faith—on the far side of certainty, anxiety, and violence.

Another sense of abiding faith can now be introduced. Rather than the more tenuous faith of the isolated and judging modern individual, weighing up the evidence for belief and religious commitment from a position of sovereign detachment, so that God might any day be found wanting and we "lose our faith," this is a more sure faith because it emerges in tandem with a more resilient self. It is not a *certain* faith, to which the anxious modern individual might cling in unreconstructed need, but it is a *sure* faith, confirmed in its living out. Hence abiding faith has a second meaning. It is a more robust, secure, *lasting* type of faith—not because it is immune to questions about belief and commitment, seeing no spiritual value in a modern, critical turn of mind, but because it transforms the knowing subject so that they can approach the evidence far more holistically and comprehensively, with an open mind and heart.

It also recovers a version of knowing that served the West well in Greek antiquity, but which has proved elusive since the modern epistemological

---

1. Turner, "John of the Cross: The Dark Nights and Depression," in *The Darkness of God*, 226–51. My Carmelite friend Fr Greg Burke, OCD, suggests that grief provides a better category than depression to account for the sense of loss regularly entailed by this inescapable spiritual process of personal transformation.

turn of Descartes and Locke, who plucked the knowing self out of the world. It can seem strange to modern Westerners given our understanding of reason—which prizes detached objectivity, and the separation of theory from practice—but the Western intellectual tradition is grounded in a far more participatory understanding of reason which, for want of a better word, sounds mystical. Plato's hugely influential contribution, at the wellsprings of Western thought, was just such a mystical vision. Knowledge (*episteme, noesis*) was not modern-style "knowledge about" but a true *theoria* leading to union with what was known (albeit a little indirectly, in the realm of forms).[2] It was, in other words, significantly *participatory*. Further, Plato is joined by the Epicureans and Aristotelians in equating wisdom with living a certain form of life, rather than with theoretical abstraction, argumentation, and the accumulation of knowledge.[3] Philosophy was a second-order reflection on actually living the good life, bearing little resemblance, for instance, to skeptical analytic philosophy in the twentieth century.

The turn to these modern forms, as we have seen, was a seventeenth-century achievement, beginning with René Descartes and cemented by John Locke. Rather than contemplatively participating in the true order of things, Descartes turned rational insight into a procedural discipline of intellectual suspicion and mastery, detached from any authoritative tradition, and regarding the world of matter in objective terms—as "expressively dead," in Charles Taylor's unsparing phrase. With Locke, the disengagement of reason from its objects also cuts the nerve of ancient longing and striving for union with the good, the true and the beautiful, in favor of what Taylor calls a "hedonist theory" of motivation, seeking rational certainty for the avoidance of unease.[4] Here is one plank of the modern therapeutic self, committed to the relief of unease at all costs, that I have described as being unhinged by abiding faith—a version of faith with its roots far deeper in classical Western thought. This imagination of the Greeks, contemplating the forms and striving after the good, the true and the beautiful, was Christianized in the New Testament and, later, by the Greek Fathers in terms of the priority of God's grace in revelation and salvation. But it was a grace that still drew us out of ourselves into union with ultimate reality, where Plato the pagan prophet also pointed, suggesting the unitive nature of abiding faith more effectively than many modern Western theologians.

2. Louth, *The Origins of the Christian Mystical Tradition*, 2–3.
3. McIntosh, *Mystical Theology*, 24 (following Hadot, *Philosophy as a Way of Life*).
4. Taylor, *Sources of the Self*, 148–49, 168.

So abiding faith, as I am calling it, might also be labeled "ordinary mysticism." It is none other than the faith of the Gospel according to the New Testament, notably in its classic witnesses: Paul, John, and their schools. It is the faith of the Greek Fathers and Augustine, so that up to the time of Aquinas the committed, rational mind was understood to inhabit God's order in the world, rather than standing separate from God and the world across an increasing gulf, so that from the late Middle Ages a more scholastic, propositional theology could become detached from spiritual practice. Hence a void emerged between head and heart, and between both these proper centers of knowing and the liturgically-shaped living-out of the Christian life which, along with reason and love, had once formed a totality. Across this imaginative gap, God slipped beyond the horizon of belief in becoming detached from spiritual, liturgical, and ethical Christian practice. Subsequently there has been no cognitively respectable home in modern Western thinking for abiding faith (though in the next chapter it will be important for my case to demonstrate that such a potential home has opened-up in post-modern Western thought).

The saints and the liturgy never stopped testifying to the reality of abiding faith, of course, though many Christians from the late Middle Ages have failed to make much sense of either, dismissing or moralizing the saints while tuning-out of the liturgy towards private devotion. As a result, the onset of modernity led to the construction of mysticism as an exotic realm of more participatory religious knowing, detached from theology and the practice of ordinary Christian faith. For rationalistically-minded religious skeptics it *proves* nothing, of course, while for some empirically-minded modern believers, "mystical experiences" constitute evidence for belief, though sourced from outside the world of rational explicability. This chapter is my attempt to take us beyond a modern stalemate, discerning a richer tradition of Christian faith that has gone underground from the late-Middle Ages—sometimes in mystical guise—only to begin re-emerging today as a more holistic epistemology makes room for it.

THE FAITH OF THE GOSPEL

We have seen how modern Western anxiety fueled a false sacred reality in the Cosmopolis, which was maintained by a fierce certainty costing many victims in the realm of "the other"—of the deviant and the foreign. Certainty and the need to shore up the self against the void of modern secularization, and under predation from a destabilizing culture of consumerism, has spawned various forms of consumer spirituality as well as unbelief. Some of these demand considerable certainty and bring their own exclusions as the price of the anti-anxiety therapy they provide. Here the nature of faith as a trust that can risk itself to the providence of God is important, rather than always seeking to make its own arrangements—at whatever cost to objective truth, to those excluded, and to our own spiritual maturing. This is an understanding of faith found in the Old Testament, and I mention two key passages.[5]

Abraham's willingness to risk the posterity that God had promised him by sacrificing Isaac is the classic instance (Gen 22:1–19). Although we are told that Abraham loved his son (v. 2), the boy's place in the narrative is clearly in the light of who he becomes—as a vehicle of God's promise rather than the fond object of a father's private affection. So the widespread moral horror that this legend inspires is mitigated somewhat if we see it as a galvanizing enactment of what being God's covenant people entails, with the focus more on identity and destiny in God's wider purposes than confined to personal relationships, which is all that is left to most modern Westerners. Such faith knows that the theological identity of covenant partnership lies at the heart of who we are. Though Abraham's psychology is not the point, nevertheless we dwellers in a more psychological age assume that his faith would have been confirmed and strengthened by being tested in this way.

A further dimension of faith in the Old Testament adds discernment and waiting to the bedrock of trust. Isaiah's account of Judah's King Ahaz provides a good example. With the survival of the kingdom at stake, Ahaz is tempted to take matters into his own hands by joining an alliance with Assyria against Israel and her allies, whereas the command of God through the prophet is for him to stand firm and understand that God has a plan across several generations, which Ahaz must not interfere with and disrupt (Isa 7). God presses a sign on him—that of the young woman bearing a son, of whom the Gospel of Matthew later makes so much (Matt 1:22–23). Ahaz must trust God's providence at work in events, waiting with an active patience that resists the temptation to try and engineer a more certain outcome.

Anxious modern Westerners, used to looking out for their own best chance in life, find such accounts to be literally incredible: that God's purposes are being worked out and God's people have to go along, so that guided by God with the aid of prophets and personal discernment they can find sufficient sureness in God's guidance for them to trust and wait. And if this sounds counter-cultural today, it was plainly never easy in Old Testament

5. See Springsted, *The Act of Faith*, 75–77.

times either. It entails an imaginative shift, in which we come to know ourselves to be more secure in God's hands than by anxiously trying to create our own meaning and purpose in life. The New Testament takes up this faith of the Old, focused in the one seen to be the fulfiller of Israel's faith.

St. Paul and Mysticism

Here I want to focus on St. Paul's testimony. Paul deepens the Old Testament conviction of Israel's favored role in covenant with God into an organic, participatory vision of Christian faith as a whole new life, caught up in a new existence, in a new Lord, a new creation, which is Jesus Christ. Paul's vision of salvation in Christ is also spoken about in terms of being indwelt by the Spirit, and as being the Church that is Christ's body—also through the sacraments of Baptism and Eucharist, which themselves grant entry into the life of Christ. And on this basis the Christian ethical life for Paul and his school (chiefly in Colossians and Ephesians) is both a gift and a task, enabled and entailed by our having been incorporated into a new realm of meaning and possibility.

After Paul this Christian mysticism took other forms, explicitly in John's Gospel—"I am the vine, you are the branches" (John 15:5a). Also, at Pentecost the ascended Jesus sends the Holy Spirit to engraft Christians into his continuing mission. In the Acts version it is the beginning of a new age, the reversal of Babel and human disunity with the reconstitution of humanity in diversity yet in mutual understanding (Acts 2:1–11; cf. Gen 11:1–9). In John's version, it is his own Spirit that the risen Jesus breathes out in the upper room of the Eucharist—the same word for spirit used in the Greek Old Testament for creation (Gen 1:2) and for Israel's re-creation, in Ezekiel's image of the valley of dry bones (Ezek 37). John's risen Jesus enlists the disciples in his own mission of judging and overcoming evil—"If you forgive the sins of any, they are forgiven them; if you retain the sins of any, they are retained" (John 20:23). Participation in Jesus is at least implicit in the Synoptic Gospels, too, where accounts of Jesus's ministry plainly co-opt the history, Scriptures, and festivals of Israel, and where he is presented as the new Israel in person—like the old Israel, Jesus is threatened in Egypt (Matthew 2), tested in the wilderness (Mark 1:12–13; Matt 4:1–11; Luke 4:1–13), and transfigured as his climactic role in Israel's story of law and prophets becomes plain (Mark 9:2–13; Matt 17:1–8; Luke 9:28–36). Likewise, the very early appearance of Christian lectionaries and liturgical seasons testifies to the Gospels being understood to apply the template of Jesus's life to every

Christian life and worshipping community thereafter. But it is with St. Paul the first Christian theologian that this possibility appears on the scene in his account of the Christian life as "ordinary mysticism."

Paul's mysticism has been a controversial idea. Debate over it reveals in miniature the problems modern Western thought has had with faith understood in terms of subjective participation rather than objective judgment. This is another reason I am devoting major attention to Paul here. The controversy over this idea began in earnest with the great theologian, missionary doctor, and Nobel laureate, Albert Schweitzer.

Schweitzer believed that Paul's mysticism was distinctive. It is different from the cultic apparatus of divine union that he identifies in the mystery religions of antiquity, and the "intellectual mysticism" he traces from John's gospel to German pietism and beyond, which he understands to be more about a blurring of self and God. Paul is different, and more matter-of-fact: we are made one with Christ and filled with his Spirit in a way that is very concrete through the sacraments, and we are enlisted in the service of God's Kingdom.

The texts that Schweitzer lists show the variety of imagery Paul gathers to describe the one reality.[6] For example, Galatians describes Christians as dead to the law through Christ, so that his life replaces theirs (Gal 2:19–20; 6:14); as baptized in Christ and hence becoming one across all former exclusive structures of identity (Jew/Greek, slave/free, male/female) (Gal 3:26–28); and united with the Son both in his relationship with the Father and in his ministry by the indwelling Spirit (Gal 4:6; 5:24–5). Anyone in Christ is a new creation, dead to what they were before (2 Cor 5:17). Beyond the power of the law to make righteous, Christians are found in Christ so that through the fellowship of his sufferings they might also share his resurrection (Phil 3:1–11). In Romans there is a strong emphasis on passing from the power of law, sin, and death to participation in Christ (Rom 6:10–11; 7:4), making possible a more fruitful life for God. Spirit language is used for the same transformation into Christ, so a new law of the Spirit applies to Christians (Rom 8:1–2, 9–11). Kingdom of God language is also used. It is described as a reality for Christians although not fully revealed before the Kingdom comes, hence the possibility of Christians falling out of the Kingdom by behavior not befitting their part in it[7] (Rom 14:17; 1 Cor 4:20; 6:9–10; 15:50; Gal 5:21; 1 Thess 2:12). Finally, all this is manifestly ecclesial in Paul's image of the Church as

6. Schweitzer, *The Mysticism of Paul the Apostle*, 3–4.
7. Ibid., 120.

Christ's body (Rom 7:4–5). Schweitzer also points to the totally realistic sense Paul has of Baptism and Eucharist effecting these transformations (1 Cor 10:1–6), as prefigured in the Exodus sea crossing and the provision of manna in the wilderness, which were the acts by which God formed God's people in the Old Testament.[8]

This is a mysticism of dying and rising with Christ that is apocalyptic and eschatological. However, because these ancient ideas about God ending the world struck Schweitzer as impossible to assimilate into modern Western understandings, this vision becomes at best for us a passionate ethical-spiritual commitment to the transformation of human society in the direction of God's Kingdom. The importance of this for Schweitzer was clear from the radical discipleship to which he devoted himself from the age of thirty as a medical missionary, seeking to transform the blighted lives of villagers in French Equatorial Africa by very practical means. It is clear from reading the last pages of Schweitzer's 1931 classic *The Mysticism of Paul the Apostle* that this vision stands behind his own extraordinary life of service.

> The conception of dying and rising with Christ brings us into an inner controversy with our own existence, which extends itself in ever-widening circles. From it we receive an interpretation of all that happens to us. It does not permit us to slip through life regardless of external events, but bids us seek in them the appointed way of passing from natural being to being in the Spirit. If we want to "live a quiet life," it attacks us with the question whether being possessed by Christ is living itself out in us, or whether it is merely a distant echo on the horizon of our lives.[9]

For Schweitzer, Paul's realistic, mystical, spiritual, sacramental, ethical, and transformational participation in Christ and the Kingdom of God, cashed out in humanitarian service, is the most authentic representation of Christ for today, in a Church which has favored a pietism that is too mystical, or else an activism that is not mystical enough. As for the problem of fitting the sheer alien frankness of its apocalyptic worldview into modern categories, he concludes that "[a]s radium by its very nature is in a constant state of emanation, so Pauline mysticism is constantly being transmuted from the natural to the spiritual and the ethical."[10] And so it was for Schweitzer himself, who wrote the preface of his book on the steamer returning up-river to his hospital in

8. Ibid., 20–21.
9. Ibid., 388–89.
10. Ibid., 385.

Lambaréné. I cannot help wondering if Christ has ever thrown down a greater challenge to the bleak antihumanism of Joseph Conrad's *Heart of Darkness*.[11]

Understanding Paul's Mysticism Today?

The *problem of faith* for modern Westerners is regularly due to a detached, skeptical starting point of "inquiry." John Locke again, and a whole tradition in New Testament studies since the Enlightenment, in which "the real Jesus" is sought.[12] The aim was to pare back many accretions of later Church teaching about Jesus, so that having rescued Jesus from his people one might choose dispassionately whether or not to believe in him. This is not to dismiss the important modern scholarly work that has aided faith's discernment, so that we more correctly understand many miracles and Old Testament precedents in the Gospels to be literary devices first and foremost. Consequently, the New Testament is rediscovered as witness and testimony to a liberating and transforming Gospel centered on Jesus, rather than flat historical reportage about a God understood to act by intervening against the grain of nature (in fact, the God of absolute power who owes more to nominalism and early-modern intellectual history than to the Gospel, as discussed in chapter 2, above). So I am not saying that the critically-minded and endlessly inventive world of modern biblical studies is to be dismissed, but only the spirit of its earlier and now increasingly discredited attempts at an objectivity that will never grasp the reality of Christ.

Newer literary studies of the New Testament demonstrate this point from the text itself. John's Gospel, for instance, presents conversion to Christ in terms of transforming encounter with him, in which he puts the questions to us rather than allowing us to interrogate him. I refer here to John's programmatic stories of people coming to faith in Christ, linked to the "signs" that structure John's narrative and the "I am" sayings accompanying them. Most notable in this respect are accounts of the woman at the well (John 4:5–42), the crowd receiving Jesus's bread of life discourse (John 6:25–40),

---

11. A steamer trip up-river to an altogether different destination, and outcome: see Conrad's great novel, *Heart of Darkness*. This story was loosely retold by Francis Ford Coppola in his 1979 film *Apocalypse Now*. The scene of a battlefield Eucharist with a tank-mounted flamethrower destroying village houses in the background suggests that someone understood Paul's vision of the new creation in Jesus Christ, contrasted with life under the old order of sin, law, and death.

12. Springsted, *The Act of Faith*, 78.

and the climactic story of a man born blind who comes to sight—that is, to faith (John 9:1–35).

Schweitzer is convinced that knowing Jesus is not a matter of *Wissenschaft*. His famous survey of nineteenth-century liberal lives of Jesus—the abovementioned scholarly genre committed to finding "the real Jesus" in order to base decisions for faith on "proper scientific evidence," yet in fact more reliably accommodating Jesus to modern rationalistic or romantic habits of mind—led Schweitzer to conclude that Jesus's apocalyptic ministry in the service of God's coming Kingdom could not be boiled down into modern categories. This prefigured the conclusions of his book on Paul's mysticism. Jesus would always pass by those detached inquirers, as one unknown. But this did not mean Jesus could not be known, believed in or served, as Schweitzer himself had discovered. In his famous ending to *The Quest of the Historical Jesus*, we see again his skepticism about understanding Jesus according to contemporary intellectual categories, combined with his mystical conviction—one he was already putting into practice—that Jesus could be known by following him in the work of God's Kingdom.

> He comes to us as One unknown, without a name, as of old, by the lake-side, He came to those men who knew Him not. He speaks to us the same word: "Follow thou me!" and sets us to the tasks which He has to fulfill for our time. He commands. And to those who obey Him, whether they be wise or simple, He will reveal Himself in the toils, the conflicts, the sufferings which they shall pass through in His fellowship, and, as an ineffable mystery, they shall learn in their own experience Who He is.[13]

The greatest attempt in twentieth-century New Testament studies after Schweitzer to understand Paul's message about being in Christ was that of celebrated German scholar Rudolf Bultmann. He intentionally advanced beyond the spirit of Locke and the mistaken idea that faith is some sort of dispassionate decision based on evidence.[14] He also repudiated another major focus of Protestant interpretation: that individual moral transgression and its acquittal by God is at the heart of Paul's testimony. Instead, he explored creatively the new existence that Jesus opened beyond the dominion of sin—understood to

---

13. Albert Schweitzer, *The Quest of the Historical Jesus*, 403. For further clarification of his sense that Jesus claims us directly without our having to share the horizon of his apocalyptic faith, or assimilate it to modern thought, see Schweitzer's autobiographical reflection, *Out of My Life and Thought*, 46–51.

14. Springsted, *The Act of Faith*, 88.

be an anxiously self-justifying state of self-deception—which involves a setting aside of the law by which righteousness is grasped at, and an overcoming of the death that awaits us all on the wrong side of God's offer of new life.[15]

Bultmann's genius was in seeking the meaning of this apocalyptic vision and its call for decision in existential terms. Gospel preaching confronts the individual with God's judgment on a life turned inwards, which must be abandoned for the new existence offered in Christ. Baptism and Eucharist are acknowledged as the necessary entry to this new reality through the Church for Paul, though for Bultmann they are subordinated to hearing the preached word and our response in faith. Pauline faith, whereby we receive righteousness as a gift, centers for Bultmann on a new knowledge and a new self-understanding. "A new understanding of one's self takes the place of the old . . . faith is decision in regard to the grace which encounters man in the proclaimed word. . . . He, the sinner who is in death, is confronted by the gospel when it reaches him with the decision whether or not he is willing to understand himself anew and to receive his life from the hand of God."[16]

This is not a rationalist's attitude toward the evidence, or a pietist's inward conviction. Bultmann sidesteps these twinned modern options, seeking to acknowledge that faith is rooted in a reality external to the believer. But the rubber still meets the road, if you like, in the modern individual's project of becoming a self.

Further, Bultmann understands faith for Paul to be manifest in obedience, holding on to the Gospel promise so that hope overcomes the anxiety characteristic of unfaith, whereby we attempt to secure our own future. So, for Bultmann, "'Faith'—the radical renunciation of accomplishment, the obedient submission to the God-determined way of salvation, the taking over of the cross of Christ—is the free deed of obedience in which the new self constitutes itself in place of the old."[17] Bultmann is also very clear that this obedience involves constant decision—Paul plainly believes that the "righteousness of faith" can be lost if we cease to live by it: "Not that I have already obtained this or have already reached the goal; but I press on to make it my own, because Christ Jesus has made me his own" (Phil 3:12). This passage, from which Paul goes on to show that faith involves the constant putting behind us of our former life, has many parallels (e.g. 1 Cor 1:8; 10:12; 15:58;

15. Bultmann, *Theology of the New Testament*, vol. 1, chapter 5, "Man under Faith," 270–345, especially 314–30.
16. Ibid., vol. 1, 269.
17. Ibid., vol. 1, 316.

16:13; 2 Cor 1:21; Gal 5:1; Phil 1:27, 4:1; 1 Thess 3:13; 5:23). The past threatens yet, paradoxically, the new future remains real. "Existence in faith," for Bultmann, "is a movement between 'no longer' and 'not yet.'"[18]

Bultmann has sought to make his own the alien apocalyptic mindset of Paul, whereby a fundamental shift of allegiance between a doomed self and the life-giving Christ takes place. The question a later generation of New Testament scholars put to Bultmann, however, concerns the very plausibility of this whole intellectual exercise—whether Paul can be explicated at all in categories making sense to the modern Westerner.

His student Ernst Käsemann wondered whether the sheer objectivity of Paul's vision could be appropriated at all in terms of changed self-understanding. Likewise, could Bultmann's emphasis on the obedience of a constantly renewed decision do justice to what Paul sees as the sheer givenness of a transfer that happens primarily from God's end rather than from ours? Käsemann also points to the plainly objective efficacy of the sacraments for Paul, with which Bultmann clearly struggles as a Protestant-minded, modern Westerner for whom human interiority *must surely* be the locus of faith.[19] For Paul, however, as Käsemann points out, faith is all about the objective status of the Christian, "therefore the sacrament mediates the new existence by giving me the new Lord, the one true *Kyrios* beyond and above all the lordships of the world. And therefore we are entitled at this point to speak at last of incorporation into the body of Christ."[20] To say "at last" is to acknowledge that there is no prior reality of the body of Christ into which the sacrament might subsequently come, so radically foundational is its role in Paul's understanding of participation in Christ.

Bultmann's reading of Paul on participation in Christ in terms of a new self-understanding is further challenged by late twentieth-century New Testament scholar E. P. Sanders. He describes Paul's participatory account of life in Christ as a dogmatically asserted primary reality that is not graspable at all in Bultmann's terms, apart from actual participation in faith. It is not based on an assessment of humanity's situation under the law, as in the Reformation period, let alone in terms of a changed self-understanding, according to more recent existentialist discussion.[21]

18. Ibid., vol. 1, 322.
19. Ibid., vol. 1, 312–14.
20. Käsemann, "The Pauline Doctrine of the Lord's Supper," 118.
21. Sanders, *Paul and Palestinian Judaism*, see Part II, 442–43, 482–84. Bultmann acknowledges the necessity of being found in Christ for subjectively understanding the

Sanders offers a helpful discussion of all the participation texts in Paul gathered under various headings—"members of Christ's body," "in Christ" (here following Schweitzer), "Christ's," "servants of the Lord"—and also the "transfer terminology" referring to a believer's new status: "participation in the death of Christ," "freedom," "transformation"/"new creation," "reconciliation," "justification and righteousness."[22] He believes that Bultmann arranges such texts unhelpfully, hence dispersing the force of testimony that they build up—perhaps so that he could better manage the inassimilable strangeness of participation in Christ as the core of Paul's vision.[23] Notably, Sanders also takes Protestant tradition to task, and the modern-style individualism that supports Reformation trends toward making personal transgression and forgiveness the heart of Paul's gospel. Instead he reads all the key texts as really about participation—righteousness is not juridical, bogged down in what the individual does or does not do prior to faith, but it too is chiefly participatory.[24]

Consequently, Sanders brings us back to where Schweitzer left off, with his conclusion about the cultural strangeness of Paul's mysticism. He acknowledges Paul's conviction that "a *real* change was at work in the world and that Christians were participating in it." However, Sanders despairs of going any further. "Although it is difficult today to formulate a perceptual category which is not magic and is not self-understanding, we can at least assert that the realism of Paul's view indicates that he had one. To an appreciable degree, what Paul concretely thought cannot be directly appropriated by Christians today."[25]

While self-understanding may not grasp the extent of Paul's vision without remainder, nevertheless the fact that Paul constantly appeals to his hearers and recalls them to their best sense of themselves and their vocation indicates that self-understanding *is* involved. Paul's testimony is to something objective that God does, as we have seen, but also to something that does require decision, trust, and perseverance to remain part of it. Both Schweitzer and Bultmann write with a spiritual mission, testifying to if not exhausting a

---

objective dilemma of life under the law, and that Paul does not preach sin to awaken the need for grace (see *Theology of the New Testament*, vol. 1, 266), but he does nevertheless set out as an explicable theory what Sanders declares to be a surd-like mystery.

22. Sanders, *Paul and Palestinian Judaism*, 456–74.
23. Ibid., 453.
24. Ibid., 502–8.
25. Ibid., 523.

reality that is real enough, even if not entirely explicable. Can we perhaps do a little better at understanding Paul's mysticism today?

Paul's Mysticism: Breaking Down and Building Up

Two things strike me as providing important clues for understanding Paul's mysticism today. First, Paul's Gospel focuses on an event first and foremost rather than a theory or a structure of being: on Christ, and him crucified. In that sense Paul's apocalyptic message is intentionally antisystemic—it is disruptive of our desire for closure that leads anxiously to all false sacred meaning making and system building. Second, the mystical reality of new life in Christ is conveyed by Paul and his school using persuasive rhetoric, and is expressly intended to be established by pragmatic means based on apprenticeship and imitation. Here, René Girard helps us once again, showing how this new form of life takes hold.

Regarding the first of these points, we can get some of the way here by shifting our thinking from content and meaning to event and process. Catholic theologian David Tracy repositions the question, latching on to the dialectical method Paul uses to commend his vision.[26] In other words, he attends to the *performativity* of Paul's texts, with their topsy-turvy dialectic of cross and resurrection hammered out again and again upon the reader, until we grasp that strength is possible in weakness, and victory in defeat, with a new life established despite evidence that the old remains to tempt us. This shifts the discussion from how the text might be rationally grasped, or what it might point to beyond the horizon of our understanding, to how its disruptive dynamics can change us—that is, we are shifted from logic to rhetoric. The text becomes the vehicle of an objective reality taking subjective root.

There is a further dimension of this performativity. Apocalyptic texts serve to detach us from counter claims in the present. This is how they *work*. They do this by demolishing the structures whereby we allocate meaning, hence mentally ordering and so seeking to control our world. Paul's text does not offer us a new structure of meaning, nor even a self-understanding that can be unpacked in terms of a worldview. Rather, it offers us an *event*—Jesus Christ and him crucified. And, as the atheistic French philosopher Alain Badiou points out, in a heartfelt tribute to St. Paul, this is the first great instance of Western anti-philosophy. That is, Paul does not offer a new philosophy, understanding,

---

26. Tracy, *The Analogical Imagination*, 281–87.

worldview, or system of meaning but, rather, the end of all these as necessary means for humans to orient their lives.

The way Badiou expresses this calls to mind the false sacred Cosmopolis that I identified as modernity's favored version of the sacred, with its sociopolitical manifestations, structural exclusions, and violent effects. All systems of meaning are like this and, for Badiou, Paul puts them all on notice. This is what I was getting at earlier in the chapter, referring to mysticism as a deconstructive agency rather than a new body of knowledge (albeit one that is sourced from beyond the ordinary). In this vein, and referring to Galatians 6:14, Badiou writes, "'the world' that Paul declares has been crucified with Jesus is the Greek cosmos, the reassuring totality that allots places and orders thought to consent to those places, and that is consequently a question of letting in the vital rights of the infinite and the untotalizable event."[27] So rather than a new self-understanding, or an old Protestant theory of sin and atonement—let alone a mystery that Paul was privy to but we moderns cannot fathom—this is an event that dispenses with the ideal of closure.

But while this Christ event does not offer closure, it still reliably transforms our imagination. So faith in Christ and being found in him brings with it the end of our systemic captivity in the false sacred, which we recognize to be our characteristic human plight. This is the same as the law, for Paul, understood as a self-justifying system that makes us the in-group at the expense of an out-group. His great apostolic and pastoral challenge was to forge one Christian Church out of Jews and Gentiles, declaring the former Jewish insiders to be what they are thanks to God's grace, rather than because of any system (any "law") in which they might boast, and mark them out to be superior, while at the same time declaring uncircumcised Gentiles, formerly outsiders, to be insiders through the same grace (Gal 3:26—4:20; Rom 1–3). For Paul the event of the cross does away with all such systems that exclude. A different type of law—a "non-system system," if you like—is revealed in human affairs. The Jewish law is no different from any other system of human meaning in this respect. All of them are challenged by an event that reorients human attention and fascination. The new life in Christ draws us in while excluding no category of persons, revealing that we have been set free from every self-justifying, false sacred reality.

Now, how does that drawing in take place? This is the second issue I am raising here. Very important for me in conceiving this book as a whole, and this chapter in particular, has been the insight of American theologian Ellen

27. Badiou, *St. Paul*, 71.

T. Charry into the rhetorical and *pastoral* nature of Christian doctrine, beginning with St. Paul. It was this engrafting, spiritually and morally formative dimension of Christian proclamation that came adrift from mainstream theology, going underground in mysticism (more on this in the next section).

Paul worked on the renewal of his Christians' minds by reiterating the indicative and imperative, gift and task nature of participation in Christ, whereby we are always becoming what we already are in Christ. Meanwhile, from another perspective, Paul offers reassurance that the Spirit is at work in us enabling our transformation. There really is a changed self-understanding, but Charry pays more attention to the working-out of it—to how it is evoked and takes root—than Bultmann did, for whom the existential decision is registered but not analyzed.[28] And here is my point. The means by which this is worked out is through the apprenticeship of belonging to a worshipping community of disciples, and being formed in that context. Charry invokes Alasdair MacIntyre's influential emphasis on the importance of induction into the formative practices of a moral community for creating faithful adherents to a moral vision. This is a particular focus of second generation Pauline proclamation, in the letter to the Ephesians.

In a fine and sonorous declaration of Paul's Gospel in Ephesians 1 and 2, the community is exhorted to see itself as caught up in the new reality of Christ while, in Ephesians 3, Paul's own leadership by example is offered. Then there is the great "therefore" of Ephesians 4:1, moving from the indicative of God's gift of salvation to the imperative of Christian transformation in accord with Paul's authoritative vision. In this way the new self-understanding is given guidance so it can take root. The context of formation in accord with Paul's vision, in Ephesians 4, is through belonging together within the Church, understood to be a community enlivened by a complimentary multitude of gifts and committed to mutual, respectful up-building (Eph 4:11–16). The specter of the former life, lived "as the Gentiles live, in the futility of their minds" (Eph 4:17b), is set out in terms of hard, bitter, corrupt, and dissipated me-first arrogance and insensitivity, which is problematic not so much because it is morally wrong but because it is destructive of the community that God is calling and enabling Christians to be, in mature unity of spirit. Ephesians 5 continues in this vein, setting out further warnings about behavior that is destructive of the body, and the arrogant self-deception that points away from new life in Christ. Here the formative importance of worship is made clear, "as you sing psalms and hymns and spiritual songs among yourselves

28. Charry, *By the Renewing of Your Minds*, 35–60.

. . . giving thanks to God the Father at all times and for everything in the name of our Lord Jesus Christ" (Eph 5:19–20). The Christian monastic vision of a thankful (Eucharistic) communal life of shared giftedness and mature, other-regarding generosity has major roots here, recognizing that the mystical identity of participation in Christ is at the same time a form of life together that needs the right conditions if it is to be reinforced and take hold.

Then comes the Deutero-Pauline writer's version of a Greco-Roman household code (Eph 5:21—6:9), about husbands, wives, slaves etc, but with mutual loyalty in the Church setting the context for its moral vision: "Be subject to one another out of reverence for Christ" (v. 21). This is not *civitas* but *ecclesia*. Ephesians ends with explicit guidance about maintaining the vision by a set of spiritual practices, described as putting on the whole armor of God, which is at the same time an invitation to know that God establishes Christians in the strength of God's power—again, we see indicative and imperative woven fine. There is one final exhortation to prayer and a reiteration of the writer's example "in chains," and of his ongoing involvement from afar through Tychicus the intermediary (Eph 6:19–22).

Ellen Charry points out that individual struggle against the vices and temptations is not what Ephesians commends. "In sum," she concludes, "Ephesians is a work in pastoral theology for the church because it explicates the morally formative power of the work of God. It recognizes that while Christian excellence is theologically grounded, it is socially constructed and liturgically reinforced and is therefore a pastoral responsibility."[29] One could also find in Ephesians a template for the role of Episcopal ministry in building up a community of faith and holding it united and accountable, as well as the Christ-centered discipleship of monastic life in community.

One dimension Charry touches on that I want to develop concerns imitation. In chapter 3, above, the mimetic theory of desire taught by René Girard was introduced, with its *interdividual* understanding of human motivation. In a real sense, we inhabit the desires of others. And those desires lead to violence when rivalry builds up between us and the model, or mediator, of our desire. Girard teaches that this envy can escalate so that mass violence is only averted by everyone agreeing that someone is to blame, and scapegoating them. Girardian theory illuminates how human linguistic and social behavior is learned and how belonging to a community shapes its individual members. Role models not only inform our actions in the community but also construct who we *are*, because they give us our desires. Hence, wholesome role models,

---

29. Charry, *By the Renewing of Your Minds*, 50–57, here citing 54.

regularly commended to the young, turn out to be of absolutely foundational importance. We can actually be colonized by their desire.

So, in the context of realizing Paul's mystical vision in the Christian community, it is no surprise that imitation is relied upon. Ephesians, which we have just been considering, as a more fully worked-out Pauline vision of Christ's mind being formed in the Church, offers both God the Father and Jesus Christ as models for our desire. In entreating us to become a kind, tenderhearted, forgiving fellowship, rather than a bitter, politicized, malicious one, the Deutero-Pauline writer knows that this new existence depends on a reliable model of desire: "Therefore be imitators of God, as beloved children, and live in love, as Christ loved us and gave himself up for us" (Eph 5:1–2a). I have mentioned how (the by-then-no-doubt-legendary) Paul's own example is also commended by Ephesians.

But there is also plenty of this emphasis in Paul's own writings. His authentic letters begin with 1 Thessalonians, and we are immediately presented with the importance of imitation for learning and commending to others the faith that Paul and his co-workers exemplified in hardship: "And you became imitators of us and of the Lord, for in spite of persecution you received the word with joy inspired by the Holy Spirit, so that you became an example to all the believers in Macedonia and Achaia" (1 Thess 1:6–7). In Philippians 3:17, Paul commends both his own example and that of others in the community who in turn follow that example, going on to identify those other Christians whose wayward desires are not to be imitated. In a similar vein, Paul commends his own example to the Corinthian Christians for imitation along with the derivative example of Timothy, sent to them chiefly as a reliable role model after Paul's own example. Paul suggests that it is through such spiritual fatherhood that the "children" are established in Christ (1 Cor 4:15–18). Later in the same letter this message is as plain and simple as it can be: "Be imitators of me, as I am of Christ" (1 Cor 11:1). The greatest Pauline call to imitation I reserve to last. It is the Christ hymn of Philippians 2:5–11, commending the non-self-regarding humility of Christ, and it begins with a mimetic invitation: "Let the same mind be in you that was in Christ Jesus." We note, too, that mimesis, and the *interdividuality* that makes us the creatures of others' desires, is also clearly involved when Christians slip away from their participation in Christ—when they follow by imitation those wrongheaded Christians against whose example Paul is always warning them.

So the theory of mimesis and interdividuality gives us a new model for understanding the power that enables Christ to make all things subject to himself, changing the body of humiliation into the body of glory (Phil 3:21)—this capacity of Jesus and his saints to capture and reorient the desires of Christians. Paul may not have been a Girardian, but he certainly did seek to build and commend the new identity in Christ through a consciously formative pastoral and liturgical strategy, involving a mechanism that is more fully explicable according to Girardian mimetic theory than Bultmannian existentialism. This theory shows how a personal example—whether in sacred narrative, hagiography, apostolic leadership, or pastoral care—can capture our imagination so that we find our lives have been fundamentally reoriented. Thus we come to imitate Christ's desire, so that his life is formed in us, as ours is drawn into his.

In this section we have found in St. Paul and his school the powerful original vision of Christian life understood in mystical terms. It is about being drawn into the life of Christ out of enthrallment with the world, sin, and the law. If Sanders was right that this cannot be reduced to a shift in self-understanding, as Bultmann brilliantly tried to do, then neither need it be left entirely unexplained. Albert Schweitzer—the missionary doctor, scholar, and saint—knew the reality of being made a prisoner of Christ and his Kingdom even if he could not fully explicate it, rightly recognizing that it is manifest in a renewed spiritual and ethical life. I have tried to push further along in understanding Paul's mysticism. This vision makes as much sense for today's homeless hearts exposed to the voracious meaninglessness of consumer culture as it did when the culture of Greco-Roman fatalism fell before the power of Christ and his resurrection.

THE RISE AND FALL OF ABIDING FAITH

This final section of the chapter is about how this mystical, participatory understanding that I am calling abiding faith provides the most helpful way of talking about mainstream Christian faith and theology from the New Testament to the rise of nominalism after Aquinas. Faith used to be seen as an integral affair, while the foreglow of modernity from the late Middle Ages to modernity's dawn in the seventeenth century brought an increasing separation of heads from hearts from forms of life, hence spirituality from theology, and contemplation from action.

The Classical Mystical Understanding of Christianity

Earlier in this chapter, I mentioned the mystical roots of Western thought in Plato (429–347 BCE), whereby the knowing mind indwelt the known object and a kinship was thought to exist between the soul and the divine. In the pagan philosophy of Neo-Platonism, Plotinus (c. 205–270) taught the journey of the soul back to God through the inner ascent of contemplation, and an ecstasy enabling us to pass beyond self-consciousness. This developing Platonic tradition was adapted and transformed by the Church, becoming a "Christianized Platonism" of knowing God through being reconnected with God.

It was not the small-group elitism of Platonic mysticism that the Fathers took up, however, nor Plotinus's "flight of the alone to the alone," least of all the whole of Greek cosmology as a system of meaning (this, as Badiou pointed out, was exactly what St. Paul did not do). Rather, it was adapted in terms of the more communal understanding of salvation in the Church which we have found in the New Testament, along with the role of Scripture, Baptism, and Eucharist in bringing Christians to knowledge of God—right from the start, in fact, with what Andrew Louth in his study of mystical origins refers to as St. Paul's "fully ecclesial mysticism."[30] The initiative of God's grace was emphasized, too, following Philo (20 BCE—50CE)—antiquity's great Jewish assimilator of Hellenistic culture—who insisted over Plato that grace was the actual basis of the soul's kinship with God. The orthodoxy of the Nicene Creed and its understanding of God as creator of the world *ex nihilo* further undermined the idea of souls occupying what we might call a "naturally immortal" realm. With Athanasius (c. 298–373), the great champion of Nicene orthodoxy, Christ's descent in the incarnation became the means whereby God's image is restored in the Christian, rather than the soul's Platonic ascent back to God. And in Athanasius, Ellen Charry identifies the basic psychology of the Fathers. "Unlike in the modern view, our dignity is grounded not in that which individuates us from others or demonstrates our self-sufficiency but in that which links us to God by virtue of his grace. Human dignity is seen in our connectedness to God, not in our autonomy. What is required is that one understand the objective state of things correctly: who God is and who we are as a consequence of his love, power and respect for us."[31]

---

30. Louth, *The Origins of the Christian Mystical Tradition*, 197. I rely on Louth throughout this section.

31. Charry, *By the Renewing of Your Minds*, 90.

So theology and the spiritual life were woven fine in this period. Origen (185–254) introduced the influential purgative, illuminative, and contemplative triad into Christian thought, capturing the personally transformative dimension of all Christian knowledge of God. But neither Origen nor the Eastern mysticism which followed him understood the darkness of purgation to be any more than a stage on the way to an achievable vision of God.

Gregory of Nyssa (c. 335–395), on the other hand, saw the darkness of God that Philo had brought to Platonism as foundational and inescapable—God could not be unveiled by mystical ecstasy but only known through living out the life of Baptism, following Christ. This is the so-called apophatic tradition in Western spirituality, that reaches a high point in early modernity with a radical Carmelite vision from John of the Cross (more of this shortly). Very influentially, this brings to the Western Church a sense that God can be really known and participated in while not being fully comprehended—a state of affairs that was still the case for Thomas Aquinas, as discussed in chapter 2, above.

This was also true of Gregory's brother, Basil of Caesarea (c. 329–379), who emphasized the sanctifying role of the Holy Spirit for coming to know God, and the use of persuasive means. Again, rhetoric not logic keeps the doorway to faith. Basil linked the Trinitarian orthodoxy he was crafting with the revealing of God that comes to the baptized through Scripture, through the liturgy that he championed and through obedient Christian life. In this he offers the antithesis of rationalism and modern desires for closure and certainty, in favor once again of participatory knowing. Ellen Charry concludes in a compact sentence that "Basilian trinitarianism is a rhetor's episcopal exercise in pastoral theology."[32]

Western monasticism began with Benedict (c. 480–547) as the very practical business of life together in a formative liturgical community of mutual love and accountability. It was centered on scriptural reflection guided by allegorical method, so the Old and New Testaments served for individual and communal discernment. Scripture breathed at the heart of monastic life, and monastic theology spoke its language.[33] This trend, flowering in the meditative reading of *Lectio Divina*, set a more scriptural and earthy tone for Western monastic contemplation than that of the Eastern Church. Likewise, apophatic Western trends toward darkness and unknowing, also the barrier thrown up by human guilt, loomed always larger than in the East.

32. Ibid., 101–19, 118.
33. See LeClercq, *The Love of Learning and the Desire for God.*

Another difference between East and West emerged in Augustine (354–430), who retained from Plato the importance of feeling and longing in the quest for God—of *affect*. These emphases contributed a more affective dimension to Western spirituality than the more objective Eastern Church culture, according to which the self is not fulfilled within itself but drawn out of itself, as in the contemplation of icons. Neo-Platonic emphasis on the ecstasy of the soul moving towards union with God gives way to God's own incarnational and salvific ecstasy towards us in Jesus Christ, while the soul ascends to God not by its own ecstasy but by the patient renewal of the Trinitarian image within the soul by the work of the Holy Spirit. Critics who blame Augustine for many modern Western ills—being focused on the individual, for instance, and obsessed with sin and salvation—can miss his emphasis on coming to participate in the divine life, as Ellen Charry demonstrates.[34] So, once again, there is no separation between theology, scriptural interpretation, spirituality, and formative communal life in this vision.[35] "In the hands-on intellectual and moral training of the church, the love necessary to know God is excited and nourished," as Eric Springsted concludes, going on to describe faith for Augustine as "a habit of the heart and mind, not an ideology; it is a practice that is at its root a form of interpersonal activity."[36]

A different Neo-Platonic current influenced Pseudo-Dionysius (or Denys) the Areopagite (c. 500). His continuing use of the apophatic, divine darkness tradition was matched by a sense of God manifest through the whole world, undergirding its created hierarchies of being. While such a vision of divine order in the world was characteristic of Greek antiquity, for Dionysius the vision was confirmed and given content by the Bible's testimony and celebrated in the Church's liturgy. It was not a vision denying the mind, which remained at full stretch toward what he called the "dazzling darkness" of God's presence, though it was a vision that ensured knowledge of God was not available to the idle and uncommitted. Once again, this non-objective, self-involving, and transforming sense of knowing God is characteristic of pre-modern faith. There is a clear influence from Dionysius on Thomas Aquinas and his sense of the incomprehensible and transcendent God who nevertheless stands near to all of creation in supportive proximity. Unfortunately the intellectualism characteristic of this approach also produced the side effect of helping to keep Christian women subordinate. "Once the mystical path was

---

34. Charry, *By the Renewing of Your Minds*, 120–28.
35. Jantzen, *Power, Gender and Christian Mysticism*, 80.
36. Springsted, *The Act of Faith*, 132–33.

delimited in the way Dionysius had done," Grace Jantzen observes, "there would not be many women who *could* walk it."[37]

The affective tradition of mysticism from Augustine influenced Bernard of Clairvaux (1090–1153)—the great Cistercian exponent of the Song of Songs—and, notably here, it appealed to a range of medieval women spiritual writers whose imagery was more embodied and hence more genuinely erotic than that of Bernard. Francis of Assisi (c. 1181–1226) also demonstrated a more embodied "mysticism of love." This served as something of a corrective to the more intellectualizing mystical trends leading from Dionysius to Meister Eckhart (c. 1260–1328).[38] The later individualizing and de-cosmicizing of Dionysius's vision in the West contributed to our modern Western sense that the mystical was somehow different from the Biblical and the liturgical.[39] This was one of a number of features that combined in the late Middle Ages to undo the mystical synthesis that had persisted from the New Testament through the Patristic era.

Abiding Faith Goes into Exile

The exile of abiding faith from Western theology and institutional Church life is intimately related to this developing sense of mysticism as a separate category. It is helpful to think of this development in terms of three historical moments. First, mysticism became a distinctive spiritual genre from the fourteenth and fifteenth centuries, with the break-up of more integral, participatory abiding faith into rational theology and affective spirituality, while the Church was transformed by a rising mood of individualism and authoritarianism. Second, *mysticism* came to name subversive and sometimes irrational currents in the sixteenth and seventeenth centuries. This mysticism involved prophetic testimony from the dark place of God's absence, against the breakdown of pre-modern social and religious structures, and the imaginative sense of God's alienation from the world that prompted the erection of modernity's Cosmopolis. Finally, in the nineteenth century, mysticism was defined in terms that remain more or less current—as the individualistic, emotivist antitype to dogmatic theology and institutional religion. For the modern Western Christian, mysticism is a reminder that feeling formed a crucial part of abiding faith, though we must not forget the real-albeit-contained

---

37. Jantzen, *Power, Gender and Christian Mysticism*, 95–109, 109.
38. Ibid., 123–46.
39. Louth, *The Origins of the Christian Mystical Tradition*, 206–7.

commitment of abiding faith to rationality, also the often uncomfortable expectation of personal transformation that abiding faith involved, along with its necessary embedding in Church and sacrament. Let me take these three moments in turn, from the fourteenth to the seventeenth to the nineteenth century, and hence to today, as mysticism in its various forms served at best as an echo of abiding faith.

First, the fourteenth century and the break up of organic, participatory faith. In chapter 2, above, I discussed the rise of nominalism and a series of changes in Church and society undermining the holistic sense of God interpenetrating our world that Aquinas had retained from Christian antiquity. This spiritual vision of life in which a transcendent but deeply involved God underpinned an imaginatively unified cosmos gave way before a rising tide of individualism, rationalism and authoritarianism, with secular and religious realms beginning the great divorce that characterizes Western modernity.

The separation of reason from feeling played a part. From Platonic roots in a yearning love for the good, the true, and the beautiful, through the integral vision of Augustine in which reason and affect both informed the transformative process of religious knowing, on to the twelfth-century monastic reformer Bernard of Clairvaux, whose mystical vision was highly affective but retained the scriptural focus and language that had marked monastic tradition from antiquity, feeling was known to be crucial for faith, though always in tandem with faith's other dimensions. The Franciscan tradition, however, opted for love, affect, and embodiment but left the intellectual dimension of faith to philosophy. Consequently, knowledge of God through love alone detached itself from reason, and a mysticism of love and feeling grew up alongside the official theology that was condemned to an increasingly rationalistic isolation. This trend opened a divide between rational skepticism and Romantic pietism that remains in the modern West.

Bonaventure (1221–1274), the great Franciscan theologian, was a major figure in shifting knowledge of God to the realm of love and feeling, while the mysticism of Richard Rolle (c. 1290–1349) represents a high point in this affective turn.[40] The mood is also linked by Grace Jantzen to female mystics—two Beguines, Mechtild of Magdeburg (c. 1207–1282) and Hadewijch of Antwerp (thirteenth century), as well as Julian of Norwich (1342–c. 1416)—who took affect much further in the direction of genuine embodiedness and eroticism than Bernard did, who remained very cerebral in

40. See, e.g., McIntosh, *Mystical* Theology, 72–75, tracing this theme in Rolle. This is a fine book on the whole area covered by this section.

his exposition of the Song of Songs.[41] Denys the Carthusian (1402–1471) is identified as a bridging figure—he knew the bifurcation was happening, and consciously made something of a last-ditch effort to hold reason and affect together in his presentation of the Christian faith.[42]

One mark of this divergence was the shift of theology from the institutional Church into the universities and away from the monastic pursuit of holiness. Monastic theology, which had been pre-eminently scriptural, liturgical, and discipleship-oriented in community, diverged from scholastic theology, which thrived in the new environment of logic, commerce, great and hugely popular centers of learning committed to disseminating the recovered wisdom of Aristotle, and ecclesial centralization of power. Most theologians in antiquity were either bishops, saints or both, which almost entirely ceased to be the case from this turn in the fourteenth century. There can be no clearer sign of abiding faith breaking apart. Consequently theology and the pursuit of holiness have drifted apart, as Hans Urs von Balthasar laments, leaving the legacy of a dry and disconnected theology unfit for guiding the people of God in faith, and a theologically ungrounded pietism inadequate for forming spiritual maturity.[43] He acknowledges great mystical writers who held the more unified position of antiquity, but their position was uneasy as the Church took on the institutionally controlling mood of modernity.

And here is the other key dimension of this medieval shift—the role of control, system, and exclusion. In chapter 2, I mentioned a range of social transformations ushering in a new era of individualism, absolutism in power, and the subordination of natural communities to that new ideological invention, the sovereign nation state. In the medieval Church, a systemic approach to truth began to emerge as the prequel to early modernity's more extensive Cosmopolis. I have already mentioned the increasingly rationalistic syllabus of university theology. There was also the shift toward clericalism and papal infallibility. The liturgy became more of an authoritarian tableaux than a drama involving the people of God—think of the priestly sacrificial spectacle of a non-communicating medieval mass. All these dimensions came together in the building of St. Peter's Basilica in Rome, which so offended Luther at the time, and remains in our own media age as a vast theatre for staging liturgies of papal power, to be beamed worldwide at Easter and Christmas. The medieval transformation of laypeople from participants to spectators, and

---

41. Jantzen, *Power, Gender and Christian Mysticism*, 133–56.
42. Turner, *The Darkness of God*, 210–25.
43. Von Balthasar, "Theology and Sanctity."

hence the decline of liturgy's ancient formative role, led to the rise of private devotions, such as saying the Rosary at mass. This heightened the individualizing, privatizing, and de-ecclesialising of spirituality, all at the expense of abiding faith.

The Reformation declared this late-medieval Church to be a false sacred reality, claiming a lay independence that unfortunately often mirrors the controlling hubris of the clerical Church that it opposed. Another sure sign of the false sacred at work is the creation of outcasts, which the mystics regularly were. For men, it was a position outside the ecclesial mainstream. For women, as Grace Jantzen argues, the mystical was an outlet for unauthorized religious creativity, since biblical exposition and scholastic theology were reserved for men. Its price for women, however, was religious enclosure.[44] Apart from which there was some danger, evident in the execution of Beguine writer Marguerite Porete (d. 1310) for a text that posterity did not judge to be heretical.[45] Likewise, the great Carmelite reformers Teresa of Avila (1515–1582) and John of the Cross (1542–1591) both suffered at the hands of the institutional Church.[46] John carried the apophaticism of Gregory of Nyssa to its most radical extreme, resisting both the extreme rationalism of Spanish theological scholasticism (he was a contemporary of Suarez) and ecclesial authoritarianism with the passivity and near-quietism of his spiritual writing.

With Teresa and John of the Cross we move on from the first, medieval moment in the retreat from abiding faith to the eve of European Enlightenment, and the *second* phase of abiding faith's exile, with mysticism emerging as a transgressive category in uneasy partnership with the dawning modern Cosmopolis. The late French Jesuit and consummate historian of ideas Michel de Certeau is an expert guide into this strange territory, identifying "the tensions and innovations that, like a barrier reef, raise the mystic wave as it nears the land on which it will break."[47]

Certeau acknowledges the emerging transgressive role for mysticism in the Middle Ages that we have considered, when ecclesial structures and habits of authority assumed more organized features and faith became more rationally systematized. At that time, mysticism began to take on the role of "other" that every controlling system needs. In the sixteenth and seventeenth centuries, however, mysticism also became the voice of those who had been

44. Jantzen, *Power, Gender and Christian Mysticism*, 193–241.
45. Ibid., 259–64.
46. Louth, *The Origins of the Christian Mystical Tradition*, 210.
47. Certeau, *The Mystic Fable*, 10.

historically disinherited by the rise of modernity, socio-economic changes and war, as a kind of Utopian reaction from the underside of history. A second dimension registered the loss of Catholic Church authority thanks to the Reformation, and the rise of modern rational doubt. Mystics therefore, in Certeau's memorable phrase, "lived the decomposition of a cosmos and were exiled from it."[48] As for the new mood of control and standardization in the Roman Church following the Council of Trent (1545–1563), as the modern Cosmopolis started to show itself, Certeau wryly comments that these mystic exiles were "filled with mourning unmitigated by the rapture of new ambition."[49]

In particular, Certeau emphasizes the intentionally transgressive, deconstructive purpose of mysticism in this period. This prompts comparison with the possessed nuns of Loudun, who I discussed in chapter 3. That episode was the outward expression of deeply felt social trauma and spiritual disorientation during the Thirty-Years War when many old certainties were collapsing and the modern Cosmopolis was in its infancy. The nuns' possession was carefully contained, stage-managed, and promoted for effect by the Church, at a time when Rome was intent on re-establishing its authority. Other contemporary occasions of possession were firmly suppressed, but this one was turned to advantage.[50] Mysticism too was repressed. And in this repression the proper supremacy of rational theology and ecclesial authority was confirmed, in coming to dominate "the other" it had helped construct and which it relied upon for its self-definition.[51]

Certeau points to various outbreaks of Christian unreason, linking them to similar occurrences from early Christian monasticism which protested the worldliness of a newly Christianized Roman Empire. He identifies various figures of the wild man in early modern European society with this disappointed, transgressive manifestation of mysticism, representing "the silhouette of untamed desire, now cruel, now seductive, issuing forth from the forests to haunt the marketplaces and homes, while a fledgling bourgeoisie learns the asceticism of a productive rationality."[52] He includes various ill-fitting religious reformers, like Jan Hus and Martin Luther. From his own Jesuit tradition Certeau adds "the little saints of Aquitaine" expelled from the

48. Ibid., 25.
49. Ibid.
50. See Certeau, *The Possession at Loudun*; cf. Certeau, *The Mystic Fable*, 87.
51. Certeau, *The Mystic Fable*, 17, 26.
52. Ibid., 205.

Society of Jesus. He also discusses a dubious Jesuit gyrovague called Labadie the Nomad, whose restless symbolic journey into Europe's deep North, bringing him eventually to rest in Denmark as a Calvinist, represented a perpetual flight from ecclesial structures and norms of belief in which he simply could not compose himself.[53] For Certeau the mystics in this period, like the fantastic creatures of Hieronymus Bosch's painting from 1503–4, "The Garden of Earthly Delights," enacted the break up of an ordered worldview.[54] Mysticism thus became the *Samizdat* literature of anti-systemic Christianity—a volatilization of meaning lamenting the loss of a more abiding faith.

The *third* moment in this account of Christianity's inability to articulate the fullness of abiding faith comes with the eventual cementing of mysticism as one version of modernity's "other" in the nineteenth century. The definitive split between things in themselves and our perception of them that Immanuel Kant had effected in his *Critique of Pure Reason* (1781), entailing God's separation from the realm of knowledge altogether and consignment to the background of ethics—of "practical reason"—opened a new path to religious knowing. With Friedrich Wilhelm Schelling (1775–1854) and the Romantic movement, feeling and emotion came to be celebrated as an authentically independent means of knowing, so that mystics joined the Romantic retinue of gifted spiritual individuals who had direct access to the sublime, apart from reason or the habituated disciplines of Christian life in the Church. So, although modernity had cut-off the path of reliable rational access to God, modern empiricism in Romantic mood replied by annexing mysticism to provide a new means to "prove" God. Mysticism became a kind of sixth sense. As Mark McIntosh memorably puts it, "language for talking about the indescribable wonder of God . . . becomes the language of having a wonderfully indescribable experience of God."[55]

The rational and the affective together, embraced in the formative habits of a worshipping, mutually accountable community, was the abiding faith of classical Christianity. "The mystical" simply referred to the embedded Christian participant undergoing transformation of life, mediated by the

---

53. Ibid., chapters 8 and 9, 241–93. A *gyrovague* was the worst sort of monk, according to the Rule of St. Benedict—a wandering troublemaker who could never settle to the mature monastic stability of life in one community. Certeau, an apparent lover of wandering, seems to think that Labadie's disappointments were sufficient justification for his long search for a Church he could belong to. I have my doubts.

54. Ibid., 49–72. Bosch's picture is in Madrid, at the Prado.

55. McIntosh, *Mystical Theology*, 68.

Baptism and Eucharist that joined them to Christ and his new creation. It involved a theological understanding of the intellect in *ek-stasis*, stretched beyond itself and the myth of exhaustive reason, but it was not the abandonment of reason for ecstatic private feeling. It was also by no means centered on the individual self and its interiority, let alone its emotional experiences. Yet this is what mysticism became. The deformation that this entails is explored profoundly by Denys Turner, who identifies an "anti-mystical" reaction to this trend as early as the fourteenth-century in the apophatic English classic *The Cloud of Unknowing* and in Meister Eckhart. Turner is worth quoting at length. He explains how the apophatic tradition deconstructs increasingly sovereign religious selves whereas experientialism seeks to re-establish them.

> Hence, the deformations of the 'experientialist' derive from the mistake of reinterpreting as a first-order practice *of* Christian piety that which is the second-order dialectic practiced upon and *within* that piety; from the error of understanding that which is a 'moment' of reserve, of denial and unknowing within worship, prayer and sacrament as if it were a rival practice which displaces that Christian ordinariness. 'Experientialism' in its most extreme forms is therefore the displacement of a sense of the negativity of all religious experience with the pursuit of some goal of achieving *negative experiences*. Experientialism is, in short, the 'positivism' of Christian spirituality. It abhors the experiential vacuum of the apophatic, rushing to fill it with the plenum of the psychologistic. It resists the deconstructions of the negative way . . . It is happy with commendations of the 'interior' so long as it can cash them out in the currency of experienced inwardness and of the practices of prayer which will achieve it.[56]

This turn to experientialism, however, is now largely unquestioned in the West. William James made mysticism a style of personal religion, while in Evelyn Underhill an undifferentiated tradition of mystical experiences emerged (though she later became suspicious of this reifying definition).[57] Mysticism according to this modern, psychologistic definition was subse-

---

56. Turner, *The Darkness of God*, 252–73, here citing 259.
57. Jantzen, *Power, Gender and Christian Mysticism*, 304–21. The James reference is to *The Varieties of Religious Experience*. The Underhill reference is to *The Mystic Way*, in which she defines mysticism as "a sequence of psychological states," viii. See also her classic work, *Mysticism*. Underhill's doubts about mysticism as an experiential category emerged in her "Preface" to its 12th ed, of 1930, viii (see Jantzen, *Power, Gender and Christian Mysticism*, 317).

quently imposed on figures from the past for whom "the mystical" would have referred to something else entirely. Indeed, thanks to the modern study of religion, mysticism was decoupled from Christianity altogether and became the ineffable experience to which certain people of all religions and none are prone, according to the writings of R. C. Zaehner and others.[58] This is how I first encountered mysticism—in a first-year studies in religion course at a secular university, presented as a psychological curiosity. Andrew Louth reminds us, however, that "what we find in the Fathers undermines any tendency towards seeing mysticism as an elite, individualist quest for 'peak' experiences; rather for them the 'mystical life' is the 'life with Christ hid in God' of Colossians 3.3, a life which is ecclesial, that is lived in the Body of Christ, which is nourished liturgically, and which is certainly a matter of experience, though not of extraordinary 'experiences.'"[59]

Grace Jantzen speculates about what Michel Foucault would make of this trend toward private experientialism. What power interests would be served by constructing a mystical tradition along these lines? The answer is that in making mysticism a private retreat from public meaningfulness, the controlling rationality further establishes itself by ensuring that yet another voice of potentially deconstructive otherness is sidelined and silenced.[60] And secular Western culture is not the only beneficiary, with yet another religious impulse more firmly privatized. There are advantages here for fostering easy, comfortable Christianity, too. The dimension of repentance and transformation that has characterized Christian faith from St. Paul onwards will always be uncomfortable, misunderstood, and unpopular. Who nowadays wants a "mysticism" that has to be worked out through organic relationships, word and sacrament in the Church, straining at the apophatic edge of meaning where we are called beyond reason and the carefully-cultivated self toward the annihilation of all such human categories in the fullness of God? In particular, there is absolutely no room whatsoever in today's "positive," popular, "relevant" Christianity for the apophatic—for the dark night that John of the Cross proclaimed. Indeed, Rowan Williams traces this denial of the apophatic right back to the rise of nominalism, where the emptying and displacement of the self in response to God's self-emptying ceased to be the heart of a unified

---

58. See e.g., Zaehner, *Mysticism, Sacred and Profane*. His link between spirituality and drug taking became a theme of 1960s spiritual writing and practice.

59. Louth, *The Origins of the Christian Mystical Tradition*, 213.

60. Jantzen, *Power, Gender and Christian Mysticism*, 326–27, cf. 345–46.

theological-spiritual vision.[61] In its place, something less integrated than abiding faith, though offering far more superficial reassurance.

TO CONCLUDE

In this chapter I have defined abiding faith as integral Christian belonging that is rational but not rationalistic, inseparable from the experience of Christian life but not purely experiential, affective but not necessarily emotional, self-involving and self-transforming but not centered on the self, and entirely ecclesial and sacramental though with more spark than the typically dry formalism of modern "organized religion" normally delivers. We noted its beginnings in the trust, discernment, and waiting of Old Testament faith, and its fulfillment for Christians when they come to dwell in Jesus Christ, as St. Paul classically testifies. The means of this transformation were explored in Paul's authentic writings and in Ephesians, with an account of its objective givenness and subjective appropriation sought in René Girard's theory of how we live in the desires of others. This was thought to provide a deeper understanding than Rudolf Bultmann's existentialist reading of Paul in terms of changed self-understanding.

Such abiding faith was then identified as the comprehensive totality of faith according to Patristic witnesses in East and West. Yet this comprehensive mystery of faith proved impossible to sustain as the Western Church's mainstream understanding of faith from the fourteenth century when new theological, ecclesial, and social trends threatened the imaginative bond between Christians, the sacramental Church, and God.

Sometimes mysticism managed to sustain an underground version of abiding faith. Sometimes it preserved the affective dimension. Sometimes it rendered apophatic witness in the face of pre-modern confusion and unease or else early-modern cultural arrogance by providing a voice of protest—often an intentionally transgressive one. More recently the breakdown of abiding faith as a culturally meaningful category for life with God has become complete. Emotional experience, in the service of modern categories of knowing, now provides a newfound "mystical" way to God, while a dry rationalism fuels what (in chapter 1, above) I called the *atheist-chic* of cultural elites. Spirituality nowadays drifts independently of theology and far away from Church. Consolation and self-realization replace the self-giving and self-loss of abiding faith. Yet the real thing has never fully gone away. Let me give some examples.

---

61. Williams, *The Wound of Knowledge*, 116–37, here citing 137.

Despite the forensic rationalism that has come to dominate conservative Protestantism, also its chronic spiritual individualism and its obsession with sin and guilt, Martin Luther (1483–1546) can now be read in line with what I am calling abiding faith. In the Finnish Lutheran context of dialogue with the prominent Finnish Orthodox Church, a new theological movement centered on the University of Helsinki is excited to be reading Luther as a mystic. It turns out that his gospel is one of union with Christ, when freed from the spirit of Kantian detachment that has dominated Luther studies.[62]

My own Anglican tradition always resisted totalizing accounts of faith in favor of retaining the ancient synergy between belief and worship, defining Church authority in terms of the pastoral nurture of Christian life, and tying personal spirituality to common prayer. Anglicanism also strives to retain the participatory mutuality of Catholic Church order at its healthiest, without the authoritarianism in dogma and institutional life that the Roman version of Catholicism has struggled with throughout modernity and especially since Vatican II. Rationalizing, controlling voices are now threatening to take us in another direction, while an individualistic liberalism relegates many Western Anglicans to a religion of therapeutic consumption rather than sacramental transformation. Still, the Anglo-Catholic push, to which I adhere, respects the high dignity of sacramental worship and reveres the beauty of holiness, retaining doctrinal allegiance to the participatory vision of Christian faith according to the Fathers that is prominent throughout the foundational writings and projects of John Keble, John Henry Newman, Edward Bouverie Pusey, John Mason Neale, and other early Tractarian luminaries of the movement.[63]

Both Anglicanism and the Roman Church are also recovering a sense of liturgical, sacramental abiding in the Gospel thanks to the twentieth-century Liturgical Movement, which has made us more consciously aware of liturgy's objectively foundational importance along with its role in Christian formation. It has strengthened our fellowship with the early Church through our reacquiring of their liturgies in modern form, while helping us show the modern world an integral vision of belief, worship, and the community of disciples through the designs of modern church buildings. I would like to think that a good modern liturgy in a catholic-minded Anglican cathedral or major church near the heart of any large city of the Western world on

62. Braaten and Jenson, *Union with Christ*.
63. See an excellent discussion of what I am calling abiding faith at the heart of the Anglo-Catholic vision, evident in these writers and others, in Rowell, *The Vision Glorious*.

any Sunday morning will show in word, song, preaching, and sacrament the reality of abiding faith, even if many of the participants are prevented by an unreconstructed modern mindset from understanding or acknowledging it.

In mainstream Western theology, abiding faith is back in the legacy of Karl Barth (1886–1968), especially among post-liberals like Stanley Hauerwas with his critique of Western individualism in the name of ecclesial abiding, liturgical worship, and the necessary role of personal transformation in theological understanding. The critical shake-up that liberation theology, feminist, and post-colonial theologies are bringing restores the link between faith, belief, and transforming worship—also the inseparability of Christ from the demands of his Kingdom that Albert Schweitzer discerned in Paul, and emphasized in both thought and life. These movements also deconstruct the controlling rationality of modernity, showing its feet of clay, and in that sense they recover the supple, non-controlling rationality of abiding faith.

In the final chapter, I will be attempting to describe an abiding faith for the post-modern West. For now, in chapter 5, I want to explore how abiding faith stands up against modern Western categories of meaningfulness. It is not the case that abiding faith means a retreat into emotional subjectivity, as if the godly vocation of an integrated Christian reason petered out in the fourteenth century. The critical mind can still come to dwell in the loving heart to serve a humble and obedient will without Christians thinking that this ancient synthesis makes them intellectual lightweights or cognitive deviants.

5

Faith's Knowledge
Abiding Faith and Modern Doubt

I have been presenting abiding faith as the characteristic form of Christian belonging and believing since the beginning—from St. Paul and the Fathers through to the Middle Ages, whereupon a less integral version of Christian reason began to detach believing from inhabiting a form of life. This version of rationality has made it hard for abiding faith to make rational sense in the modern world.

Religious skeptics regularly deploy a narrow and aggressive understanding of reason to demolish claims for faith. Some believers respond in kind, seeking to outdo their critics by banishing any insufficiently hard-headed form of knowing from their defense of faith, in various forms of rationalistically-minded apologetics. In their desire for the certainty which modernity and its system has provided for religious skeptics, these rationalistic believers become what René Girard would call mimetic doubles of the unbelieving hardheads who oppose them. Or else believers abandon the rationalistic justification of faith for more subjectively based versions in the spirit of the Romantic Movement, including those who opt for out-and-out experientialism. But this, too, represents modernity at work, over-reacting against the narrowing and totalizing of reason's otherwise proper claims that are characteristic of rationalism, and overloading human subjectivity with the burden of proof.

In this chapter I want to show how we can move beyond these standard versions of faith-under-the-spell-of-modernity, to reclaim the fuller form of knowing that abiding faith entails. And, interestingly, the spirit of the times can help us. From the second half of the twentieth century it has been easier to situate abiding faith in the thought world of philosophy and the sciences. The modern myth of rational closure has been punctured by reflection on how we actually know things, from philosophy of literature to softer accounts of science to post-modern reflections on culture and meaning as diverse human creations. So today it is necessary to acknowledge the role of emotion in rational decision-making, and imagination in scientific theorizing, and any number of tacit assumptions as the precondition for reasonable action. Reason and intuition, objectivity and subjectivity, theory and practical wisdom are recovering the synergy that linked them in antiquity, but which came apart under modernity's drive to rational closure. We are learning that it is no longer rational to think that way. Abiding faith emerges as rational but not rationalistic, and experiential without isolation in subjectivity. It is holistic, participatory, and imaginatively satisfying, or it is not faith in Jesus Christ. It is certainly not a rigid system of meaning and a straitjacket of obedience, however, because that would not be faith in Jesus Christ either (more of this in the final chapter).

THE SCOPE OF ABIDING FAITH

Let me set the scene for this section by identifying some dimensions of abiding faith that need to be accounted for, especially the way it grasps and realigns the mind by a variety of means in religious conversion and the life of faith—though typically involving transforming encounters with the risen Jesus Christ, in which exposure to the Christian form of life is the mediator. I will be drawing on two English bishops whose writings help illuminate the nature of faith, and a landmark Australian short story about abiding faith and conversion. I will then offer some reflections, mostly Girardian, to help unpack the nature of faith emerging from these sources.

We begin with a thoughtful and comprehensive account of his faith by an English theologian and bishop, David Jenkins, teased out into seven strands. Significantly, he does not offer an overly neat formula, consciously resisting the simplistic yet determinedly rationalistic propositionalism of the fundamentalists—the "certainty-wallahs"—who opposed him during his controversial tenure as Bishop of Durham (recall the mention of this in chapter 1). Yet neither does he emerge as the liberal relativist that these critics claimed. Instead, Bishop Jenkins gives as good and clear a sense of what constitutes the abiding faith of a serious modern Christian practitioner (albeit a theologically sophisticated one) as you would get anywhere.

First there were experiences of two complimentary faith communities for Jenkins the schoolboy—a Crusaders group characterized by warm Evangelical fellowship, with a Bible study exploring and commending the life of faith, but also Anglo-Catholic influence at a harvest camp in wartime where the mysteries of the Eucharist were opened up for him by a devout and enthusiastic young curate.

Second—and here Jenkins struggles to capture a vision that took hold of him in his youth—a sense of "universalizability" grasped him, as he began to appreciate the Christian account of God's Trinitarian being and God's purposes of love focused in Christ, at the same time that he found himself beginning to inhabit a life of love, purpose, and hope.

Third, Jenkins mentions decades of encountering lively Christians from around the world who continually convinced him that God was a going concern and very much involved in the day-to-day events of people's lives. In particular he remembers a leisurely day of ecumenical discussion in Indonesia where he first sensed the basic unity of Christian faith around the world, and found a confidence about God's hand guiding the Church and its mission—a confidence that sustained him during his subsequent anxieties as a leader of institutional Christianity.

Fourth, there is Jenkins's brief and restrained mention of fifty-three years married to a woman whose faith continually impressed him, and everything that life together with their four children had meant, in a passage marked by profound gratitude.

Fifth, he makes joint mention of participation in worship and in theological work, under the category of "enlargement." Both have opened for him a sense that faith is something unsearchably full and rich that continues to reveal new aspects and depths.

Sixth, Jenkins refers to a range of personal experiences in prayer, liturgy, and life that seem to evoke a coherent reality. These he admits will not convince anyone else, but they have meant everything to him. None of it is spectacular—just the sense of being taken up into a praying beyond his own in the liturgy, which is Christ-specific, but also less-focused moments of wonder and stillness. Jenkins recalls one memorable occasion, on a walk in the wooded grounds of his official residence at Auckland Castle during a particularly stressful period of public controversy, when, to his surprise as a modern rationally-minded theologian, he found himself caught up in a moment of unearthly radiance in the midst of a field of violets, during which he heard a cuckoo—the very thing Prime Minister Margaret Thatcher had criticized him for being when he opposed her hard-line policies during the miners' strike. This brief experience left Jenkins feeling worshipful, elated, and liberated (he does not draw the conclusion that if this experience came from God, then God was having a joke at the expense of Margaret Thatcher).

Seventh, he mentions a lifelong journey of growing into the Bible itself as a mystery of revelation, and the sustained habit of Bible reading and reflection as binding together the whole seven-fold cord of faith.[1]

What do we notice here? There is certainly the sense that a rational conviction has emerged and deepened over time, which is diverse in its elements and cumulative in its effect. The role of Christian witnesses (and their diversity), of participation in the Church's life, of Scripture and doctrine, prayer and worship, also religious experience and broader life experience, including periods of stress and challenge, have all been grist for the mill, with no single aspect proving dispensable. Yet even for a theologian and bishop the account, while articulate, is also hesitant and falls well short of closure, with a reserve evident in the presentation that is significant. This is not a reality Jenkins possesses in the sense of controlling it, yet he is caught up in it and at home in it. I notice especially that Jenkins seems theologically uncomfortable with the personally-focused presence and action of God that is implied by his account, but he does not resile from it because the logic of his life-narrative seems to require it. Jenkins seems to have found his personal meaning through this journey of faith, and he receives it as a gift, yet this sense of meaning is also challenged, refined, and deepened.

I am struck by the abiding faith nature of Jenkins's life and witness. This is the account of an individual coming to himself within a form of life mediated by a community, its sacred texts, beliefs, and practices, though the realities it evokes are clearly not confined to those structures. The logic of the whole account points through and beyond the form of life, even though none of this is accessible apart from that form of life. As for belief in the claims of Christianity according to this account, it arises, takes form and expands as the more-encompassing reality of faith takes hold in Jenkins's life, while at every stage his belief also shapes and interprets the faith that emerges. This warns us about imagining faith too simply as a superstructure built on belief, though the faith sketched out here is also plainly inseparable from belief.

---

1. Jenkins, *The Calling of a Cuckoo*, 157–68.

Conversion

When we consider how people come to faith, there are strong resonances with what we see in David Jenkins's personal account of what it is like to live and grow in faith. Another English bishop, John Finney, provides a helpful study. It is surprising how non-theoretical a typical adult journey to faith can be. The widespread Evangelical understanding that begins with the acceptance of Christian belief, whereupon one joins the Church and faith becomes a form of life, is by no means typical. Rather, belonging regularly precedes believing, with Christian friends, time spent in faith communities among believers and their practices and, in particular, the ministry of influential clergy all proving decisive. Forming new and firmer beliefs is of course involved, but typically they cohere around changed images of God and a more mature grasp of what faith entails. Hence, for instance, God becomes more personal and the challenges of life, such as suffering, become more integrated into the life of faith, while at the personal level converts regularly testify to heightened self-worth and assurance. Significant theological doubt is not widespread, though Finney identifies regular low-level doubt (e.g. about taking the Adam and Eve story literally) that does not threaten to undermine faith. The sense throughout is of a reality being experienced that is plainly linked to the narrative and practice of faith in the Church, around which the imagination and the self are being reconfigured.[2]

Let me give an extended example, in a compelling but harrowing account of conversion to Christian faith by one of Australia's leading fiction writers. Tim Winton sets his short story "The Turning" in the caravan (i.e. trailer) park of a remote fishing town "down South" in Western Australia. There we meet working-class mother Raelene. Her partner, Max, is going nowhere as a deckhand in the fishing business and spends his days ashore drunk, stoned, and running to fat, also regularly venting his knife-edge temper on Rae. She wants to escape but lacks options, and even the mental categories that would allow her to imagine a different, fuller life. Until she meets Dan and Sherry—a good-looking, educated, practicing Christian couple who move into town. They are well up the social ladder from Raelene and Max, as Dan is the owner and skipper of his own fishing boat. This makes their interest in Raelene all the more surprising to her.

Despite Rae's cynical suspicion that they might be closet weirdos, Dan and Sherry prove to be thoughtful, genuine, and remarkably patient with Rae's

2. See Finney, *Finding Faith Today*, especially chap. 9, "Is There a Change?" 73–92.

increasing presence in their home and their lives. Rae finds herself drawn to whatever it is that her new friends have, but which she plainly lacks. Dan and Sherry even study the Bible together, including Rae in conversation about human nature, eternal life, and ethics, all discussed very naturally. She finds herself warming to the figure of Jesus as he emerges from these conversations, even though the idea of sacrifice gives her goose bumps and a lot of Bible stories do not make sense.

Yet these stories are obviously working their way into her unconscious, and Rae finds her imaginative life beginning to register an effect. Walking home along the darkened beach on a moonless, cloudy night, Rae has a religious experience. It synthesizes a heightened sense of nature, her own life story, and her growing imaginative connection with the narrative and symbolism of the Bible, also giving symbolic expression to her inchoate yearnings.

> Rae found herself walking with her hands outstretched, overcome by the apprehension that she was about to stumble on something on the smooth, empty beach. She became breathless, panicky and just as she started muttering aloud, talking herself down from the queer spin she was getting herself into, a patch of stars opened up low in the sky ahead of her and stopped her in her tracks. At first she thought of a shimmering bit of cloth, like a piece of the dress her mother once got from a bloke she almost married, but the image didn't last because she went on to thinking of candles and lamps and campfires and she felt woozy for a moment as if she was in the clouds herself and looking down through the gaps to see the fires of a thousand desert camps. There were lights impossible to count and around them, in her mind's eye, people huddled, all of them searching like herself. Afraid, wondering, looking into their fires, with the sky a blank over them. She didn't know why she thought of deserts and campfires except for the reading she'd been doing, all those name-strangled stories from the Old Testament had left her cold.[3]

Later, in bed, Rae remembers a remote happy childhood time with families night fishing, and beach campfires, and the dim memory of her father singing, all somehow tied up in the pain of her life today, and the Bible. Rae's psychological processing had yielded what might popularly be called a mystical experience, but this was really the deep inner work of a form of life

---

3. Winton, "The Turning," 149–50. Reprinted with the permission of Scribner, a Division of Simon & Schuster, Inc., from *The Turning* by Tim Winton. Copyright © 2004 by Tim Winton. All rights reserved.

and a worldview preparing to take hold. In this spirit, and despite Sherry's distaste for such religious kitsch, Rae acquires a little snow-dome featuring Jesus walking on the water, with his hair flying and his manly chest exposed. When shaken, the cloud of particles released is not snow but, rather, tiny white doves. Rae keeps the little snow-dome by her bed, and it becomes the symbolic key to her looming conversion.

Rae quizzes Sherry about the "born-again business," asking what it feels like, but is unsatisfied by Sherry's dreamy account of a moment "Like . . . like I was butter and there was this knife opening me up. That's the best way I can describe it."[4] Rae knows she has come close to belief, moved as she has been in her friends' company, and during the beach experience, but also by the goodness and consistency of Dan and Sherry, who under Rae's close scrutiny would surely by then have revealed any "awful secrets" marring their Christian claims. But while they possess a quality that makes Rae jealous, their faith still eludes her.

Until the climactic scenes of the story, when circumstances force Rae's hand. Discovering Rae's absences from her weekly darts night at the pub, and not knowing that these evenings have been spent with Dan and Sherry, Max accuses Rae of seeing another man. He violently assaults Rae and demands the other man's name. Significantly, Rae has just been telling the story of Jonah and the whale to her daughters at bedtime, and despite noticing Max's sweat and stink on the bedclothes where they were lying, she realizes she is no longer afraid of Max. Rae finds herself standing up to him, and it dawns on her that *Jesus* is her new man—"he's bigger than you, Max, so be careful."

> Raelene hit the van so hard it felt as though her eyeballs would spurt from their sockets . . . She was powerless but for the smile that stung her mouth, sharp as a split lip. She had a name for him, her secret man. He was just the shape of a man but he was all man to her and any moment, when she got her breath back and her tongue steady, she'd spit that name in his face and see him explode . . . But the moment never came. Everything just stopped, like the power going off.[5]

Yet for Rae the power was in fact just being turned on. Seeing how bruised and torn her head was after her beating, and further disfigured by the sutures, Rae talks the nurse who treats her into cutting the rest of her hair off,

---

4. Winton, "The Turning," 153.
5. Ibid., 156.

around the clumps that Max had pulled out. Like the military recruit's standard buzz cut on arrival at basic training, this symbolizes action and resolve, and standing on the brink of a new identity. Max's next attack catalyses Rae's conversion, and ends the story.

> In the spill of light at the bedside she saw the little dome and her man upon the waves. She said his name, too, said it aloud with love enough to send a shudder through Max as he pushed her down. She knew she was safe from him now, not safe from tonight but gone from him altogether. He smelt of death already, of burning, of bile and acid. He was crying and she did not pity him. He was gone and it didn't matter when. Everything was new. In her dome it snowed birds as the van rocked, birds like stars. The moment Max speared into her and tore open her insides she was full of hot and certain feeling. She was free. She had already outlived him.[6]

This brutal spearing image of being anally raped is obviously a counterpoint to the "knife into butter" of Sherry's more piously gentle and intensely private experience of conversion.

"The Turning" for Rae was the final coalescence of the Christian form of life as she was learning it mimetically from Dan and especially Sherry, who was a model for her of a different way of being a woman. The Bible is absolutely central to the transformation, as Rae begins to soak in its strange world like a tea bag, and take its worldview into herself, re-narrating her life in a process that for her was largely unconscious. In particular the figure of Jesus is crucial. Note, for instance, that he is presented as walking on the water, which evokes Elohim moving over the waters of chaos in Genesis 1 to create order. With the primal violence of Babylonian cosmology in mind, against which Genesis tells a non-violent creation story, Jesus' walking on the water as it is presented in the Gospel (Matthew 14) follows Jesus' challenge to King Herod's violent worldview—enacted at the dinner during which John the Baptist is violently murdered and his head brought in on a platter. What follows immediately in Matthew 14 is a quite different dinner where Jesus is host, at which the multitudes are fed and united in peace. To further emphasize the contrast being highlighted, Jesus is then portrayed as walking on the sea. This Eucharistic image of the feeding, followed by the baptismal image of Jesus walking on the water, represents a doubly-symbolic challenge to the primacy of violence in the Kingdom of the false sacred. Consequently, Raelene's Jesus walking on the water in her snow-dome is a symbol of the new

6. Winton, "The Turning," 160–61.

world into which she has been summoned, beyond Max's control and the hegemony of violence that he represents.

A further Girardian observation may be helpful here, on the attractiveness of the figure of Jesus in Rae's snow-dome, with his chest bared and his hair flying. For Girard it is our model or mediator desiring another that awakens our own desire for that other, as we have seen. Where another desires themselves—fancies themselves, as we might put it in the vernacular—then the desire they have for themselves can awaken that same desire in others. They are the model as well as the object of desire.[7] This is the mechanism driving coquetry, according to Girard, whereby the desire of admirers is awakened by the narcissistically self-confident adornment and demeanor of the coquette. Rae's Jesus figure is self-consciously attractive, and that plays a part in awakening her desire. We need not be shocked by the sexual overtones in this desire for Jesus on Rae's part. There is clear testimony to near-sexual love and longing for Jesus in the history of monasticism and especially monastic preaching on the Song of Songs, and in the Gospels. Think of Jesus's approving the "woman of the city" who washed his feet with her tears in front of the Pharisees, dried them with her hair, and anointed them with ointment. Plainly the salvation of this "kind of woman" did not entail the sacrifice of her sensuality (Luke 7:36–50).

Another thing René Girard would notice about Raelene's snow-dome is the release of tiny white doves when it is shaken—biblical figures of sacrifice, but also pointers to the end of sacrifice (think of Noah's dove, in Gen 8:11). Rae, too, had moved beyond the status of victim.

The Intelligence of the Victim

We recall from the last chapter the importance of imitating the faith of others for St. Paul. David Jenkins, like everyone else of abiding faith who reflects on their experience, can point to this shaping by the desire of models—in his case, the Evangelical Bible students, the enthusiastic Anglo-Catholic curate, his own wife, and the many contacts in ministry over a lifetime from whom his faith took form and strength. Likewise, Raelene's story is one of learning a new desire from a new model. No longer for Raelene the dysfunctional and competitive rivalry for rough male attention learned mimetically from her mother and contemporaries. With Sherry this rivalry was starved of oxygen and hence overcome. Likewise Rae's desire for the masculinity of her lost fa-

---

7. See the discussion of Freud on narcissism in Girard, *Things Hidden since the Foundation of the World*, 367–82.

ther was transformed into a desire for Jesus, away from the ersatz masculinity of the bruisers to whom she had always been drawn. Again, Sherry and Dan were her models for this shift of desire. Hence a key obstacle was removed from her life.

The Girardian "interdividual psychotherapist" Jean-Michel Oughourlian describes this as, typically, the key breakthrough: "Complete healing and ultimate wisdom," he writes, "will be found in the renouncing of all *rivals* and *obstacles* in order to keep only models."[8] Sherry went from being Rae's potential rival to her model, once Rae realized that Sherry was not in competition with her. And Jesus displaced the obstacle of a distorted masculinity that she had desired in Max. The power of her former existence is overcome by a new life in faith, with new models and new desires supplied by faithful Christians and the Gospel itself. I suggest that Bishop David Jenkins underwent a similar experience during that fateful walk in the grounds of Auckland Castle, no doubt struggling inwardly with the desire of any establishment figure for the public accolades regularly accruing to others in his position, only to be declared a pariah and a cuckoo by the Prime Minister. Yet he found himself freed from the potential bitterness and victimhood of that situation, including the likely emergence of envious hatred toward the models of his desire who retained the approbation that he had lost. Rae found the same thing, liberated at once from Max's power and the suffocation of her former imaginative world even though her appalling physical ordeal was not quite over.

English Catholic priest James Alison, who is René Girard's leading theological interpreter, talks about faith in Jesus in terms of "the intelligence of the victim." It is not a pious and mystical thing confined to personal attitudes. Rather, it is a re-narrated personal identity, involving release into a new world of models who form that identity—in the Church, the tradition, and the Gospel.[9] No longer is the individual either as able or as willing to play the role of victim in an imaginative world of misplaced desire, rivalry, and scapegoating. What Alison describes is essentially what I am calling abiding faith. Such faith is something that happens to us, so that we are changed by it even before we come to understand it—hence the inarticulacy that regularly accompanies a faith that is nevertheless quite genuine.

Faith is a break-in whereby God lifts us out of whichever false-sacred system has entrapped us, with its inevitable conflicted rivalries for self-definition. The place of shame, from which every form of human desire naturally resiles,

---

8. Oughourlian, *The Puppet of Desire*, 245.
9. Alison, *Knowing Jesus*, see especially "The Intelligence of the Victim," 33–59.

is found in fact to be bearable and habitable, as Jesus signally demonstrates in his resolute embrace of the cross.[10] His victory there is a victory over the power of every false sacred reality. Bishop David Jenkins and Tim Winton's character Raelene both found that place, and the intelligence of the victim. It placed them beyond the power of their former rivals, who became nothing to them. The next step of course is becoming so free of their power that even sympathy towards these former rivals becomes possible. Rae was not quite there, understandably contemptuous towards Max's tears of self-loathing as he enacted the grim ritual of his own entrapment in the false sacred. But give her time. Beyond her life with Max, I do not think Rae's future would have been defined by a continuing state of bitter victimhood in thrall to his memory. That obstacle had been removed. Jesus, her new model, would have done in her the same work he did on the cross, forgiving his own tormentors.

This is what abiding faith is like. It is a form of life that entails a worldview. But it is not a static form of life. Rather, it has to incorporate change and growth, as we see in the account by Bishop Jenkins and the story of Raelene. Nor is abiding faith able to conceive its worldview as a closed and infallible system, after the pattern of every false sacred reality. Again, I will have more to say about all of this in the next chapter. For now, I want to put my case that abiding faith cannot be accounted for in terms of rationalism—or of its twin, the withdrawal of faith from reason. Seeing it primarily as a form of life is the surest way to account for faith's stubborn resistance in the face of religious skepticism.

ABIDING FAITH AS "PARTICIPATING KNOWING"

What would Richard Dawkins make of Bishop Jenkins's nearly-stumbling but nevertheless sure account of the form of life that is his faith? What would he make of Tim Winton's story, "The Turning," with its account of a complete liberation, transformation, and empowerment for one of life's countless chronic victims? Would he "get it"? Dawkins is today's most popular religious skeptic, and I introduced him briefly in chapter 1.[11] I am returning to him now as an example of a particular attitude, augmenting his account as necessary from elsewhere among the stock arguments beloved of religious skeptics.

---

10. Alison, *Undergoing God*, see especially "Introduction: Of Concavities and Tent Poles," 1–14; and "Deliver Us from Evil," 73–83.

11. Dawkins, *The God Delusion*.

The Rationalistic Repertoire of Religious Skepticism

Dawkins offers a naturalistic account of biological and human origins. He speaks from deep conviction about the way nature is obviously built up "from below" rather than emerging "from above" in one deft stroke as a finished whole. He rejects the narrowness of a religion that resiles from this richness and complexity of nature, and of human life that forms a part of nature. It is as if he suffers from displaced religious wonder, and his severe case for reason seems driven by a sense that religion regularly fails to appreciate the world properly. As a Christian I sympathize with these concerns. I am also pleased by Dawkins's avoidance of a standard skeptical argument that actual scientific training tends to dispel. I refer to the natural dimension in philosophy of religion's so-called problem of evil. Dawkins is scientific enough to know that the world has emerged and life has evolved as it is, wonderfully and terribly but certainly all of a piece, so he does not discount God in the same way as those skeptics who think the world could and should have been better constructed, so cancer and earthquakes do not happen. Up to this point in Dawkins' case, modern faith can endorse and assimilate his challenges. Less so with what follows, however, much of which faith feels obliged to challenge.

Dawkins is critical of religion *per se* and not just fanaticism, outraged by all the bad things regularly done in God's name. This is a standard critique, and one shared by many believers—though, rather than leading to religious skepticism, it regularly inspires troubled Christians to reform the Church. As for human evil, which is the other dimension in philosophy of religion's problem of evil—that God might somehow have avoided in creating humans, without removing something essential to human life—Dawkins seems to reserve his charges of human evil for religious people only. He spares tyrannous atheistic regimes from criticism, taking a buoyantly confident, Enlightenment view of human perfectibility.

At least we are spared the now old-fashioned debate in skeptical analytical philosophy questioning the meaningfulness of religious statements, as mid-twentieth-century advocates of the "verification principle" did, arguing that all meaningful statements were either empirically verifiable or tautologous (ironically, the principle itself proved meaningless by its own criteria).[12] Dawkins simply questions the existence of that to which religious statements refer. Nor is he impressed by the newer currents in philosophy that view

---

12. The key material is much anthologized; see e.g. Diamond and Litzenburg, *The Logic of God*.

science chiefly as a dimension of human culture, with a powerful method but surely not the only one suitable for supporting worthwhile human meaning. Instead, he is a hard rationalist who feels that faith is a poisonous distraction from the noble business of seeking objective truth and living with proper human autonomy in the modern world.

It is notable, however, that Dawkins studiously avoids accounts of faith that share his wonder in the pursuit of cutting edge science. Many believers thrill with him at everything the evolutionary theory has revealed, and welcome naturalistic accounts whether they be of human origins, consciousness, or behavior. Yet none of these things are considered incompatible with faith, when it understands God to be at work through the within of things in a way that is compatible with the open universe of today's science.[13] Many believers also share his concern about inadequate models of authority in the Church while remaining pleased—like Dawkins and all serious scientific practitioners—to be part of an authoritative community of fellow practitioners that helps to keep you honest.

In all, Dawkins has reacted in kind to the way Christianity has regularly presented itself since Descartes and the Enlightenment, in rational terms based on universally-acknowledged truths and general wisdom. This rationalistic version of faith has suffered, however, as scientific advances closed-off various gaps in our account of natural processes through which God had been thought to direct things in the world. Subsequently the rational defense of faith has retreated into accounts of the human self, with moral obligation or fundamental trust or a sense of order or experience of the sublime invoked to establish a sure and certain departure point for faith in God—though none of these have proved compelling for skeptics, either. Nor indeed for many modern believers, from Pascal to Kierkegaard to today, who are convinced that the life of faith into which Christians are drawn through Jesus Christ brings its own sureness beyond what any "rationally provable" argument, human condition, or definitive experience could provide. Yet for Dawkins, as for most skeptics today, the justification of faith entirely on rational grounds is now the default position which they must oppose, and the Church is being disingenuous if it opts for anything different.

---

13. See Cowdell, *A God for This World*. This is a line popularized by the leading particle physicist-turned-clergyman, John Polkinghorne, for instance in *Science and Providence*.

Faith and Rationalism

Having learned nothing from the fate of sterile rational apologetics in the Enlightenment, many Christians today try to be just as resolutely rational in their defense of faith as the religious skeptics are in its dismissal. Under the useful category of "cognitive-propositional" approaches, George Lindbeck in his influential account of doctrinal types[14] indicates a range of largely conservative positions. The verities of Scripture, Church tradition, or authoritative Catechism, clearly expressed in propositional form, underpin the Christian account of faith according to such perspectives. In the Catholic tradition, naturally accessible truths about God's will in creation and human life are augmented by further propositions about Jesus and the way to salvation, while Protestantism may vary this mix by declaring human reason to be stained by sin and unreliable apart from its rehabilitation in the light of faith. But such Protestantism ends up asserting an equally "cognitive-propositional" version of faith, though in theory drawn from the Bible alone and declared immune to rational challenge. This represents a particularly hard version of a trend that takes various forms across the spectrum of Christian faith, and is known as *fideism*—faith without dependence on reason.[15] Yet such versions of faith can be highly rationalistic in expression even if their foundations are not sunk in reason alone. I will take a moment over these inherent weaknesses of the rationalistic approach in general, then go on to consider the shortcomings of a "cognitive-propositional" account of abiding faith in particular.

Rationalistic apologetics gets nowhere with religious skepticism. Anyone who has watched a creation-science advocate debate a scientific rationalist knows that, and in such obsessive encounters Girard's mimetic doubles come to mind—that is, twinned figures locked into a rivalry that defines them, who mirror one another's behavior. Hence the rationalistic account of faith regularly fails in terms of Christian witness. At a time when the hegemony of reason is widely challenged in post-modern philosophy, when the regular political connivance of truth with power has become a mainstream suspicion in the West, when for all their obvious blessings science and technology increasingly prove to be blind guides, and when the planned rationality of managed modern life is producing homeless hearts more reliably than it is yielding instances of human perfectibility *a la* Dawkins, a more broadly-based

---

14. Lindbeck, *The Nature of Doctrine*.

15. For a helpful discussion of the range and history of fideist positions, and a contemporary defense of one such, see Evans, *Faith Beyond Reason*.

account of Christian faith is surely called for. Important developments in the philosophy of science have also weakened the claims of science to be the objective arbiter of truth.

The myth of rational objectivity has been unseated thanks to Thomas Kuhn's discovery of scientific paradigms, so that scientific truth is what emerges by consent of the academy as much as by experiment and hypothesis.[16] The inevitability of (unfounded) tacit assumptions woven all through the substructure of scientific thought has also been revealed, thanks to the reflective scientific practitioner Michael Polanyi and the philosopher Karl Popper.[17] As a result of such newer insights, scientific facts are regularly acknowledged to be "theory-laden." Ironically, the spirit of authentic science can now point the way for us beyond "cognitive-propositional" accounts of Christian faith, and beyond their skeptical dismissal.

There is also a new appreciation of feeling in philosophy nowadays, as a necessary part of how we even begin to make rational sense of the world. Feelings orient us to particular persons, events, and even scientific conclusions, they sustain the interest necessary for rational attention to take hold, and they reveal the truth of situations where we might never have pulled the facts together otherwise, or correctly weighed their import.[18] Emotional intelligence,[19] pre-cognitive pathways of perception awakening our brainstem to danger before our thinking frontal cortex registers it,[20] and the deep relationship between mind and body that is now emerging from popular psychology to become the stuff of empirical science[21] all point to a richer model of cognition emerging into the light of intellectual respectability. No longer is it only feminist critics of hard rationality (as conscripted by patriarchal authority) who champion the fact of bodily knowing,[22] but the synergy between bodily and mental states long known to folk wisdom—and acknowledged to some extent during the Enlightenment[23]—is now beginning to have its nervous

---

16. Kuhn, *The Structure of Scientific Revolutions*.

17. Polanyi, *Personal Knowledge*; Popper, *The Logic of Scientific Discovery*.

18. Here I have been particularly helped by Watts and Williams, *The Psychology of Religious Knowing*; Wynn, *Emotional Experience and Religious Understanding*; and Nussbaum, "Love's Knowledge."

19. See Goleman, *Emotional Intelligence*.

20. See LeDoux, *The Emotional Brain*.

21. See Sternberg, *The Balance Within*.

22. See Ind, *Memories of Bliss*.

23. See Porter, *Flesh in the Age of Reason*.

pathways and biochemical substrate brought to light.[24] Any good working scientist knows the power of intuition and insight to advance their work, and philosophy is beginning to surrender its mannered distaste for feeling, beyond its long-standing preference for a dry and adversarial approach to truth.

"Cognitive-propositional" approaches also sell-short the lived reality of abiding faith. I mention two significant blind spots.

For one thing, it is significant that faith can be genuine without being articulate. Finney's account of adult conversion reminds us that ideas are not usually the key thing, yet a rationalistic account of faith insists that they are. Charles Taylor and Robert Bellah make a similar point (as noted in chapter 1, above). They acknowledge that modern Westerners retain a persistent sense of moral and spiritual obligation despite a culture confining their imagination to the therapeutic agenda of individual meaning making, focused on ordinary life, work and family, with a reduced sense of belonging to any wider communal reality. For Taylor the strongest of these intuitions still summon people to an identity, a form of life, and a narrative giving shape to it, *but all of this is typically fuzzy in its articulation.* He concludes that reducing this broader reality of imagination and lived commitment to the bare terms of intellectual assent to God's existence is to derive and abstract one aspect from a reality that is far more comprehensive.[25] Robert Bellah believes that people intuit these depths but normally cannot name them—"they cannot think about themselves or others except as arbitrary centers of volition. They cannot express the fullness of being that is actually theirs."[26] Without a "second language" for faith matters, beyond the modern West's "first language" of technical, utilitarian individualism, it is hard to put today's experience of faith into adequate words. So there is something here that is real and significantly life-determining but it is regularly found to be inchoate, which is hardly compatible with a cognitive-propositional account.

Another challenge for the cognitive-propositional approach is the acknowledged fact of transformation and growth in faith. We have a classic account of this growth thanks to James Fowler, inspired by earlier investigations of moral development in children and adults.[27] Fowler's journey of faith ranges from the early faith-stages ("Undifferentiated," "Intuitive-Projective" then

24. See Sternberg, *The Balance Within*.

25. Taylor, *Sources of the Self*; see part I, "Identity and the Good," 3–107, especially 75ff.

26. Bellah, *Habits of the Heart*, 81.

27. Fowler, *Stages of Faith*.

"Mythic-Literal") of children—along which the influence of parents and other early models slowly declines in influence—through the questioning typical of teenage years, during which "Synthetic-Conventional" faith is challenged by the experience of growing up and beginning to ask questions. If faith continues to develop, this stage gives way to the "owned" faith of the "Individualistic-Reflective" period, and perhaps then to a more mellow "Conjunctive" faith that faces and assimilates the challenges of adulthood. With further maturing a "Universalizing Faith" can take root in advanced years when anxiety and any desire for too-complete closure are typically let go.

Fowler's typology clearly pictures faith as a journey of transformation, assimilation, and surrender, where the same objects and practices can come to mean different things and be articulated in different ways as we grow older. This clearly refers to a form of life, a shifting and expanding narrative of identity that is variously related to the facts of life as they reliably present themselves through the life cycle, manifesting continuity along with change. The situation is complicated—if you are a rationalist seeking closure, that is, otherwise it is enriched—by the contribution of more recent perspectives extending Fowler's work. I mention three.

First, it is suggested that there is a different faith experience for women. Nicola Slee argues that women's faith has distinctive features, challenging Fowler's account of faith's movement toward a mellow, "Universal" end point as too isolating and masculine in its conception. She traces a typical (albeit educated) Western woman's journey of faith from "alienation" to "awakening" to "relationality," so that identity in solidarity with other women eventually emerges out of a patriarchal environment in which women's identity and freedom are regularly undermined. She emphasizes an "epistemology of connectedness"[28] manifest in "a dominance of concrete, visual, narrative and embodied forms of thinking over propositional, abstract or analytical thought" and "a dominance of personalised and relational forms of appropriating faith over abstract and impersonal means."[29] Here is an account of faith's transformation hammered out in the gendered distinctiveness of socio-political reality, which is distinctly incompatible with "cognitive-propositional" treatment. *Second*, the faith experience of men has attracted similar attention, in tandem with widespread reflection on masculine maturity more generally. The American Franciscan Richard Rohr is one who unerringly identifies the shortcomings of modern Western life in its failure to form emotionally whole and integrated

28. Slee, *Women's Faith Development*, 135.
29. Ibid., 79.

men. He invokes a combination of tribal wisdom, depth psychology, and theological insight in his ministry of men's spirituality and masculine initiation. The archetypal images of "warrior," "wise man," "lover," and "king" serve to name areas of disorder and potential growth that Rohr identifies both in life and faith, linking our failures in these areas to the psychological, social, and environmental malaise of modern Western life.[30] *Third*, there is also a distinctive faith experience among the elderly. My colleague Elizabeth MacKinlay offers a more evidence-based approach than Fowler to the particular spiritual task of what she calls "the last career." The challenge is to find ultimate meaning, becoming reconciled to one's life story and also to one's impending death (the chief tool for this is provided by the natural trend toward reminiscence typical of that stage in life).[31]

In all these cases—general, feminine, masculine, and aged—faith appears as more of a synthesizing, evaluating, meaning-and-identity-creating form of life than as a list of propositions—the sort that a skeptic ticks off as nonsensical, while a "cognitive-propositional" Christian apologist responds by affirming them in mono on behalf of a faith that is actually experienced in stereo. The next step towards an adequate account of faith takes us some way beyond the "cognitive-propositional" account in the direction of a feeling dimension that it neglects.

Faith and Experientialism

George Lindbeck has a second category for understanding the nature of doctrine that he calls "experiential-expressive." The primary locus of faith shifts to the inner-human world—either of human cognition, meaning making or religious experience. This is a reaction against the rationalistic excesses of modernity and, in the case of religious experience becoming the sole basis for faith, this account becomes the Romantic obverse of Enlightenment rationalism. It can be identified in pietistic versions of Christianity, which arose in Europe after the Thirty Years' War with a bias away from the doctrinal controversies that had led to so much violence. An "experiential-expressive" approach is also characteristic of liberal theology wherever a deep human spiritual awareness is invoked to provide a surer basis for belief and faith, as is often the case in liberal Protestantism from Friedrich Schleiermacher

---

30. Rohr, *Adam's Return*. See also Moore and Gillette, *King, Warrior, Magician, Lover*.
31. MacKinlay, *The Spiritual Dimension of Ageing*.

(1768–1834) onwards.[32] An important variation is found in mainstream Roman Catholic theology since Vatican II, which grounds faith in deep structures of human knowing. Hence Karl Rahner and his "transcendental anthropology"—a vision of human beings constituted fundamentally as "hearers of the Word," with an unthematic horizon of transcendence woven into all human activity.[33] Also Hans Küng, basing his account of faith on a "fundamental trust" which is the tacit background of all human knowledge and enterprise.[34] All this offers an advance on the "cognitive-propositional" case, helping to disclose just why it is that beliefs appeal and faith takes hold. It finds echoes in today's greater intellectual openness to feeling, intuition and tacit assumptions in human knowing more generally—things that rationalism can neither fathom nor tolerate.

Yet wherever this reaction against the positivism of reason takes the form of a positivism of feeling—a thoroughgoing experientialism—it reveals liabilities as an adequate basis for abiding faith. One liability is that experientialism is readily challenged for being cognitively irresponsible. Religious skeptics like Dawkins typically declare such reliance to be a subjective retreat from proper scientific objectivity, smiling bemusedly while concluding that there is nothing of substance remaining. Another liability is that it cannot help tending toward relativism. Indeed, many "experiential-expressive" theologians tend to be religious pluralists, such as John Hick[35] and Wilfred Cantwell Smith,[36] seeing divergent religious beliefs as different expressions of the same root experiences (of "the real" for Hick, and of "faith" according to Cantwell Smith—understood as a basic human state prior to both belief and practice). Hence religions resemble different software packages that can be run on the same computer hardware.

Further, the naturalistic accounts of faith's various aspects that have been advanced by skeptics (and welcomed for their clarifying power by many theologians) have an answer for religious experience. These range from Sigmund Freud in *The Future of an Illusion* (1927), declaring faith to rest on wish fulfillment, through to Jean-Francois Lyotard suggesting that the sublime—which has widely been acknowledged as religiously suggestive—really only represents

32. See Schleiermacher, *On Religion*.
33. See Rahner, *Foundations of Christian Faith*, parts I–IV, 24–137.
34. Küng, *Does God Exist?* 442 77.
35. For his mature position on religious pluralism see Hick, *An Interpretation of Religion*.
36. See e.g., Smith, *Towards a World Theology*.

our sensing the inherent limit of our powers of representation.[37] Don Cupitt comfortably interprets transcendence in these post-modern terms for his non-realist theological project, as representing nothing more than the experience of our own transience and contingency.[38] In such cases, the experience can be affirmed as real enough while the belief built on it is denied. This approach cuts the objective nerve of religious truth altogether. It finds consistent support in late-twentieth-century philosophy of religion, as a means for retaining the enjoyment and comfort of religion without the anxious burden of maintaining its link to objective truth. It represents the most radical form of fideism, too, in that any decision to construct either this faith or that on the basis of experience is essentially arbitrary and volitional.

I mentioned Don Cupitt in chapter 1 as the example of this religious non-realism with whom I am most familiar, and so again here. I can testify from my own personal experience, as a young graduate student and priest, that the "experiential-expressive" path in liberal theology, with its reliance on subjective states, can quickly lead to the loss of all objectivity in faith. For me the study of existentialist theology—in which Gospel and salvation are regularly cashed out in terms of a transformed self-understanding (as we saw in our discussion of Bultmann in the last chapter)—led me to Jungian psychology and spirituality, where God's objective existence outside the unconscious is essentially optional. From there it was a short step to Don Cupitt, and hence to the brink of atheism—albeit in the form of a non-realist version of Christianity. I only returned from that brink (after four years) when it *clicked* for me through a combination of insight, wider theological reading, a religious experience (not dissimilar to Raelene's beach experience) and an "adoption reunion" with my natural mother that the logic of abiding faith demanded something beyond non-cognitivism and its re-badging of belief as software. The Canadian philosopher Paul Janz accurately names the spiritual and existential choice that pressed itself on me with great force at that time, concluding that "the overall choice for realism over anti-realism . . . is most essentially the choice to be at home in the world rather than to be a stranger in it."[39] I found myself able to relativize my doubts and trust my instincts again, rather than mistrust all the things that participation in a Christian form of life was telling me.

37. I am grateful here to the discussion by Bauerschmidt, "Aesthetics: The Theological Sublime."

38. Cupitt, *Life, Life*, 30.

39. Janz, *God, the Mind's Desire*, 97.

Faith does indeed grasp and reprogram the mind, as we saw in the Jenkins account and the Tim Winton story, also in the last chapter's fast-forward through abiding faith across Christian history. Even Pascal's famous account of his life-changing night of religious experience was freighted with belief ("God of Abraham, God of Isaac, God of Jacob, not of the philosophers and the learned . . . *God of Jesus Christ*"),[40] and this from a major critic of propositionalism in matters of faith. Faith works as a piece, as we see in so many authentic accounts, with belief woven into experience, and experience following upon forms of life, and forms of life maturing belief and making it explicit. Faith and belief are not superstructures built on the bare hull of experience.

Nor can our regular need for trust in the life of faith be accounted for if faith is solely an "experiential-expressive" phenomenon, rooted in inner states—ones presumably that are positive, affirming of the self, and conducive of a coherent life-narrative. It is precisely in the absence of such positive reinforcement that faith comes into its own. So, for example, religious skeptics harping on the problem of evil regularly fail to dissuade Christians from their faith, because the logic of that faith sustains the paradox of believing in God's providence while at the same time acknowledging that faith regularly faces gaps in confirmation. It was to explain this stubborn persistence of faith as it is actually lived, despite the challenges of religious skepticism, that an English philosopher of religion and Christian believer, Basil Mitchell, came up with his parable of the partisan and the stranger.[41] A partisan in wartime meets a stranger and, after a night of inspiring conversation, becomes convinced that he has met the leader of the Resistance. Subsequently, however, his faith is tested when he sees this stranger going about in Nazi uniform, even arresting members of the Resistance, while on other occasions the partisan sees him leading Resistance forces in successful attacks on the enemy. On balance the partisan remains convinced that there is an explanation for the aberrations in a grander purpose that he does not presently understand, so disbelief is held at bay by the action of trusting faith. The absence of knockdown experience proves not to be terminal. This recalls how the psalmist's lament regularly gives way to a statement of faith based on the remembrance of God's past faithfulness, making up for the loss of any present sign of that faithfulness—for instance in Psalms 22 and 77.

---

40. See Pascal's celebrated "Memorial."
41. The parable appears in Mitchell's contribution to "Theology and Falsification."

In similar vein, religious biography regularly reports that periods of dryness, spiritual disorientation, and temptation to doubt are absolutely standard in the life of faith, as Christians strive and wait for the assimilation of negativity and confusion to take place. John of the Cross stands as a great witness to the role of "night" or "the dark night," which refers to suffering in the key of bewilderment. This is an encounter with God that takes us beyond the realm of experience in a movement that may end in peace and inner certitude, but in which there is no unproblematic "experience" of God.[42] This particular witness, in the sixteenth-century Spanish religious culture of religious esoterica and experientialism (alongside a very rationalistic scholasticism), stands as a warning on the cusp of modernity that modernity's key definitions of faith are problematic. Regarding spiritual experience, John of the Cross emphasizes the importance of continuing to pray, bringing the spiritual dryness and sense of God's absence to prayer, so that faith carries on when experience is lagging. And it works.

Interlude: Is Religious Skepticism Evasive?

Before going on to Lindbeck's next category for defining doctrine, linking it explicitly to the Christian form of life, let me return to the religious skepticism that rejects faith in both the forms I have been discussing. Faith almost unfailingly refuses to commend itself to the skeptic either as a "cognitive-propositional" undertaking, or in the "experiential-expressive" account (where it is deemed to be fanciful and wish-fulfilling). Interestingly, as a Christian believer I can acknowledge (as Lindbeck does) the incompleteness of these approaches as an adequate account of belief and faith, while retaining faith. So what is it about abiding faith that proves inaccessible to the religious skeptic?

The English philosopher John Cottingham is clear that religious skepticism does not attend to the phenomenon of Christian faith in a way that can hope to appreciate the primarily hermeneutical rather than analytic mentality of belief, the primacy of practice, and the whole-of-life perspective entailed by faith, so that "to insist on approaching it with complete analytical detachment may be less a sign of intellectual integrity than a stratagem of evasion, a refusal of openness and vulnerability, and hence a flight from acknowledging all the dimensions of our humanity."[43]

---

42. I am indebted here to Matthew, *The Impact of God*.
43. Cottingham, *The Spiritual Dimension*, 71.

In chapter 1 I addressed Dawkins' critique briefly with the help of Nietzsche and his follower Max Scheler, the latter interpreting modern philosophical reductionism as the sign of a slave revolt in morality: "the *ressentiment* of the vitally unfit against the fit, of those who are partially dead against the living."[44] American theologian Russell R. Reno would agree, suggesting that the skeptical arguments really mask an underlying fear of the Christian Gospel and a resistance to it.

> To put the matter bluntly, the problem with traditional Christianity does not rest in the fact that the so-called modern mind is too sophisticated, too scientific, too worldlywise to believe. Rather, the problem is that we do not want to believe. We want a "gospel" that affirms our increasingly fragile self-images. We want a "gospel" that helps us maintain stable and unchanging relationships in a world full of threatening forces that might sweep us away. We do not want repentance. We do not want transformation. In short, we do not want what Christianity teaches.[45]

This is a strong critique, and hard to prove other than on a skeptic-by-skeptic basis, though I have heard people assess Dawkins's ultimate motivations in these terms. It is sufficient to say that the religiously skeptical approach is not scientific, critical or rational enough to grasp the complex and multi-layered reality of abiding faith, so it will of necessity come up with a corrupt account of what it purports to study. John Cottingham spells this out.

> Religion has been isolated as an object for dissection, scrutinised as a set of abstract doctrines, abstracted from the ethical commitment that makes it truly meaningful. It has been cut off from the spiritual praxis that makes it live, from the psychological and developmental story it links to our quest for self-understanding, from the linguistic domain of symbolic understanding and the multiple layers of significance that are its natural means of expression, and from the liturgical and sacramental tradition that sustains it. So lopped and trimmed, it is hardly surprising that a formerly flourishing plant appears to many as a sickly specimen, fit only to be disposed of as quickly as possible.[46]

It must be acknowledged that any evasiveness on the part of religious skeptics is echoed regularly among believers. There are both "cognitive-

---

44. Scheler, *Ressentiment*, 116.
45. Reno, "*Pro Nobis*: Words We do Not Want to Hear," 49.
46. Cottingham, *The Spiritual Dimension*, 171.

propositional" and "experiential-expressive" versions of this evasiveness. The rationalistic Christian mindset, dismissive of emotion, feeling, and experience as untrustworthy and unworthy of faith's objective ground, regularly dismisses more experiential Christianity, either pietistic or charismatic. But there is a cost. The dearth of good spiritual direction at the conservative end of Reformed Protestantism, for instance, where growth in faith is regularly reduced to sustained obedience interpreted statically and legalistically, highlights a pastorally-impoverished narrowness inadequate to nurturing growth in robust, psychologically-integrated faith. There is a complimentary narrowness found among some of the more pietistic or charismatic Christians, also regularly among those who gravitate to the self-definition of "simple faith." Difficult questions of integrating experience with belief, and both with the life of discipleship, are evaded. An example. In the novel *Brideshead Revisited*, Evelyn Waugh's character Sebastian Flyte, all Oxford bags and ironic childlikeness, describes himself as a resolute believer. Asked why he believes, Sebastian gives as an example the Almighty's obvious intervention following an urgent prayer to St. Anthony of Padua, whereupon a taxi driver returned Sebastian's accidentally-abandoned teddy bear "Aloysius." A notorious conversation with the Anglican private-school-trained skeptic Charles Ryder gives the feel.

> 'But my dear Sebastian, you can't seriously *believe* it all.'
> 'Can't I?'
> 'I mean about Christmas and the star and the three kings and the ox and the ass.'
> 'Oh yes, I believe that. It's a lovely idea.'
> 'But you can't believe things because they're a lovely idea.'
> 'But I *do*. That's how I believe.'[47]

Poor Sebastian with his too-fragile faith ends up being unable to live in the real world, while Charles Ryder ends up finding a faith fit to sustain him in wartime, and prayer—"an ancient, newly-learned form of words"—as part of a new form of life in the practice of Christian discipleship.[48]

Abiding Faith as a Form of Life

All such intimations of a more integral description of faith—the sort that religious skepticism programmatically fails to plumb—brings me to the most comprehensive account of abiding faith, which is in terms of a form of life.

---

47. Waugh, *Brideshead Revisited*, 102–3.
48. Ibid., 394.

George Lindbeck finds in this broadest of perspectives his own favored understanding of doctrine, as a "cultural-linguistic" phenomenon. Faith thus understood is a culture, a language with doctrine providing its grammar and syntax, and the practice of a community first and foremost.

Ludwig Wittgenstein (1889–1951) provides the main philosophical basis for this approach. The meaning of words is found in their use, according to the later Wittgenstein, and that use is discovered by attending to forms of life. He envisaged rather limited undertakings called "language-games" in which people learn how to use words confidently, such as the practice of naming things. Many tacit assumptions are woven into these language games, which are not questioned. As Wittgenstein observes, "the *questions* that we raise and our *doubts* depend on the fact that some propositions are exempt from doubt."[49] Indeed, he says, regarding such unquestioned propositions, "that I should stand before the abyss if I wanted so much as to try doubting their meanings . . . shews that absence of doubt belongs to the essence of the language game, that the question 'How do I know . . .' drags out the language-game, or else does away with it."[50] This puts paid to rationalism's insistence that it fearlessly tests every belief at the bar of reason. Rather than conviction resting on individually provable certainties expressible in propositional form, conviction is the poised, assured, convinced action whereby we negotiate a form of life. "To say of man," Wittgenstein concludes, "that he *knows* something; that what he says is therefore unconditionally the truth, seems wrong to me.—It is the truth only inasmuch as it is an unmoving foundation of his language-games."[51] Cultural anthropologists attuned to Wittgenstein led the way in interpreting whole cultures and religions in this way, such as Peter Winch[52] and Clifford Geertz.[53] As for Christianity, belief in God is foundational to the language game of Christian faith in the same way that belief in the Greenwich Meridian is essential (but tacit) for the language game of telling the time. This so-called Wittgensteinian fideism shows how "cognitive-propositional" and "experiential-expressive" accounts of religious truth are essentially secondary, emphasizing the form of life with its "cultural-linguistic" structure as primary.

49. Wittgenstein, *On Certainty*, #341.
50. Ibid., #370.
51. Ibid., #403.
52. See, e.g., Winch, "Understanding a Primitive Society."
53. See, e.g., the celebrated essay by Geertz, "Thick Description."

PART II: BELONGING, BELIEVING, AND BEHAVING

Indeed, in the hands of Wittgenstein's inheritors among the non-cognitivist philosophers of religion, such as R. B. Braithwaite,[54] D. Z. Phillips,[55] and Don Cupitt (at least in his middle period, through the 1980s),[56] any referent for Christian truth beyond the practice of Christian life is declared unnecessary. While this sort of "cultural-linguistic" approach *can* lead to skeptical conclusions about God's objective reality, however—the so-called non-realist account of theology—it also delivers enough benefits to Christian orthodoxy for it to be worth the risk, according to Lindbeck and the post-liberal school in theology. For tough minded post-liberals like Stanley Hauerwas and William Willimon—as for Kierkegaard—a solely objective, belief-oriented account of faith, let alone a more emotive, experiential one, would betray the call to discipleship by driving a wedge between faith and discipleship (quite apart from failing to convince a religious skeptic).[57] Not for them the separation of belief from practice in modern Western Enlightenment thought, and experience from both, hence putting asunder what genuine faith joins together. For post-liberal theologians, it is worth the risk of slippage toward a non-cognitive account of faith to preserve this essential link between belief and practice—a link that also serves to undermine religious skepticism, declaring it to be off target because it is not engaging with the lived reality of faith but only with its rationalistic shadow.

The attractiveness of a form-of-life approach stands behind today's uptake of the Catechumenate as a natural means whereby Christian communities in all the mainstream Churches are beginning to address the formation of believers through intentional immersion in the Christian community, with a focus on linking the liturgy with the practice of discipleship as the proper context for exploring and learning Christian belief. An acknowledgement of the role of models (or mediators) in the commending of faith by example is evident in the lay-led nature of this process—laity acquiring the faith primarily from laity—and in the intentional provision of a lay mentor for each candidate. The catechumenal process properly replaces modernity's characteristic version of preparation for adult Christian initiation, which was normally based on

---

54. See, e.g., Braithwaite, "An Empiricist's View of the Nature of Religious Belief."

55. See, e.g., Phillips, "Religious Belief and Language Games."

56. See Cowdell, *Atheist Priest?* Cupitt takes Wittgenstein into his project explicitly in *The Sea of Faith*, 213–28. Cupitt later came to question the worthwhileness even of the idea of God, concluding that religious practice was better off without it.

57. See e.g., Hauerwas and Willimon, "The Modern World: On Learning to Ask the Right Questions."

doctrinal instruction by the clergy via a Catechism or other Christian education material. The recovery of the Catechumenate from Christian antiquity, however, sees believing and experiencing as woven together with belonging and participating. This approach is even making inroads into Evangelical Christianity, where acknowledged doctrine or else felt experience had previously been understood to come before entry into the Christian form of life.[58] Today's Emerging Church movement throughout the Western world extends this transformation of Evangelicalism. Something like this seems to be envisaged by Wittgenstein himself, in his own account of how religious belief functions, and how people are in fact captured by faith.

> It strikes me that a religious belief could only be something like a passionate commitment to a system of reference. Hence, although it's *belief*, it's really a way of living, or a way of assessing life. It's passionately seizing hold of *this* interpretation. Instruction in religious faith, therefore, would have to take the form of a portrayal, a description, of that system of reference, while at the same time being an appeal to conscience. And this combination would have to result in the pupil himself, of his own accord, passionately taking hold of the system of reference.[59]

I now want to explore more closely how the form of life I am calling abiding faith commends itself, generating its own worldview by a combination of reason and imagination. In this it will also become clearer how those who inhabit the "participatory knowing" characteristic of abiding faith have always understood themselves to be participating in the truth.

ABIDING FAITH AS "PARADIGMATIC IMAGINATION"

In the immediately preceding discussion I was trying to show what abiding faith is and is not like as a form of knowledge, and how religious skepticism consistently misses the point. The version of faith that it attacks is not the fully-orbed reality which converts and sustains people as a form of life with wide-ranging connections to the whole of human experience, interpreted in conversation with Bible, Church tradition, liturgy, and Christian witness. Belief is regularly defined, defended, and attacked as if it were a foundational reality, according to the rationalistic and experientialist approaches, as deployed by Christian conservatives and liberals respectively. The rationalistic

---

58. See e.g., Abraham, *The Logic of Evangelism*; and Webber, *Ancient-Future Faith*.
59. Wittgenstein, "Ethics, Life and Faith," 302.

account starts with facts about the world and God (derived from natural and revealed theology, authoritative tradition, and/or Scripture) and assesses human feelings and thoughts in the light of those, while the experiential account begins with this or that inner reality and construes the objective world according to a starting point in the mind. Wallace Matson splits up the history of Western philosophy into these standard, foundational options, which he calls "outside-in" and "inside out."[60] This yields a helpful table.[61]

	Liberal	Conservative
knowledge	experiential foundationalism inside-out	scriptural foundationalism outside-in
language	expressivism	propositionalism

Both approaches, when applied to faith, invite religious skepticism to challenge their foundations. And both prove inadequate to explicating the nature of abiding faith, which builds experience and the objective givens of Scripture into its structure, but is not *founded* upon them—as if faith is a building and one or the other (or indeed both) are its foundations. The American theologian Nancey Murphy suggests that we can begin to move beyond this deep impasse in contemporary theology, which for my purposes is also doomed to give an inadequate account of faith, by changing the key metaphor. Instead of a *building*, abiding faith is more like a *web*.

Hence we move from a foundational to a holistic epistemology (or theory of knowledge). This shift helps us better account for the comprehensive way in which faith as a form of life works internally and relates to the world externally. The later Wittgenstein was invoked in the last section to show how it is that forms of life are not actually based on objectively proven foundations in knowledge at all, and also the way meanings of words and concepts are best looked for within forms of life. Nancey Murphy points to an influential philosophical paper written in the year of Wittgenstein's death, 1951, as cementing these conclusions and finishing foundationalism as a theory of knowledge. Willard V. Quine's "Two Dogmas of Empiricism," over which I remember laboring in undergraduate philosophy, demolishes these two foundations—the first propositional and the second expressive. Both knowledge and concepts, outer fact and inner experience, are better understood as integral to a form

---

60. Matson, *A New History of Philosophy*, vol. 2, 275–76; cited in Murphy, *Beyond Liberalism and Fundamentalism*, 28.

61. Murphy, *Beyond Liberalism and Fundamentalism*, 37.

of life making its way in the world. Quine imagines human knowledge on the analogy of a web, in contact with experience only at its edges. Inside the web, as it were, our beliefs and concepts shift and mutate in a holistic way to address the facts of experience encountered at the edges. It is not as if each belief is mapped onto one occasion of experience, and it is not as if concepts are immune from change, because we constantly re-jig them so the web of meaning continues to fit the external facts of experience. With apologies to *Star Trek,* and especially to Dr McCoy, "it's empiricism, but not as we know it."[62] "A conflict with experience at the periphery occasions re-adjustments in the interior of the field . . . Re-evaluation of some statements entails re-evaluation of others, because of their logical interconnections—the logical laws being in turn certain further statements of the system . . . But the total field is so underdetermined by its boundary conditions, experience, that there is much latitude of choice as to what statements to re-evaluate in the light of any single contrary experience."[63]

Instead of foundations, this is about the fit of a worldview to experience. It recalls Thomas Kuhn and that central concept of twentieth-century philosophy of science, the paradigm, which is an account of empirical reality that shares a holistic epistemology with Quine's web of meaning approach. Its rational claims are not foundational ones. Rather, the paradigm commends itself to practitioners in terms of the accuracy of its theoretical predictions, the scope of the paradigm in accounting for a large range of evidence, its simplicity, and its fruitfulness in predicting the outcomes of future investigations. This helps deal with the specter of relativism, which stalks non-foundational accounts of knowledge. There could be many webs, according to Quine, but Kuhn reminds us how science ends up with the "best" paradigm possible at the time, in terms of its power to make meaning more coherently, comprehensively, *and persuasively* than others. This is very like the mentality characteristic of abiding faith.

Paradigms and Faith

An important thing about paradigms is that they change, collapsing in the face of chronically ill-fitting facts of experience for which they cannot make room, so that in time a new paradigm emerges with greater power. Different paradigms will also seek out and address different facts of experience—it

---

62. The famous line was, of course, directed to Captain James T. Kirk by his ship's surgeon: "It's life, Jim, but not as we know it."

63. Quine, "Two Dogmas of Empiricism," 42–43.

is not as if the different webs are all connected to the same pinning points in experience. Hence different worldviews regularly lead to people talking past each other, and finding gaps in one-another's version of reality. Still, comprehensiveness and fruitfulness are powerful criteria for the paradigm's *rationality*, even if its truth cannot be proven and is always being renegotiated. Nancey Murphy points to the philosopher Alasdair MacIntyre in this connection, referring to worldviews in ethics rather than science. He argues that the capacity to incorporate a rival account is the mark of a rationally compelling worldview, offering the example of Thomas Aquinas enfolding the newly-recovered Aristotelian system into the Augustinian tradition—a successful takeover of a potential competitor.[64]

Faith on this model of web or paradigm is able to show its many-sided character, its mixture of observation, theory, experience, tacit assumption, its own innate logic—all features that we have noted—and its capacity to convert people by winning them over. This is how a paradigm change occurs, as insight builds to flashpoint, after which the details are increasingly worked through once the scientific community is operating, reasoning, and researching in the new way—that is, when a new form of life for that community is being inhabited. Likewise, we have seen that conversion to Christian faith is both a breakthrough and a process of adaptive growth, where Scripture is constantly being re-appraised in conversation with experience, and vice versa.

Conviction builds up, according to this account. Basil Mitchell explores this building-up in his discussion of rational religious conviction as a *cumulative case*. This cumulative account is not what Antony Flew acerbically describes as "the Ten-leaky-buckets-Tactic," however, because the "evidences" are not disconnected. Rather, they are cumulative in terms of their connections one with another, not just in terms of the quantity of evidence they muster.[65] Mitchell illustrates this with a naval example. In the same way that indefinite but increasingly consistent sightings of a hostile coast from a fogbound warship will eventually lead a prudent officer of the watch to draw away, even though the navigator has sworn that his dead reckoning and star sightings put them well clear of land, so the rational intelligence registers a series of

---

64. MacIntyre, *Three Rival Versions of Moral Enquiry*, 103, cited in Murphy, *Beyond Liberalism and Fundamentalism*, 108.

65. Flew, *God and Philosophy*, 141; cited in Mitchell, *The Justification of Religious Belief*, 40. Mitchell points out that if the leaky buckets are put inside one another and the holes are not aligned, they certainly can hold water (see 160 n2). In other words their contribution is genuinely cumulative.

observations mutually reinforcing towards a conclusion until at last, when the possibility of a new interpretation of the facts constellates, and perhaps with the encouragement of some urgency (as on the bridge of that warship), faith takes hold.[66] This is exactly what we saw in Tim Winton's short story, "The Turning," about Raelene and her conversion.

It is important to remember the form-of-life aspect to all this, evident in the way Kuhn discusses scientific revolutions and how a new paradigm catches on.[67] It is not always a switch of gestalt, as it were, imposing itself on the investigator—like the famous line-drawn duck that suddenly becomes a rabbit in response to our sustained gaze,[68] then promptly switches back again—but neither is it simply the sober accumulation of evidence until at last the perspective changes. It is a bit of both and more besides, because scientific investigation is first and foremost a form of life in a community of practitioners. As the increasingly-tottery old paradigm is abandoned by one after another of the investigators, they act as models for the as-yet-unconvinced, with attachment to the model (or mediator) of their desire proving significant in prompting colleagues to follow the new lead. Or else "conversion" is resisted by those who hold out in favor of the older paradigm, remaining loyal to those who were their models in "inhabiting" it.

This helps explain why paradigm change starts with younger scientists who are less socialized into ways of thinking characteristic of the established paradigm. They are more willing to acknowledge its failings, and seek their models among younger colleagues probing its weaknesses. Rivalry with the old guard in this respect would complete the picture of Kuhn in Girardian style that I am painting here. In the same way, the transformation to faith happens as a form of life changes in response to new models—typically, as new accounts of reality are lived-out by a new group of associates who become models for our desire. The former solutions sour and cease to work, often leading to a period of unease and uncertainty until the old questions are resolved in new and more compelling ways, and until the crises that the old form of life did not avert are dealt with more effectively in the new vision that is coalescing, while previously unappreciated aspects of life are enticingly revealed to the fresh eyes that an emerging new paradigm provides. All this

---

66. Mitchell, *The Justification of Religious Belief*, 112–13, cf. 69–71 on Kuhn and conversion.

67. See Kuhn, *The Structure of Scientific Revolutions*, 147–59.

68. See Wittgenstein, *Philosophical Investigations*, 194, improving on the earlier version of Joseph Jastrow.

fits what we saw in the accounts of Bishop David Jenkins and Raelene with which this chapter began. Rational synthesis, cumulative effect, moments of breakthrough—and all this under the influence of models of desire—is what faith is like, and it works paradigmatically. It is a rational synthesis that acts persuasively as part of a new form of life taking hold.

Two further insights fit this account more closely to the reality of faith precisely as *Christian* faith. *First*, as we have seen, the dispassionate and uninvolved perspective of the skeptic and its religious mirror image in the rationalistically-minded believer is unequal to the essentially participatory nature of faith. So the properly rational nature of Christian conviction cannot be done justice to if we think of that conviction merely in terms of a reasonable conclusion or inference from evidence. It is more of a significant personal surety, experienced existentially rather than disinterestedly. *Second*, it is also the case that paradigms, as with the webs of meaning imagined by Quine, carry with them logical rules and connections proper to the paradigm or the web. So in the same way that the logic of a romance novel demands a happy ending for the couple, so the logic of the story of God incarnate demands that the world of experience must be taken seriously.

Some Christian paradigms or webs of meaning refuse to do this, however, anxiously refusing to engage with great swathes of experience. Fundamentalists leave whole areas of historical fact, scientific consensus, and widely undisputed conclusions about the facts of human sexuality entirely out of consideration, true to the nature of paradigms in the way they sift and select the evidence they engage with. A truer or *better* Christian paradigm, however, on the model of Alasdair MacIntyre, will be one that encompasses more of life, more of reality, and is more faithful to the incarnational logic of Christian orthodoxy—that is, more creatively and openly engaging Scripture and tradition with the facts of life. Fundamentalism can be likened to what the philosopher of science Imre Lakatos called a *degenerative* research program, nervously clinging to a theory that is plainly failing to account for more and more of the evidence that experimental applications of the theory throw up, provoking increasingly anxious and fruitless twists and turns on the part of inquirers. By contrast the *progressive* research program, as Lakatos described it,[69] is increasingly successful, and particularly in accounting for new discoveries. A progressive, non-anxious Christian orthodoxy, incorporating both reason and experience, Scripture, and tradition—welcoming the widest possible

---

69. Lakatos, "Falsification and the Methodology of Scientific Research Programs"; cited in Murphy, *Beyond Liberalism and Fundamentalism*, 100–102.

realm of human reality without closing down due to the fear of otherness—is both vigorous as a form of life and most true to the logic of the incarnation.

Faith and Imagination

The role of what the American Anglican theologian Garrett Green calls the "paradigmatic imagination" further aids our understanding of how faith works as a web of meaning or paradigm. I also think that Green improves on the classic account of John Henry Newman—he is better on revelation and less problematic on religious certainty than "the Anglican apostle to Rome." So in this final section of the chapter, I will reflect on these two significant accounts, exploring imagination as the key faculty in abiding faith, through which the mind of Christ is formed in those who belong to him. But first a historical word about imagination in theology, which has proved a contested category.

Imagination remained linked to reason at the origins of modernity, preserving from antiquity an understanding of rational knowledge in terms of the subject indwelling the object of knowing. The Anglican "three-fold cord," with reason acknowledged alongside Scripture and tradition in theological method, actually preserves this fuller account of reason—carrying over from Richard Hooker (c. 1554–1600) and John Milton (1608–1674) their sense of a necessary complementarity between intuitive rationality and the lesser, discursive rationality.[70] This is why Anglican recourse to reason retains a fuller, more intuitive, poetically-tinged edge to this day.[71] But this account was sidelined as modernity's Cosmopolis took shape, with a new preference for the analytic use of language in Bacon, Descartes, and Hobbes contributing to the characteristic set against the imagination typical of Enlightenment thinking. This bias emerged fully with John Locke, according to the helpful account of imagination and Enlightenment provided by Paul Avis. Locke combined "Bacon's empirical method, Descartes' critical principle of clear and distinct ideas, and Hobbes's passion for precision and suspicion of metaphor."[72] The *Philosophes* shared this suspicion of the imaginative, as did the utilitarian Jeremy Bentham (1748–1832), with his obsessive striving for logical clarity.[73] The legacy of this attitude flourished in much twentieth-century analytical philosophy and religious skepticism which, if my suspicions are correct,

---

70. Avis, *God and the Creative Imagination*, 41.
71. See Countryman, *The Poetic Imagination*.
72. Avis, *God and the Creative Imagination*, 19.
73. Ibid., 20–21.

actively resisted abiding faith because it slips the traces of the controlling modern mindset—and especially in abiding faith's incorrigible insistence upon the symbolic, the poetic, and the sacramental.

The imagination was reasserted in modernity's reaction against its first, rationalistically-tending phase, represented by the Romantic Movement. The highest exponent of this trend was the poet and theologian Samuel Taylor Coleridge (1772–1834), who took-up the more fully-orbed account of reason, ascribing reason's capacity for grasping the order of things to "the imagination, or shaping or modifying power: the fancy, or the aggregative and associative power: the understanding, or the regulative, substantiating, and realizing power; the speculative reason—vis theoretica et scientifica, or the power by which we produce, or aim to produce, unity, necessity and universality in all our knowledge by means of principles a priori."[74]

The distinction (but not division) in Coleridge between primary and secondary imagination[75] in human beings—the former echoing God's creativity and the latter, at one remove, constituting human creativity—is related to how Cardinal Newman understood imagination and revelation, and more latterly Garrett Green. Newman points the way forward to Polanyi and the late-twentieth-century rediscovery of a more holistic epistemology that I discussed in the previous sections, where trust is woven together with knowledge, and participation in a form of life provides the substrate for understanding. Garrett Green helpfully clarifies why this tradition never really caught on in nineteenth-century theology. He thinks it was because "imaginative skeptics" had given imagination a bad name—those who imaginatively reinterpreted Christianity in an atheistic direction rather than simply declaring it to be in error, as rationalistic skeptics do. Green blames Hegel, and the young-left Hegelians Marx and Feuerbach, for scaring theologians away from imagination because of the supposed risks for orthodoxy that it posed.[76]

Still, the tradition has been vindicated, as the post-modern critique of rationalism has shown. We are now open to the role of intuitive grasp and tacit assumptions throughout the natural sciences—those former bastions of hard-headed reasonableness which have begun to yield before the claims of holistic epistemology. To Cardinal Newman's significant but also unhelp-

---

74. Coleridge, *Biographia Literaria*, 160, cited in Avis, *God and the Creative Imagination*, 41.

75. Coleridge, *Biographia Literaria*, 160.

76. Green, *Imagining God*, 24–27.

Faith's Knowledge   171

fully freighted account of imagination and faith I now turn, and then to the sharper version of Garrett Green.

John Henry Newman (1801–1890), in *A Grammar of Assent* (1870), seems to be incorporating this fuller theory of knowing based on the imagination into a modern scholastic account of faith with Augustinian roots—that is, with a guiding concern for sin and redemption, and for insisting on the Church's teaching authority for preserving believers from error. Certain of Newman's assumptions strike me as problematic and unnecessary, also representing a bridge too far in terms of the arguments he provides. For instance, Newman emphasizes the natural revelation of God, chiefly through the conscience, as an unquestioned starting point. That natural revelation works on natural knowledge and experience—and especially the knowledge of suffering, which serves for Newman as a sort of spiritual eye-opener. Then special revelation adds particular doctrinal content into the mix. All of this is pulled together by the faculty of imagination, which is the ring master in Newman's epistemological circus. And all of it is largely assertion. Newman's zeal as a convert to Roman Catholicism is also evident in the way he believes that imagination under the hand of God will lead the believer inexorably to the full truth of Catholic dogma—not just its Eucharistic doctrine of the real presence (which Anglo-Catholics regularly share), but also the full panoply of Marian dogma and the Papal Magisterium—provided that a starting point in strongly incarnational faith is present. Otherwise, the imagination, acting on inadequate spiritual premises (such as the Protestant starting-point of Scripture alone), will lead faithfully to erroneous conclusions.[77] Here it is hard to follow the balls in Newman's juggling act, for instance knowing exactly where it is in the work of imagination that the guiding hand of revelation takes hold. But if Newman's polemical purpose as an apologist for his adopted Church is set aside, his account of religious knowing through imagination contributes a valuable analysis of Christian faith more generally.

I mention two key aspects of his case. *First*, Newman distinguishes between "notional assents" and "real assents"—the former are broad and shallow, involving forms of knowing such as profession, credence, opinion, presumption, and speculation, while the latter are deeper, narrower, and more personal, covering beliefs, convictions, and certitudes.[78] The "real assent" is clearly the one with imaginative force, and indeed Newman called it

77. Newman, *A Grammar of Assent*, 198–99.
78. Ibid., 30–31, 47, 86–92.

"imaginative assent" in an earlier draft of the *Grammar*.[79] The authority of witness is significant in "real assent," as in Newman's loaded ecclesial image of a child's assent being keener and more energetic when it is supported by the authority of his mother.[80] Here I think of the Girardian model or mediator whose desire becomes our desire, and also a verse of Newman's hymn "Firmly I believe and truly," with words from *The Dream of Gerontius* (1865), capturing the role he gives to authority in guiding the imagination:

> And I hold in veneration,
> For the love of Him alone,
> Holy Church as His creation,
> And her teachings as His own.

Newman also acknowledges the cumulative nature of "real assent" when it comes to faith, listing the various elements that dispose towards it, including imagination, sensibility, horror at sin (Newman's conscience again), the mass and other rites, meditating on the Gospels, hymns and religious poems, dwelling on the evidences, parental example and instruction, religious friends, strange providences, and powerful preaching, noting that the synthesis is personal in every case[81] rather than formulaic. Here we see many aspects of abiding faith recalling our discussions earlier in the chapter. Note also Newman's contempt for rationalism in favor of a fuller basis for Christian faith. "Logic makes but a sorry rhetoric for the multitude," he writes, insisting that "man is not a reasoning animal; he is a seeing, feeling, contemplating, acting animal."[82] Here is "real assent" at work, employing a holistic, participatory form of knowing that brings a unique form of certitude. Newman declares that certitude to be irreversible,[83] manifest for instance in the faithful Catholic's refusal to question creedal orthodoxy.[84] This is a special sort of imagination for Newman, into which God's guidance and reassurance is somehow woven.

---

79. Cited in Avis, *God and the Creative Imagination*, 8. Perhaps Green's account of nineteenth-century concerns about imagination as a theological category explains Newman's reluctance to retain the word so centrally in his account.

80. Newman, *A Grammar of Assent*, 34–35.

81. Ibid., 85.

82. Ibid., 90.

83. Ibid., 169–70.

84. Ibid., 159–62.

This brings me to the *second* important thing to note about Newman's account. He identifies a category of knowing called "the illative sense,"[85] which is variously described but consistently conceived as truth-seeking intuition at the heart of human imagination. Whether it be the quality of genius that sees through complexity to the simple solution, like that of Isaac Newton in physics or the remarkable military ability of Napoleon to imagine quantitatively and together all the different elements of a battle unfolding in real time—along with more widespread accomplishments such as practical sagacity, wit or eloquence—the thing in common is that step-by-step reasoning is swept aside in favor of an unerring grasp that is immediate, intrinsic, quite sure of itself and, in particular, quite personal.[86] "His mind does not proceed step by step," Newman writes, "but he feels all at once and together the force of various combined phenomena though he is not conscious of them."[87] So the illative sense pulls together the elements of religious conviction, also furnishing the wit necessary to recognize special providences, should they have been provided by God.[88] It is the key to conversion for those rightly disposed, which for Newman means those with hearts open rather than closed. "I say plainly I do not care to overcome their reason without touching their hearts," he declares, with his chief criticism reserved for the influential apologetics of Archdeacon Paley, who reasoned from the evidences to the existence of his watchmaker deity (in a way that remains characteristic of much popular Anglican divinity, lay and clerical). Newman has no time for speculative tomfoolery, but only existentially serious inquiry. "I wish to deal, not with controversialists, but with inquirers," he writes.[89] Here then is the imagination that creates religious certitude. Newman never seems to resolve the tension between this process of holy knowing—essentially a heightened version of a natural faculty—and his proviso that theological reason is sustained by more than human imaginative power.[90] Nevertheless, abiding faith for Newman ultimately means being grasped imaginatively.

> Such imagination; creating a certitude of its truth for direct enumeration, too personal and deep for words, too powerful and concurrent

---

85. Ibid., chap. 9, 270–99.
86. Ibid. On the personal nature of this sense, see 301, 320.
87. Ibid., 261.
88. Ibid., 333.
89. Ibid., 330.
90. Ibid., 299.

PART II: BELONGING, BELIEVING, AND BEHAVING

> for refutation. Nor need reason come first and faith second (though this is the logical order), but one and the same teaching is in different aspects both object and proof, and elicits one complex act both of inference and assent. It speaks to us one by one, and it is received by us one by one, as the counterpart, so to say, of ourselves, and is as real as we are real.[91]

Turning finally to Garrett Green's account, we find the insights of Newman into the role of imagination in faith confirmed, but also the relationship with special revelation clarified and the necessity of certainty in Newman's account moderated—the Anglican restraining the excesses of the ex-Anglican, as it were. For Green, "'Faith' is the nearest analogue in Christian doctrine to the philosophical concept 'paradigmatic imagination.'"[92] Psychologically, it is primarily *pattern recognition* to which he is referring. Imagination is not the ground of special revelation for Green, but the place where it happens.[93] And this imagination, where revelation takes place, is also cumulative, holistic, and self-involving, according to Green, incorporating the believer's identity into Christ—all of which typifies what I am calling abiding faith.

> God does not appear, on this interpretation, to address the intellect, the feelings, or the conscience separately; and it does not require a subsequent theory to relate the various human faculties to each other and to revelation. Imagination is not so much a particular faculty as the integration in human experience of the various human abilities and potentialities. The integrative function of imagination in apprehending patterns of meaning externally also allows an integral response on the part of the imagining subject. To imagine myself, for example, as the random product of the forces of physical nature, or as a member of the master race, or as destined to fail at everything I attempt, or as a sinner redeemed from death and hell by the sacrifice of Christ—each of these images calls forth a total response, having intellectual, emotional, and volitional aspects.[94]

The specific nature of the revelation that grasps Christians through their imagination, along with reforming that imagination, is the "form of Christ," the image of God, according to Green, which is discerned in Scripture. Green

---

91. Ibid., 379.
92. Green, *Imagining God*, 144.
93. Ibid., 40.
94. Ibid., 151.

closely follows St. Paul here, but also Origen, both of whom were discussed in the last chapter as champions of abiding faith. This means being transformed by Christ in imitation of him, involving imitation of St. Paul's own example (1 Cor 11:1). It means Christians being transformed by the renewal of their minds (Rom 12:2), whereby they emerge as a new creation in Christ (2 Cor 5:17).[95] Origen's emphasis on the future aspect of this is important, and contributes to the strength of Green's account over Newman's by not demanding dogmatic certainty of faith in the present. Origen believed that while we retain the image of God, God's likeness has been lost by sinful humanity. But that likeness is being restored in Christ on the way to its full revealing in the eschatological future. In the interim, however, the life of faith is necessarily tentative and unfinished.[96]

Green's account addresses three problems that arise for form-of-life oriented, "cultural-linguistic" approaches to faith. *First*, there is the charge that they are constructions of the human imagination, on the non-realist model. Green thinks that such human constructions of God are in fact idols, whereas his insistence on revelation as a given ensures that the "paradigmatic imagination" retains theological objectivity.[97] *Second*, he denies the related charge of fideism, insisting that his account positively welcomes challenges that the rational modern mind has brought to the interpretation of Scripture and doctrine, so that "critically trained Christians can . . . in good conscience be literalists of the second naiveté." "Fully aware that there are other ways of construing the Bible and the world," he continues, "they are nevertheless persuaded that the most realistic way to view the world is through the spectacles of scripture" yet, unlike modern foundationalists, both skeptical and religious, "they recognise . . . that there can be no 'direct' or 'neutral'—that is, no nonimaginative—access to reality."[98] *Third*, Green addresses the problem of faith and certainty with a theology of the cross, insisting that God captures but does not compel the imagination of the faithful, which is "the only kind

---

95. Ibid., 101.

96. Ibid., 104.

97. Ibid. I am aware that a fine, extended discussion of revelation through the "form" of Christ is offered by Hans Urs von Balthasar in *The Glory of the Lord*, the first series of his great trilogy. I liked the critical edge Green brought, however, linking paradigms and imagination. It was also very late in the chapter to introduce von Balthasar's seven volumes.

98. Green, *Imagining God*, 143.

of conquest that leaves them free."[99] This argument is explicitly based on Luther, Kierkegaard, and Bonhoeffer, and in this characteristically Lutheran emphasis on the Gospel's revelation of God's power hidden in powerlessness is a fitting critique of Newman's insistence on an infallible revelation, certainty, and Church. Instead, Green is content for the whole thing to be self-authenticating in its living-out. He concludes that "Christians will find provisional confirmation of the story's truth in its continuing ability to illumine their own lives and the world around them."[100]

TO CONCLUDE

This chapter has been an attempt to see how abiding faith fares in the light of modern religious skepticism. The rationalistic and experiential responses to this skepticism appealed to one or another version of philosophical foundationalism to authenticate faith in the critical environment of modernity, but were in fact reactions in thrall to the spirit of modern skepticism—and vice versa, as more recent skepticism assumes that Christianity is based entirely on (erroneous) history, (unbelievable) Scripture, and (unreliable) experience. They did not do justice to abiding faith as a multi-stranded, evaluative, self-involving reality, as illustrated for instance by the two highly suggestive contemporary accounts of faith with which the chapter began—those of Bishop David Jenkins and of Tim Winton's character Raelene, from his short story "The Turning." Nor did such foundational approaches prove adequate in light of today's newer holistic epistemology, which blurs the distinctions between inner and outer, fact and interpretation, objective and subjective, on which such foundationalism relies. Here the discussion focused on George Lindbeck in theology, with Ludwig Wittgenstein and Thomas Kuhn in philosophy. The scientific paradigm provided the best image for the sort of worldview that abiding faith entails, with imagination explored as the key to faith's characteristic form of knowing. In a discussion of John Henry Newman and the contemporary theologian Garrett Green, imagination served to explicate the way abiding faith does its work—by capturing-yet-liberating the Christian, and forming them in the likeness of Christ. Green also helped to show how faith's personal certitude, on which Newman insisted, could be understood non-dogmatically and non-violently in keeping with the type of God we see revealed in the cross of Jesus Christ. This is not faith according to the rules

99. Ibid., 147.
100. Ibid.

of modernity's Cosmopolis—a quest for certainty rooted in control, which in turn reflects fear of the other and issues regularly in violence. Abiding faith, on the contrary, is calm, large-souled, and life-giving—not at all anxious, peevish, and defensive.

Having seen in this chapter how abiding faith can hold its own in today's contest for intellectual respectability, the final chapter to follow will show how abiding faith can and does play out today, as an alternative both to the homeless heart and to the false sacred.

Behold, I Make All Things New
Vision, Self, Spirituality

The title of this chapter recalls words from Revelation 21—words of the revolutionary lamb in whose presence the new heavens and the new earth are revealed, the heavenly Jerusalem.

This is a city where violence, manipulation, selfishness, and lies have no place, for the age of deprivation matched with "me first" self-assertion is over. The age of tribalism and war is over, too, with the nations and their claims relativized in the light of this city, while kings line up to surrender their former glory. It is a system of God's imagining, "a city not built with hands." This is why the heavenly city is structured in such a wonderful and mysterious way, with a typology of ancient mineralogy invoked to convey its extraordinary and polyphonic solidity—a structure entirely beyond and different from the systems of meaning that regularly govern human theory and practice. And there is no temple in the city, because the God of the slaughtered lamb is in its midst. Hence there is no more need for sacrifices to establish human order and peace with God. That is, the false sacred is at an end. No wonder it is a place where every tear from humanity's bitter travail is wiped away, along with that core imaginative principle of the old order, which is death. No wonder God's dream for humanity brings an end to the mourning, crying, and pain that life in the kingdom of shame and death demands—of violence and scapegoating, of frailty fearfully and anxiously shored up at the expense of the despised other. And this great vision with which the Bible draws to a close has its foretaste, wherever the Spirit of the slaughtered and resurrected lamb is at work.

In this final chapter, I want to look at three dimensions of that foretaste, which take us beyond the power of human meaning systems and the false sacred they regularly entail. Beyond the certainty, anxiety, and violence of modernity's Cosmopolis, we will explore the gift of God in Jesus Christ for the transformation of human existence under three headings: vision, self, and spirituality.

VISION: FROM SYSTEM TO GIFT

In chapter 2, I presented a case for understanding modernity as a system of meaning combining a cosmology with a political order—a Cosmopolis—in keeping with similar undertakings throughout the human cultural enterprise, as revealed for instance by anthropology. This Cosmopolis arose at a time of European uncertainty and anxiety in the sixteenth century and was variously developed to provide stability and reassurance. Its powerful rational, technological, and economic hegemony, its supreme cultural and political confidence, and its recreation of God in its own image made this wonderful and terrible human creation thrive for three hundred years. The twentieth century brought its implosion, however, with the spectacular redistribution of economic power in a new global era, and in the unleashing of a corrosive cultural pluralism that destabilized the rational certainties of modernity. The post-modern philosophical turn redescribed modernity as a human power-structure rather than a rational inevitability. In particular, victims of the Cosmopolis began to emerge. Feminism identified a patriarchal agenda at the root of modern Western life, from its cultural and economic exclusions to its disembodied metaphysics. Likewise, critical voices arising from modern Europe's "other" in the colonies created viable cultural alternatives by a blurring of distinctions, hybridizing the dominant culture with their own. Minority and marginalized voices of every sort demanded and received their place in the sun, out of the shadow cast by modernity's Cosmopolis.

Prophetic Christian voices joined in, identifying the false sacred tendencies of human culture wherever the ill-fitting other in whatever form is sacrificed to the security-providing idol that is modernity's system. From Nietzsche onwards, the collapse of the god of this Cosmopolis followed upon the system's own crisis. René Girard has been my prophet of choice in this discussion, for the simple power of his mimetic account of human desire driving system-building, his explication of how violent exclusion serves as social glue, and his breakthrough understanding of how Jesus began to unravel the sacrificial mentality necessary for human cultural creation.

Faith Is Not a System

Claims to encompass the totality of meaning are at the heart of Western modernity and of Christianity, whether conservative or liberal, wherever it shares the totalizing spirit of modernity's Cosmopolis. Yet these totalizing claims are slipping. The Hispanic American feminist theologian Mayra Rivera makes the simple but telling point that whenever "the system claims to comprehend all, the recognition that there are victims—people whose needs the system does not satisfy—reveals the limits of the system."[1] There is also the little matter of this whole drive toward certainty in Christianity regularly failing to deliver the goods. According to Kierkegaard, the greater our insistence on certainty, proof, and metaphysical completeness in matters of faith, the more certain it is that the inwardness and quiet certitude of genuine faith are lacking.[2] In such circumstances, Kierkegaard knew that the anxiety of formless possibility would remain unrelieved, demonstrating the hollowness of grand system building in modern philosophy and Christian faith. All this is misconceived, and especially the great intellectual system of Hegel that Kierkegaard disdained. Its prompt upending into atheism by Marx and Feuerbach provides as good a warning as any about the limited converting power of such systems.

Rowan Williams echoes this concern about fearfulness lying at the root of certainty claims in theology today. He singles out theodicy for special mention (which has both conservative- and liberal-theological versions)—the attempt to give a rational account of natural and human suffering and evil, so God's power and goodness are both vindicated. Interestingly, Williams twins this undertaking with the anti-realism I mentioned in the last chapter, which he sees as a kind of obverse to such totalizing faith. One account—the theodicy enterprise—urgently seeks to reconcile the ill-fitting complexity of existence with God's goodness and power, while the other, antirealist account dismisses God altogether, leaving only the optional practice of religion, as a corresponding attempt to be rid of too much complexity.[3] Neither system is adequate according to Williams, here honoring his teacher D. M. MacKinnon who

---

1. Rivera, *The Touch of Transcendence*, 70.
2. Kierkegaard, *The Concept of Anxiety*, 138–46.
3. Williams, "Trinity and Ontology" (1989). In *On Christian Theology*, 148–66.

insisted that the surd-like nature of so much in experience refuses complete closure to ethics as well as theology.[4]

Williams observes that the best sign of all this theoretical unresolvedness in our understanding of God is the fact that Christians are driven to the Trinitarian confession. The Trinity is not a system of belief but, rather, a mystery preserving God's freedom from systemic imprisonment. Indeed, this Trinitarian confession is highly political, supporting the post-modern vision of meaning in terms of the "polyphony" and un-control it endorses, in the face of modernity's totalizing dreams of closure.[5] This control extended to the modern Western preference for a generic divinity underwriting, among other things, the power ambitions of modern nation states. However, the Trinity is a perennial spanner in the works of all such divinities assigned to Cosmopolitical duty.

Such a polyphonic spiritual vision saves us from the binary oppositions that structure so much modern thinking—including Christianity when it misappropriates apocalyptic categories, applying them to struggles within history rather than understand them as providing a perspective on the whole of history. The biblical witness of apocalyptic literature is a perennial reminder that God is *beyond* the oppressive power structures of human history, so that faith cannot be reduced to the claims of any particular human system, let alone its black and white oppositions. However, the apocalyptic mindset has been too-readily taken over as a principle *internal* to history and national destiny, as Catherine Keller points out concerning her own nation, the United States. I touched on this in chapter 2, above. America has an apocalyptic vein in its national story, claiming God as America's champion against whichever excluded evil empire.[6] The Cold War and now the War on Terror are powerful examples of oppositional rather than polyphonic thinking, into which a Trinitarian (rather than Unitarian) view of God is less apt to be conscripted. The Gospel is liberating precisely because it is Trinitarian, relational, inclusive, and open outwards.

Nor is Jesus himself able to be annexed by systems of closure, despite the mentality that could conquer indigenous empires under his banner or devise

4. MacKinnon, "Ethics and Tragedy," 206.
5. Cunningham, *These Three Are One*.
6. Keller, *God and Power*. Peter Beinart suggests how America can recover international respect and still prevail in the War on Terror, by taking responsibility for improving conditions in poor Muslim countries, recalling the example of the Marshall Plan and other successes by American liberals in postwar foreign policy; see Beinart, *The Good Fight*.

a bumper-sticker proclaiming "Kill a Commie for Christ." I offer a recent example, illustrating the conservatives' insistence on making Jesus in their own image. At our place we have recently enjoyed a fine NBC TV series on DVD entitled *The Book of Daniel*, about a painkiller-popping New England Episcopalian priest called Daniel (Aidan Quinn) and his adventures at home and in the parish—with a wife too fond of martinis, a gay son, an embezzling brother-in-law, an anxiety-radiating female bishop, and a church-school building project in the hands of the Mafia. Most notably, a thirty-ish Jesus (Garrett Dillahunt) regularly appears in costume at Daniel's side as a wise guide and support, very frank, quirky, and Jewishly humorous. Indeed, at Morning Prayer earlier today—the day of writing—I found myself imagining how Jesus appears to Daniel in this program when the set reading from Acts 9 portrayed the Lord appearing to Ananias in a vision, and persuading him against his better judgment to go and lay hands on the blinded Saul.

Anyway, *The Book of Daniel* shows—sometimes quite movingly—how ordinary family dynamics, discipleship, and the demanding, persevering life of faith play out together in the real world. My point here is that the show was pulled off American television mid-series after an avalanche of complaints from a scandalized, religiously conservative public and canned forever, apart from its 2006 release on DVD. Its Jesus was "a namby-pamby frat boy," according to one blogger, while the image of a loving Christian family helping each other through the ups and downs of life was just not Christian enough. This reaction represents the nexus between certainty and anxiety about which I am concerned, requiring a more remote, religious, disapproving (in fact, violently disapproving) Jesus.

Jesus need not and should not, however, be conscripted for Cosmopolitical duty, just as God rightly understood is not that sort of god either. The widespread conservative Evangelical worldview of today—quixotically unscientific, widely misogynistic, and invariably homophobic—has dubious connections to Christ. Instead, a non-imperial understanding of Christ emerges as a constant feature of "Christology from below" in its many forms during the last quarter of the twentieth century. Jesus' face is found among faces of the poor, women, African Americans, and gay people riding the postmodern wave towards recognition and justice, as a voice of the oppressed rather than a plank in the ideology and the system that oppresses them.

Rowan Williams points out that the finality of Christ is precisely not the triumph of totalizing meaning but, rather, the unique revelation of a non-hegemonic, self-disposing God. It is salutary to remember that Jesus's crucifixion was at the hands of a controlling religious system. Hence following Jesus cannot mean hiding out in another one just like it. Rather, his finality and hence his authority is as a particularity on which every human system of meaning has to choke, because Jesus will not be swallowed by any of them.[7] René Girard's own account of Jesus's finality is complimentary with that of Williams—in Jesus the nature of human meaning making is shown to be implicated in violence and scapegoating, as his own crucifixion quintessentially demonstrates. Hereafter, this universal trend loses traction because Western culture is now alert to its nature and working, thanks to Jesus revealed as the Christ.[8]

Jesus's empty tomb is a further sign that the risen one cannot be pinned down. The empty tomb is a tease and a warning, according to Williams: "he is not here."[9] Consequently, Christ is free in the Spirit to judge all who would enroll his Easter triumph in whichever ultimately self-serving and oppressive Christian program of theory or practice. Williams ends this particular discussion with some musings about the role of theology being to hold this space of divine freedom open, resisting its premature closure—not as a relativistic denial of Christ's definitive witness but precisely because that definitive witness has a particular nature, which is away from certainty, anxiety, and violence. This raises the wider question of human meaning making in the light of Christ. What is appropriate and what is not?

Modest Metaphysics

There is scope for debate about the right relationship between metaphysics and theology if this vision of faith beyond anxious and violent-tending control of the world's complexity is correct. If faith is not to slip the traces of wider rationality altogether as fideism recommends, than what is its proper relationship with various overarching philosophical accounts of meaning?

In the last chapter the trend emerging was to see meaning in tentative terms—empirically related to the world of experience as a web of understanding, paradigmatic and imaginative, commending itself as part of a form of life and, by its coherent thoroughness, attending with respect to the world's complexity. But not with any presumption to absolute definitiveness and timeless theoretical closure. Too-ambitious metaphysics trips over the complexity of

7. Williams, "The Finality of Christ" (1990). In *On Christian Theology*, 93–106.

8. Girard, *Things Hidden since the Foundation of the World*, 249–53.

9. Williams, "Between the Cherubim: The Empty Tomb and the Empty Throne" (1996). In *On Christian Theology*, 183–96.

reality, which serves as a salutary reminder to theology that it should not aspire after theoretical comprehensiveness, as D. M. MacKinnon points out.[10]

One option is to cut the metaphysical nerve altogether and declare the whole undertaking to be ill-conceived and inappropriate. Gianni Vattimo is a contemporary Catholic philosopher who inherits from Nietzsche and Heidegger a critique of the nexus between belief in God and controlling rationality, viewing all objective metaphysical claims as tainted by the false sacred. Vattimo interprets secularization as the wholly appropriate and desirable fruit of Christ unpicking the false gods of the system, whose deserved end is atheism. This is the return of true religion, however, beyond the god of the system who has died.[11] The suppression since Nietzsche of the great controlling individual will that God became from the late-Middle Ages recalls the kenosis (i.e. self-emptying) of God in Jesus Christ, which is at the heart of the Gospel. It is this vision that for Vattimo links together a kenotic understanding of God, weak ontology in metaphysics, and non-violence in the socio-political order. Vattimo is a Girardian. He highlights one possible aspect of working out a full Girardian account of modernity. This is central to what I plan to investigate in my next book, and resolve in my own mind.

A less radical solution (or version of the same solution) is to shift metaphysics in a more relational, less individualistically-oriented direction, as the feminist and liberation theologians teach us. Likewise, the Trinity is currently being mined for resources in this very cause—pointing beyond the controlling 'I' towards a lighter metaphysics that can embrace (without controlling) the diverse and ill-fitting from the perspective of the relational.

I am aware of one attempt along this line that is quite comprehensive. The Canadian Christian philosopher Paul Janz offers a form of critical realist metaphysics that denies philosophical closure while affirming the claim of objective reality, and the role of the human mind in world-making, but also the challenge of Christ through revelation to every pretentious false sacred —along with the need for right participation if something like the truth is to emerge. Janz is also influenced by MacKinnon's discussion of the need to incorporate the ill-fitting complexity of existence, typified by the tragic, and for philosophy to moderate its idealistic tendencies accordingly. And he is in tune with the holistic epistemology that emerged at the heart of faith's mentality in the last chapter, linking the objective hold of our minds on the world with the subjective component of world-making, combining correspondence and

10. MacKinnon, "The Conflict between Realism and Idealism," 164–65.
11. Vattimo, *Belief*; also *After Christianity*.

coherence approaches to truth. The really notable thing here, however, is the way Janz includes the gift of meaning that comes from revelation, which is only accessible to the rightly-disposed individual—the sort of thing discussed at the end of the last chapter under the heading of faith and imagination. Reason certainly does not give us the world, according to Janz and in keeping with the whole tenor of this discussion. But the world is given to reason in a suitably Christian way if sensory data are augmented by the human classifying logos of rationality along with the counter-logos of revelation. This resets the whole question beyond the distortions that a despairing identity bring to whatever meaning humans make in the world. Here of course we are talking about the power of sin. Janz writes, "the real detachment that must occur here is precisely the detachment from the false self, that is, from the despairing way of being human, from the autonomous way of being human, and the movement toward a creaturely way of being human."[12] His indication that this openness beyond the false sacred represents an appropriately creaturely stance points forward to what I will be exploring in the next section under the heading of "self," and what emerges for us in the light of this new attitude.

I want to address one final problem before drawing this section to a close. It is necessary to beware the sectarian impulse, whereby Christianity overreacts to the perceived threat of contamination by an alien mindset through seeking a purer version of itself. This purer version can become just one more instance of the false sacred—itself becoming a kind of law that works by excluding the unsuitable and ill-fitting, like every other cultural manifestation of the false sacred. In particular, and despite the advance that his "cultural-linguistic" proposal represented over other Christian accounts of faith's mentality, George Lindbeck and the post-liberals can go too far in aspiring to a pure Christian culture. How can we honor this zeal for discipleship without it becoming zeal for the law?

Two answers. First, we are reminded by the American theologian Kathryn Tanner that cultures are flexible, cumulative, adaptive, and changing, or else they cannot survive. The post-colonial experience provides many examples of this. She insists that faithful Christianity has always meant inhabiting the wider culture, though in a different spirit, rather than achieving a "culturally pure" Christian Church.[13] While affirming Lindbeck's broad approach to the storied nature of Christian identity, American Catholic theologian Terrence Tilley insists that the most authentic tradition of the Catholic Church is

12. Janz, *God, the Mind's Desire*, 218.
13. Tanner, *Theories of Culture*.

hopeful, incarnational, open, and world-affirming—all of which militates against the sort of purism that he insists arose late in the day with papal infallibility—and it is an evolving tradition, so that it is sometimes only with hindsight (contra Newman) that the truly Catholic emerges.[14] This is a gentle reminder that a genuinely Christian culture is not obsessive about border violations. Bruce Marshall gives a number of examples of the way encounter with wider culture has changed the Church's sense of the plain meaning of Scripture over time.[15] He demonstrates internal transformations within the Christian web of meaning, of the sort that the holistic epistemology outlined in chapter 5 absolutely requires. Rowan Williams is another who positively welcomes engagement with alien perspectives as perennially fruitful for the Church, enriching rather than diminishing its faith.[16] Surely this is one of the most attractive things about abiding faith—its large-souledness, beyond peevish superiority and fearfulness toward the world.

Second, there will be implications for apologetics. For example, Christian apologetics could help Western culture get over its current ruling myth of therapeutic individualism by showing that many noble and worthwhile commitments and trusts are actually sustained by participation in narratives and traditions, hence opening a wider cultural window of explicability for the Christian version of abiding faith as a storied identity. This approach, which American post-liberal theologian William Werpehowski calls "ad hoc apologetics," is certainly a better option than standard liberal Christian apologetics, competing for meaning on the same ground with therapeutic individualism, offering nothing better than an alternative theoretical account of personal meaning.[17] That standard liberal Christian style of apologetic bypasses the whole lived, participatory, form-of-life reality of abiding faith, virtually ensuring that Christianity will appear in a boring and second best light alongside whichever lively secular alternative. Faith is not just more of the same—it is not just a system of human creation in competition with other such systems. Rather, it is better understood as a gift from God centered on a form of life.

---

14. Tilley, *Inventing Catholic Tradition*.

15. Marshall, "Absorbing the World: Christianity and the Universe of Truths."

16. Williams, "The Judgement of the World" (1989). In *On Christian Theology*, 29–43.

17. Werpehowski, "Ad Hoc Apologetics," 301.

Meaning as a Gift

It is poignant to read English Catholic theologian James Alison on the problem here, which is being able to receive identity as a gift rather than forever bewail its absence, or else pathetically pursue it, or even violently assert it in the face of private doubts. In a 1999 lecture to a gay San Francisco audience, he was at pains to deconstruct his own billing as a gay activist, making his regular point that if a homophobic culture and Church are wrong—if they have fallen for a false sacred reality that requires gay scapegoats to shore it up—then it would be a tragedy for the gay community to be locked into opposition with that very homophobia, feeding off it and defining itself in a perpetually reactive mode. This would be domination by the false sacred even in the act of protest against it, and a clear case of Girardian mimetic doubling. Instead, Alison affirms the authentic being, and *the right to be*, of his audience, in an atmosphere of anger over the recent murder of a bay area gay couple by some religiously hot-headed young rednecks.

Alison's lecture is a little classic of pastoral wisdom, and radical in his characteristically tongue-in-cheek appropriation of the conservatives' preferred sources of authority. For instance, he points to the central tenets of Catholic faith—creation, incarnation, and resurrection—and there he finds identity and meaning as a gift from God. Specifically, the Council of Trent, and in particular its resistance to Protestant Reformed notions of total depravity (that is, that our human being is distorted in every faculty by sin), emerges as an unlikely champion. Human beings are God's good creation, including gay people who are told regularly in Church and society that they are defective heterosexuals and that they must not claim to be otherwise, as if it is alright to be as they are. Likewise, the resurrection of Jesus is God reclaiming the place of shame as the launching pad for a world-transforming mission, which saw the frightened and paralyzed disciples empowered with a boldness reflecting a new confidence in being, that was anything but reactive and oppositional. The liberation of knowing oneself to be created by God, and of being caught up in the resurrection, gives an identity that would otherwise have to be made by some exclusion—of gays by the homophobic, and the homophobic by gays. In this vision of identity as God's gift, Alison also finds his own priestly commission reaffirmed, toward all the victims of false sacred realities that entrap both the culture and the Church.

> And beneath and in the midst of that I see the Sacred Heart of Jesus, palpitating and bleeding with pain and love because these

are his brothers: the weak ones, the fatherless ones, the shepherdless ones, the murderers and traitors and the simply confused, who can, oh yes who can, be nudged into a story of being held in being beyond all the flailing around, the bravado, the cover-up of a life out of control. And he's saying, and it cuts me to the quick: Feed my sheep, feed my sheep, feed my lambs.[18]

Only this faith as a gift, the opposite of a human system or idol, will cure the false sacred and the binary back-and-forth of violence that it mandates. This is about a God who gives being, rather than an idol of human construction originating in a system of self-assertion and exclusion. Such idols are bound for their own twilight, as the French Catholic philosopher Jean-Luc Marion points out.[19]

Marion is concerned to preserve the freedom of this gift from being annexed to human control. He subtly dismisses extreme Reformed Protestant bibliolatry, insisting on the divinity of the Holy Spirit ensuring that the divine word transgresses the text. Accordingly, he makes a traditional Catholic argument for the Eucharist as *the* great site of unalloyed gift. The logic of God's gift in the incarnation points to the real presence of Christ in the Eucharist as pure gift, beyond the text and beyond theoretical explanation. Here Marion identifies a problem with Vatican II–era attempts to redefine Christ's presence in the Eucharist in terms of *transignification*, in the hands of Edward Schillebeeckx and others. This move shifted emphasis away from Aristotelian physics and the invisible transformation of the "whole substance" of the bread and wine into the "substance" of Christ to a more recent understanding of meaning as constructed symbolically in human language and communal practice, so the "significance" of bread and wine change at the consecration, becoming what the people of God intend rather than what the baker and vintner intended. At the time such a shift no doubt helped to emphasize a role for the whole assembly in celebrating the Eucharist, as against a former clericalized and even bureaucratized version of Christ's Eucharistic presence.[20] *Inter alia*, Catherine Pickstock warns of other consequences when modernity gets its hands on liturgy, corrupting it with its own spirit of stifling closure. She points to the older rites retaining some of the mystery that modern rites risk forfeiting in their relentlessly forward moving, voluble clarity, losing the

---

18. Alison, "On Finding a Story," in *Faith beyond Resentment*, 194–208, 208.
19. Marion, *God without Being*, 37.
20. See, e.g., Edward Schillebeeckx, and his fine discussion in *The Eucharist*.

sense that liturgy is primarily about God's gift rather than human togetherness and shared meaning.[21]

The problem with transignification, Marion realizes, is that it makes Christ's Eucharistic presence an act of human meaning making rather than an objective gift of God's making, hence his rehabilitation of traditional Catholic teaching on the real presence. Here we have the clearest expression of Christ present, apart from human constructions, as God's loving self-donation. Thus, Christ remains an active subject in the Eucharist rather than a passive object in the control of a human institution—which is what the Reformers wanted, too, as Rowan Williams points out.[22]

And it is this gift which grounds the logic of faith, according to Marion. "But if a relation of mastery governs the confession of faith," he warns, "restricting it to busy militancy and/or to conquering heresy, we are miles away from what we are seeking—to absorb the discourse of faith in the 'logic' of charity."[23] The truth of faith is for Jesus to confirm, and so it cannot involve what Marion refers to as "the idiotic prolepsis of a blunt certitude."[24] It is in fact better than that—it is the stuff of personal certitude rather than the certainty of systemic hegemony. According to Marion, as for Alison, "[t]his . . . is the pretension of an absolute qualification, the certitude of an election, the assurance of having neither explanation to give nor account to settle, nor, at the extreme, words to make heard."[25] If faith were a system, promising more certainty than this, it would not offer this quiet certitude. Kierkegaard has warned us that such religious certainty does not cure anxiety. A system will not do it for us. But a gift will.

SELF: FROM ANXIOUS INDIVIDUAL TO ECCLESIAL PERSON

In chapter 3, I introduced the Girardian vision of human life as *interdividual*, which means living in the desires of others rather than being a coherent, autonomous self in our own right—an individual. It is from these *interdividuals* that religions and cultures are made and defended by the scapegoat mecha-

---

21. Pickstock, *After Writing*. This is an argument with which I have some sympathy, but also some significant reservations: see Cowdell, *God's Next Big Thing*, 138–42.
22. Williams, "The Nature of a Sacrament" (1987). In *On Christian Theology*, 197–208.
23. Marion, *God without Being*, 186.
24. Ibid., 71.
25. Ibid., 189.

nism. It is a constant of post-modern anthropology to question foundational individuality, however. René Girard offers but one example.

Beyond the Modern Western Self

The modern version of the self goes back to Descartes who distinguished between outer and inner, mind and matter. But that distinction has been subjected to sustained criticism since the mid-twentieth century. In the last chapter we saw in the later Wittgenstein, and holistic epistemology more generally, an acknowledgement that networks of mutual trust and accountability, with unexamined assumptions undergirding forms of life, challenged modern conceptions of the individual as the ultimate, fully-conscious rational arbiter of meaning and truth. The mid-century Oxford philosopher Gilbert Ryle famously dismissed the Cartesian account of minds with a radical empiricism called "linguistic behaviorism," arguing that the mind was an unnecessary abstraction from the observed behaviors and dispositions of people.[26] The "real you" is not some inner state, whether presently existing or to be "awakened" in the Romantic manner, but it is simply a way of talking about what you do and how you live your life. The inner-you, the real you, is fragile. As one Australian hospital registrar put it wryly in a press article, reflecting on his daily struggle to salvage lives from this terrible fragility, "I have not had a brain injury, therefore I am."

The dependence of the "inner me" on all sorts of "outward reality," not just my damageable body and brain, is now a widespread insight of postmodernity, with anthropologists, sociologists, geographers, and even economists able to give a plausible and even far-reaching account of why we are as we are. Advertisers in service to the commodity form program the "inner me," also, as computer programmers write instructions in code for machines to follow. It is not an insult to the human animal to talk like this. The real insult is to make do with an unworthy, limited, hijacked "self" when something better is on offer. This is the point I want to make in this section: that there is a gift of self that might just make up for our having to surrender the modern myth of the "inner self"—that inarticulate, unreliable, manipulable fair-weather friend who comes and goes from our lives.

God is certainly in on this whole drama of transforming the mythical modern Western self into a real and substantial dweller in a liberated form of life. Indeed, Christian theology has proved highly responsive to this postmodern anthropology of the de-nucleated self. It helps to account for what

26. Ryle, *The Concept of Mind*.

abiding faith means. As St. Paul knew, abiding faith means being shifted from dwelling in sin, the world, and the flesh to abiding in Christ. Modern Western culture and its therapeutic individualism seeks and promises a secure and authentic self maintained across the changes of life, but our reflection in chapter 1 on the homeless hearts of modernity gives the lie to this claim, and especially in light of the commodity form and its chronic destabilizing effects. Ironically, the Gospel of grace, whereby we come to abide in Jesus Christ, delivers an identity for a lifetime far more reliably than what the American theologian Russell Reno calls "me-first humanism" can provide—"we endure as continuous beings," he writes, "because Jesus is 'for us' as the power of incorporation."[27]

Emergent Trinitarianism provided another dimension of this healing, liberating orthodoxy, presenting the divine persons in particular but not individual terms. That is, it emphasized the relations of the divine persons one to another, holding together their unity and diversity in terms of mutual self-definitions—Son of the Father, Father of the Son, Spirit of the Son, of the Father, begotten, proceeding from, etc. Hence a graciously mutual relationship of love is a better model for God's being than the mighty, willing individual of modern theism and atheism. Indeed, the inscrutable almighty and the inward modern Western individual prove to be Siamese twins, sharing one univocal being, as became clear in chapter 2. If we are to be more like the real God, however, then we are better understood in terms of our relationships than in individual terms. According to the African Anglican theologian John Pobee, an African Descartes would have insisted that *Cognatus Sum, Ergo Sum*— "I have relatives, therefore I am." This prioritizing of relationship sounds strange and upside down to the modern Westerner, though clearly it is a widely-held sentiment in non-Western cultures. On a polyphonic Trinitarian model, then, it is better to view us as *particular yet inter-subjective nodes in a web of communication* than as isolated individuals.[28]

Rowan Williams is a Christian of global influence who is staking everything on this being true. This theological platform informs his leadership as Archbishop of Canterbury at a time when mutually antagonistic self-definition is the order of the day around the Anglican Communion, and identities are in lockdown for both conservatives and liberals. Archbishop Williams gently reminds the Communion that a better and more secure identity is available in mutual openness and vulnerability. The message of creation, he says—that

27. Reno, *Redemptive Change*, 11.
28. See Cunningham, *These Three Are One*, 121–230.

who we are is created by God—includes the gift of an identity, so we do not have to make one for ourselves. And we certainly do not have to invoke God as a bulwark for securing an identity in this or that fantasy of impregnability.[29] Rowan Williams laments the variety of troubles we get into in the modern West by trying to make our own identities—as Romantic victims, by insisting on our rights and refusing accountability, by post-modern bricolage without limits. We have lost our souls, he concludes, because we have lost the iconic eye—the non-competing "other" who assays us with the demanding otherness of grace, calling an identity into being.[30] God does not offer us any easy security, however, keeping risk and vulnerability at bay—as we might try to do by outward achievement, inward withdrawal, or by shutting out the ill-fitting. The resurrection reminds Rowan Williams of how Jesus dismisses all these strategies and comes through regardless thanks to God.[31] The Archbishop's agenda for the Anglican Communion, insisting on the courage to face difference without fear and to maintain openness, is based on how God gives the gift of identity—by having us go up against a resistant world, not by trying to master it or escape it. In this struggle, of remaining open to otherness rather than seeking to foreclose on it, an identity is discovered from God that we do not have to make for ourselves or protect.[32]

Saintly Influence: Edith Wyschogrod and James Alison

Beyond its denial of a settled inner self, or even a dormant "Sleeping Beauty self" that needs to be awakened by another, post-modern anthropology tends to view the self as a gift of the other. The demanding other actually *creates* the self, rather than merely awakening it from dormancy. Episcopalian theologian Mark McIntosh discusses a range of such post-modern accounts—of how human selves emerge, and ultimately in Trinitarian terms: as a relational God makes relational selves in God's own image through relationships. Emmanuel Levinas, Edith Stein, and Simone Weil are among the key thinkers he examines but it is the American Jewish philosopher and ethicist Edith Wyschogrod

---

29. Williams, "On Being Creatures," in *On Christian Theology*, 63–78.

30. Williams, *Lost Icons*.

31. Williams, "Interiority and Epiphany: A Reading in New Testament Ethics," in *On Christian Theology*, 239–64.

32. Williams, "Resurrection and Peace: More On New Testament Ethics," in *On Christian Theology*, 265–75.

that I want to stay with, and her account of what constitutes sanctity in post-modern culture.[33]

Wyschogrod defines the post-modern saint as a radical altruist who is captured by the suffering other, serving that other's need at whatever cost to their own selves—and with no scope for any resentment, either, because the other is not experienced as demanding, in competition with the self and its needs. Wyschogrod imagines a radically de-nucleated self which finds its centre in the other, apart from any ideological cause being served and with no expectation that serving the other will be beneficial. Her "Saints are 'native speakers' of the language of alterity, poets of the imperative."[34] This is a powerful insight, drawing on Emanuel Levinas's attention to the immediate moral claim upon us of "the face" of the other—an "epiphany" prior to self-conscious reflection; a moral beacon in the post-modern void of wider meaningfulness.[35]

But because there is this lack of wider meaningfulness, according to post-modern theory, society's institutions are viewed as anything but the objectively valid carriers of meaning that modernity saw them to be, while power is understood to corrupt truth itself. Against this backdrop of suspicion Wyschogrod struggles to account for how sanctity conveys itself. Somehow saints make something possible for others by themselves standing free from the cynical, self-serving norms of power. Wyschogrod illustrates this by reflecting on a modern hagiographic narrative by Henry James, in his 1902 novel *The Wings of the Dove*. In this story, the cynical Kate and her partner Densher aim to fleece the rich, saintly, lovelorn but terminally-ill Millie so they can fulfill their own dreams, only to find the plan spoiled by the transforming savor of Millie's memory on Densher. The influence of her saintliness, the "wings of the dove," overshadowed and transformed him, so he could no longer follow through on the plan. In Wyschogrod's discussion we come close to mimetic awareness, though the influence of her saints is not through straight mimicry but through a transforming effect more generally. Likewise any role for the Church is viewed suspiciously because, for Wyschogrod, "[i]nstitutional structure and saintly will are rival sources of power."[36]

---

33. McIntosh, "Love for the Other and Discovery of the Self," in *Mystical Theology*, 211–42.
34. Wyschogrod, *Saints and Postmodernism*, 183.
35. See, e.g., Levinas, "Ethics as First Philosophy."
36. Wyschogrod, "Saintly Influence," in *Saints and Postmodernism*, 31–60, 37.

I suggest that her aim of protecting the saintly impulse from mediation —as a pure, uncorrupted, post-modern *given*—is achieved more effectively if we take a Girardian approach. The altruistic desire of a saint would then be seen as derived mimetically from others and in turn handed-on mimetically. In Wyschogrod's own example, from *The Wings of the Dove*, the saintly Millie replaces the avaricious Kate as model for Densher's desire.

But this would only be possible if the saint had first themselves been freed from unworthy models of desire, escaping mimetic fascination with the false sacred—the Girardian name for all the things Wyschogrod seems rightly to fear in the unreliable and controlling mindset of modernity. Likewise, abiding faith means drawing our being no longer from others who are living under the sway of the false sacred—chiefly under the power of the commodity form and the life agenda it imposes on the modern West—but, rather, from those who have come under the sway of Christ and his non-rivalistic desire. The de-nucleated self that emerges has the marks of Wyschogrod's saint alright: it is free from the need to be right, to be against others in order to become a solid self (hence it is no longer chronically defensive and resentful toward others); and it is not always trying to put things right, which is an oppositional profile still dominated by former models of desire who have become obstacles to that desire. This new self is a loving, non-activist, non-ideologue self, who has received its self from the other. But not from the object of its altruistic attention, as Wyschogrod would have it. Despite their altruism, her saints have a kind of vampire-like relation to the object of their compassionate attentions. Instead, in a Girardian account, some worthy new model awakens the altruistic attention, in a chain of influence that can be traced "backwards" through the saints and also "sideways" to Scripture, liturgy, and contemporary Christian fellowship, with the root of that "saintly influence" to be found in Jesus himself. St. Paul makes this very clear in addressing his own place in the chain of influence, concluding that, at its source, "the love of Christ urges us on" (2 Cor 5:11–14).

This is a new quality of self discovered by surprise, as James Alison explains, "given to me as a 'real me' in a series of new desires for new projects which share the huge affection and gentleness towards others that I have found myself receiving."[37] This is a lower-temperature account than Wyschogrod's, according to which the "possession" of the saintly subject is by the object of its ministrations. My instinct is that Wyschogrod's understanding of sanctity, while rightly affirming a de-nucleated self, is a potential candidate for

37. Alison, "The Strangeness of this Passivity," in *On Being Liked*, 131–46, 144.

obsessional attachments and self-denial to the point of self-hatred, which Simone Weil and some earlier women saints (I think for instance of Margaret Mary Alocoque) may have demonstrated. Alison's account of sanctity is more ordinary, more widely accessible, and not quite the overheated "miracle of alterity" that Wyschogrod requires.

A good example of how a Girardian account of saintly influence might play out is given by the Australian philosopher and ethicist Raimond Gaita, in his personal account of a hospital ward of dehumanized, incurable patients who received at best the condescending attentions of well-intentioned psychiatrists. Until the nun who regularly visited these incurables began to transform Gaita's and the psychiatrists' sense of the dignity of these patients through her demeanor with them, including her body language and inflexion. This revealed both something about the patients and about the false consciousness of those who had professed to really care for them.[38] Seen from a Girardian perspective, I suggest that this is a straightforward account: the nun as model has been constrained by the love of Christ (the motto of the Sisters of Mercy, if I am not mistaken) and in this model finds her "self," so that others in time come to share Christ's compassion for those on her ward by coming to share her desire. She is "possessed" by Christ, however, and not by the unfortunates on the ward. They do not give her a self, as Wyschogrod would have it, but they certainly do not forfeit any benefit because of that. The nun's "self" is as much for them as that of a Wyschogrod saint would be, and they are perhaps spared some unwanted consequences because her self is more stable, drawn from a wider nexus of models.

The Role of Others in Making the Self

Let me now try to spell out where I have been going in this discussion of the self. Abiding faith entails a new self, beyond that created by others who are under the power of the false sacred. This new self has to emerge by a process of conversion away from the desires of others toward the desire of Christ—the ultimate "other"—so our self is created by the influence of his self. To clarify what I mean by "other" in this Girardian vision I am offering, I draw on James Alison's helpful threefold distinction. We are normally shaped by the desire of the *customary* other who we encounter in our normal environment, and we define ourselves (with greater or lesser antipathy, even violent exclusion) against the *removed* other. Conversion to Christ means that we receive our self

---

38. Gaita, *A Common Humanity*, 17–19.

as gift from the *utterly* other, whose otherness is manifest in standing free of all human systems of meaning making that rely on exclusions typical of the false sacred.[39] Jesus is fully human of course, *but not typically human*. In the light of this clarification about the various meanings of "other" involved in making the self, my point about the self accompanying abiding faith is this: *instead of anxiously controlling the other in order to secure our self, we become selves who are free to embrace and welcome the other*. This is what abiding faith entails, as a new self in a new form of life emerges from the grip of the false self.

Let me tease this out a little more carefully. We become the selves we are because we internalize the *customary* other, also because we reject the *removed* other whom we fear and despise. This is the normal human state, where the false sacred holds sway. But thanks to Christ, the *utterly* other—who, against all expectations, is utterly *for* us, and who *likes* us—we are freed from the control of being defined by the *customary* other, and from having to control and repress the *removed* other. And in becoming free from the *removed* other, we are also freed from any ongoing fascination with them (i.e. either opposing them or having to be their savior—the latter I think constituting a risk for Wyschogrod's post-modern saint). The presence of the *utterly* other as the key to all this is the main difference from Wyschogrod's account which, as I have indicated, takes us in a potentially overheated direction, dissolving the personal boundaries necessary for establishing emotionally healthy, caring relationships.

There is a decidedly positive role for the Church here. Alison acknowledges with Wyschogrod the institutional distortions of Church life, but is protected by his Christian eschatological sensibility from unrealistic expectations of the actual, historical Church. He is not as perplexed by the impurity of institutions as she apparently is, as we see in her suspicion of saintly influence being institutionally mediated.

This brings me to my final point here about the self that accompanies abiding faith. It is no longer an individual self, as modernity would have it—we know from Girard's *interdividual* account that individuals are in fact confabulations from the desires of others. So how might we name the new, "post-individual" self? The Greek Orthodox theologian, Bishop John Zizioulas, helpfully describes the path to salvation as that from *individual* to *person*, and from *biological* to *ecclesial* existence. Hence we are freed from the programmatic self assertion of our competitive biological nature to become persons able to embrace the other. This is a profound image: from isolated,

39. Alison, *Knowing Jesus*, 14–15.

threatened, defensively-yet-self-assertively fragile *individuals* to poised, secure, relational *persons* whose essentially relational identity is a gift of our essentially relational God, the Holy Trinity.[40] James Alison also finds this to be a powerful image for what he is trying to say. Rather than disparage the biological, however—because original sin in his account is not about our biological nature but, rather, the Girardian "basic state of human nature" which is living in the desires of others—Alison prefers the phrase "an-ecclesial existence." Hence the transformation of which Zizioulas speaks becomes for Alison the shift from *an-ecclesial* to *ecclesial* existence.[41] What is that existence like?

SPIRITUALITY: FROM IMMATURE NEED TO MATURE COMPASSION

The vision of abiding faith that I am developing entails being liberated from the false self which has lived in thrall to the desires of others for security, identity, and belonging, in mindsets and groups reflecting the controlling power of the false sacred. It brings a new ecclesial existence and a holiness that is not at all remote and standoffish—if it were, it would be just more of the same. There are both contemplative and active dimensions. "I am free as I find myself finally unencumbered by idolatry, false desire and vanity," as the English theologian John Webster expresses it, "and therefore enabled to fill out, actively to occupy and expand the role to which I am appointed."[42] It is the gift of a new way of being beyond modernity's—and much modern Christianity's—addiction to violent-tending mastery. So it is marked by loving and *patient* openness to God and to others, no longer feeling self-righteously disappointed with life's lack of closure and with others' natural limitations.[43] It is a quietly-and-securely inhabited holiness that you might call *chilled*. It is silent and centered, but not quietist and dissociated.

In particular, it is beyond the kind of *certainty* that goes with modernity and mastery, and with all their unwelcome geo-political manifestations, as Catherine Keller points out against the backdrop of American life today, where

> many people come to faith precisely in order to escape uncertainty. And the modalities of fundamentalism across the religions will

---

40. Zizioulas, *Being as Communion*, 27–65.
41. Alison, *The Joy of Being Wrong*, 162–63.
42. Webster, *Holiness*, 94.
43. See the fine discussion by Dutch-American Jesuit theologian Frans Jozef van Beeck, in *God Encountered*, especially 3–145.

continue to promise certainty. They offer a cure for the ambiguity of life. Oldstream Christianity . . . cannot ever compete on the terrain of certainty. There we simply lose. Indeed we might despair at a so-called Christian public who supports a politics of religious certainty—even . . . presidents who claim to know and do the will of their God-Father. This certainty has permitted the new messianic imperialism. But given the manifest failure of its projects, we need not despair. Its certainty proves certainly wrong. Its promises of stability and order are exposed as reckless boasts. And many who had been blinded by the light of a false certainty learn to see in the dark. The space opens wider, then, for Wisdom, in whom we learn the humbling old knowledge of our own ignorance. . . . This unknowing throws us back upon faith, not as an absolute kind of knowledge, but as the trustful courage that we require precisely *because* we cannot have certainty.[44]

I want to examine some aspects of this spirituality from two perspectives. First, how this plays out as we are mercifully (if painfully) relieved of our fascination with the false sacred—involving an interlude in which I share some personal experience in this area—and, second, how very world affirming all this becomes.

Healthy Attachments

James Alison is the best available guide on these matters, in my view, with his sharp analysis of how we are so readily trapped in group-think, and how the group even controls its dissidents. He observes how the law acts as a system of goodness, defining the in-group at the expense of the out-group. The generic divinity of social cohesion and "moral values" is regularly an avatar of the false sacred and a genuinely atheistic charade, not at all like Jewish monotheism in the Bible that was harder on the in-group than on outsiders. The violent cosmology of Babylon, rejected by (at least one person in) post-exilic Israel in the peaceful creation story that begins the Book of Genesis, returns whenever Christianity descends into the psychodrama of us-against-the-wicked-other—which we regularly see, for instance, in the misogyny and homophobia of much conservative Christianity. This is a belief in the violence of cosmic dualism rather than the Gospel, according to Alison.[45] However, Jesus occupies the place of shame and shows there is no outside (i.e. to the

---

44. Keller, *God and Power*, 149.

45. Alison, "Monotheism and the Indispensability of Irrelevance." In *Undergoing God*, 17–32.

jealously-guarded inside) that makes any sense, so solidarity with the outsider rather than a relationship with them characterized by obsession and rejection marks the onset of spiritual maturity. We have moved beyond the virtual prison of bogus faith based on a closed system of goodness. "We are being shown that we start off from a skewed reality, that what we call normality is in fact out of kilter, and true reality is much more alive than anything we know; so much so that we need training and new hearts and new eyes to be able to glimpse it along with that gift of being able to relax into spaciousness and being held by a power greater and more trustable than our own, which we call the gift of faith."[46]

Alison helpfully illustrates the way group belonging demands its exclusions with the Gerasene demoniac story, following Girard's own treatment of this passage (Mark 5:1–20). The community under Roman occupation is dependent, implicated, and compromised but, rather than face this unwelcome truth about itself, and the risk that would pose to business as usual, they take this strange and weak member of their community and load all their disquiet about the unwelcome other onto him, before casting him out to do his anthropological duty. By restoring the demoniac to normality Jesus provokes a crisis of self-definition for the townspeople—no wonder they want Jesus to leave. He shows how God rehabilitates the "bad influence" and calls for its reintegration, and he leaves the former outsider there with them so they have to find a new way forward together, beyond the dysfunctional group belonging that once demanded somebody's exclusion.[47]

But it is not as easy as we might think to break free of group belonging. What if we reject and distance ourselves from the in-group itself, having woken up to its poor self awareness and culturally-captive theological vision? What if we came to despise the Church, or at least its gatekeepers, because we have felt excluded? Many a gay Catholic like Alison has taken this path. Yet this is to remain in thrall to the very system that has excluded them. This is the sad fact of much activism, and adolescent rebellion, and the sort of lonely-hero pose that makes us prefer the margins because we find there a horribly congenial place of perpetual exile, beyond acceptance by the institution—and by ourselves, too, about whom we are so plainly ambivalent.

---

46. Alison, "Reconciliation in the Wink of a Hippo." In *Undergoing God*, 100–19, 113.

47. Alison, "Clothed and in His Right Mind," in *Faith Beyond Resentment*, 125–43; following Girard, "The Demons of Gerasa," in *The Scapegoat*, 165–83.

Interlude: The Parson's Tale

Alison calls this subtle delusion "[t]he self-canonization of the self-victim."[48] It is something to which I can testify from my own experience. In the last couple of years I have managed to offload an unresolved pattern of behavior which dogged me during the previous busy but lonely decade, which involved three successive senior ministry appointments in three cities. Each was a "culturally-complex" situation involving programmatically entrenched dysfunction, where a lot needed doing by a deft, disciplined, and self-aware leader. I marched in full of confidence, but each time I was tripped up by my own unconscious psychological baggage.

I was, for instance, too eager to change things in accord with my own vision, without being sufficiently alert to the opposition I was causing. I was not sensitive enough to manage the systemic complexities in each situation in a way that makes real leadership of change possible. Some sensed the agenda of personal need that I brought to each of these ministry situations. This unsettled a few and undermined my authority with others, while awakening yet others to a state of rivalry over whose needs would be met—mine or theirs. Each time I found myself embroiled in serious conflict, becoming frustrated and angry in the face of programmatic resistance, in the end veering close to pastoral disaster.

By the middle of the third appointment I woke up to myself, however, and it all ended well, but only thanks to a wise guide who introduced me to the work of Girard and Alison, also patiently and deftly helping me to understand the mimetic rivalry and to identify the models of desire that had, unbeknownst to me, been ruling my life. I came to realize that I was inadvertently perpetuating a childhood sense of feeling unwelcome that came from growing up as something of a cuckoo in the nest of an adopted family. I was unconsciously but constantly seeking signs of support, or else pushing the boundaries with people in order to find out who I could really trust. I was also seeking some control of my environment as a salve to a persistent but largely inchoate sense—not untypical of adopted children as they grow up—of being in the power of strangers who failed to acknowledge my worth, aspirations or feelings. Consequently I always gravitated to the outsider's role because I did not know how to live securely, and hence non-adversarially.

At last I began to learn the lessons of abiding faith, becoming absolutely convinced that faith hinged on the transformation of this false self rather than merely resolving the religious skepticism that had haunted me at an earlier

48. Alison, *Raising Abel*, 184.

stage of life. I came to realize how that prior struggle with doubt, which I mentioned in the last chapter, was primarily about issues of personal trust and that its resolution would not come intellectually, apart from trusting self-investment and acquiring "the intelligence of the victim." I realized that my drive toward theological writing had been motivated by the same unconscious personal need. Whether it was a search for certain belief in God's objective existence against the challenge of anti-realism, or the uniqueness of Jesus despite religious pluralism and skeptical historical Jesus studies, or God's action in the world as understood by latest science, or the Church's future at a time of galloping secularization—all of which I have written books about—have been questions more to do with personal issues of finding a basic trustworthiness in life than with objective pursuit of the truth. These books were none the worse for that, mind you, and which author does not have a personal story to tell? However, it is good to get in touch with one's deepest motivations.

This tangling-up of belief with unresolved personal need had another aspect for me, too. God, Christ, Gospel, and Church, while earnestly believed in, also served as props in an angry project of self-definition against the sort of barely-theological folk Christianity and habituated, low-temperature, social-and-therapeutic agenda that is so widespread in the Church. I realized that this represented unresolved anger against an adopted family who shared this mindset, transferred to those among whom it stubbornly persists in the Church today. Thus I inadvertently ensured that the Church would remain a place where I did not feel at home.

All this helped me realize that belief is part of a package, inseparable from a form of life, for good or ill. Abiding faith, however, is the liberation from that false self and the recovery of right belief, beyond the certainty and anxiety that regularly accompanies belief for the false self. These days, with nothing really to prove, and no longer manufacturing opponents who I can then obsess about and make a life-project out of opposing, I have passed beyond needing to salve personal hurts through the exercise of ministry. I am learning to live in the ecclesial institution and actually to like it, able to love its people as they are, and do what I can to make things better, while becoming far more able to stand back in unwinnable situations. Perhaps not surprisingly, with greater patience and poise, I am bolder yet calmer in facing opposition and am, I hope, emerging as a more effective change agent.

Yet all around us in the Church, people with unresolved personal issues as bad as or worse than the ones I eventually woke up to remain in positions of authority. Alison testifies to the painful liberation he experienced from his own "marginaholism," when his whole life-project at the time collapsed, yet he discovered that there was life on the other side of it. The place of shame did indeed prove habitable for him, because his false self that had been dominated by fear of ending up in that place had literally died.[49] This is truly to discover self as gift, beyond the false self of the self-creating victim.

This leads to a much less anxious, more accepting form of life in the Church. We come to feel less scandalized by others in the Church because we no longer see ourselves as having "the right stuff," at the expense of those who are theologically shallow, inept or wrongheaded, for instance, or of lackluster clergy superiors and bishops, or of hidebound and controlling laity—or anyone else who disappoints us and *against* whom we can create a dramatic life story either as a hero or a victim. This is a potentially-unending, self-centered drama that robs us of fellowship with the real God and the real people of God—to whom we are joined not only in baptism but in all the same foibles, really. I testify personally to the power of this false self, and its seductive deceptiveness, but also that God really does act mercifully toward all concerned in overcoming it—this unconscious occupation of the false sacred, in my case by one who was zealous-but-in-fact-empty. Abiding faith can take the place of brittle ideology, issuing in a calm and compassionate ecclesial abiding that is pure gift though by no means necessarily passive and do-nothing.

So a proper attachment to the institutional Church is crucial to a mature spirituality of abiding faith. For instance, we achieve a greater autonomy of person, with appropriate boundaries, as we go from immature and unhealthy attachments marked by "*fusion* with family, friends, religion, and culture, precisely for the sake of relationships of intimacy that are deeper, more complex, more inclusive of diversity."[50] Autonomy here, in a discussion of spiritual maturity by the American feminist theologian Joann Wolski Conn, is not oppositional and self-sufficient along the axis of modern individualism but, rather, an almost certainly painful and costly detachment from unhealthy and false attachment towards a more mature capacity for self-donation. James Alison calls for "self-critical institutional living, a sense of sociological suspicion towards any and all institutional claims but without a rejection of how we are in fact dependent on institutions," concluding that this sort of stance "seems to be coming upon us as a normal way of living the faith."[51] We cannot

49. Alison, "Confessions of a Former Marginaholic." In *On Being Liked*, 65–77.
50. Conn, "Toward Spiritual Maturity," 255.
51. Alison, "Honesty as Challenge, Honesty as Gift: What Way Forward for Gay and Lesbian Catholics?" In *Undergoing God*, 177–88, 184.

expect too much from the institutional Church of which we are a part, or we will miss the miracle of inclusion and grace-beyond-the-pale that it actually represents.

For the Life of the World

An important sign of not being against—of not being defined by an oppositional binary relationship with something or someone we despise—emerges in how the Church views and interacts with the world. The righteous Church that condemns the world is well known, as is the one earnestly trying to improve the world. Too often today's Church, resiling from its former hegemonic harshness and concerned about its loss of "clientele," sets about trying to help, or else it competes with the world, essentially setting up shop alongside the secular in the business of therapeutic individualism. But this earnest, helping Church cannot help the world to know its own blessedness in the presence of its creator and redeemer *who loves the world*, which is the unique service the Church *can* provide for the world. Rather than compete against a cashed-up consumer culture with its hooks into everyone, however—essentially, on that culture's own terms—the Church can dare to celebrate the glory of God embracing the world in Jesus Christ through word, sacrament, fellowship, and theological reconnection of the modern imagination with God, hence allowing some of the joy of heaven to shine out. This is the conclusion of American Orthodox theologian Alexander Schmemann, responding to 1960s attempts at adapting God to secular modernity with a call for the Church to recover its sacramental vision, helping the culture find God in the world rather than trying to add value to the world, as if God is absent from the world.[52]

This leads to the liberating discovery of being able to live in the world without fearing it and closing out the actual life of creatures—including the complexities and inevitabilities of their sexuality, for instance, and of their weakness more generally, both of which lead so unhelpfully to the obsessions of guilt. This was the plea of former French Dominican Jacques Pohier when he left the order and the secure clerical world—from which he came to feel that so much unwelcome detail was systematically airbrushed—to find a job and a place to live, as James Alison also had to do after he and the Dominicans parted company. Jacques Pohier decided that God was not in the business always of completing the partial and justifying the absurd. He found he could no longer support disapproving Church attitudes on what he had come to

52. Schmemann, *The World as Sacrament*.

see as plain facts about the beginning and ending of life, also official denials of much obvious truth revealed by contemporary Biblical studies.[53] Rowan Williams writes warmly of Pohier's painful journey, arguing for contemplative attention to the unfamiliar, and being prepared to settle for inarticulateness—against the over-confident volubility of a faith that has everything worked out. Such is an entirely appropriate witness to the Christ who mandates our embeddedness in the world.[54] And that embeddedness is witnessed-to by the constant presence of God's Spirit who is not episodically present on behalf of an absent God, but who is constantly invested in the human struggle.[55]

So rather than fleeing the world, or else embracing its agenda without remainder—without over-or-under-valuing the world, that is—abiding faith entails a newly-graced life within the world that God loves. God's revelation inhabits the human story as its host,[56] because only through subversion and redemption within that story is the false sacred exposed and defeated. That way we come to know the real God, and the world truly becomes our home.

---

53. Pohier, *God—In Fragments*. See also Alison, "Confessions of a Former Marginaholic," in *On Being Liked*, 65–77.

54. Williams, "The Judgement of the World" (1989). In *On Christian Theology*, 29–43.

55. Williams, "Word and Spirit" (1980), in *On Christian Theology*, 107–27.

56. Alison, *Raising Abel*, 30–33.

Conclusion

In drawing this wide-ranging discussion to a close, it may help if I give an extended summary of the whole argument as it has developed, then offer a final brief account of the major lessons I have learned about faith and doubt.

The homeless heart is a widespread modern Western reality. The tribal faith of pre-modern times, in which belief dwelt at home in a world that revealed reliably the reality of God, and in a society where the Church and its practices were integrally interwoven, has given way. The ties of *religio*, binding that world together imaginatively as well as practically, have now slipped from the human heart. The resultant sense of homelessness has been exacerbated by the end of community as the unquestioned context for human life, leaving a highly associational and voluntary version of belonging where Westerners once abided together in communities of mutual obligation—regularly at home if not always at ease. Under the pressure of globalizing economic forces and the culture of consumerism invariably accompanying them, the late-modern self is decomposed and recomposed by market forces to an unprecedented extent. In this way homeless hearts are further destabilized, and denied the purposeful, lifelong identity and solidarity that characterized much Western life well into the twentieth century.

Faith is now a choice, among the various worldviews and lifestyle options currently on offer, and associated more or less with traditional creeds and Churches. Spirituality is fully integrated into this consumer culture, to the extent that even embracing or rejecting faith is now caught up in the manipulation of self-image, as a discussion of "atheist chic" and "atheism-lite" sought to reveal. In all, tribal faith has given way to individualized faith. This does not mean that in the millennium and a half of pre-modern Christianity there were no faithful individuals, nor does it mean that there is no resurgent tribalism in the faith that modern individuals adopt—today's growth industry of fundamentalism puts paid to that misconception. But it does mean that the way individuals approach, hold, and practice faith is now different. Nowadays it provides resources for the individual of a take it or leave it sort.

The individual has become the model of both humanity and God since the rise of nominalism in the late Middle Ages when God's transcendent presence throughout Western humanity's integral existence in the world began to give way. Instead, the divine and human individuals fought against each other for *Lebensraum*, while new structures for human abiding arose. Chief among these was the cosmic-political system that annexed God to the ordinary life project of modern Western individuals who prized "life, liberty, and the pursuit of happiness," echoing in microcosm the self-interest typical of individual nation states. It is not as if there were no self-centered people or regimes before the seventeenth century, but there was not the same nexus between faith, the control of meaning, social order, and the personal life project.

The modern Cosmopolis was an example of the system building that typifies all human cultures and religions, as anthropology shows, and which René Girard explains with unparalleled theoretical power. It helps account for the downside of modernity that appears among its victims. Exclusion of the deviant and the foreign—as exposed by Michel Foucault, feminism, and also by post-colonial and other contextual theoretical movements "from the margins"—reveal to the Girardian eye a clear pattern of mediated desire, rivalry that escalates into the violence of indistinguishable mimetic doubles, and the maintenance of in-group cohesion by exclusion of the other in the regularly violent mechanism of scapegoating. This is a false sacred reality, universal in its scope, and certainly manifest in the Cosmopolis of modernity—also in the universal reach of the commodity form in more de-regulated post-modern conditions, which may represent a new Cosmopolis emerging.

Instead of individualistic faith as a participation in the controlling mood of Cosmopolis, however, there is a different and decidedly strange-sounding version of faith on offer. It is to be found in St. Paul and St. John, then in the Fathers and saints right up to the Middle Ages. I call it abiding faith because it captures the Pauline mysticism of abiding in Jesus Christ, and coming through Baptism and Eucharist to a new self beyond the control of false selves in thrall to the false sacred—to sin, the world, and the devil. This means a new relationship with the powers that be and the social order of the day, through belonging to a new nexus of human identity-formation, in the Church. Trust and belief as well as personal experience are key dimensions of abiding faith, but it turns on the fact of *participation* as the key to knowing. The testimony of antiquity to knowledge as participatory—as entailing a relationship between the subject and object of knowledge—is preserved, though in Christian hands the emphasis is on the action of God the Father reaching out toward the world in Jesus Christ to establish that participation.

However, such participating knowing ceased to commend itself from the late Middle Ages as theology and spirituality, theory and practice, inner and outer began to drift apart. Faith as belief, and trust across an abyss of disconnection from God, sat uneasily with a special sort of Christianity called mysticism, which was supposed to offer a more direct connection. Today mysticism is part of the spirituality industry, which in turn risks becoming a wholly-owned subsidiary of the commodity form.

Because the modern order could eventually sustain itself with a sufficient sense of meaning without God, so that faith became a personal preference, atheism emerged as a major cultural possibility for the first time in modern history. Yet religion has refused to go away—it continues both in its stubbornly false sacred forms, but also as the bearer of a transformed self that will always be God's counter-witness to the false sacred. Yet this stubborn perseverance is currently attracting a lot of skeptical attention, with all religion tarred by association with the false sacred after 9/11.

Nevertheless, this skeptical attack proves to be off-target. Abiding faith turns out to be of a form entirely compatible with the participating knowing and paradigmatic imagination that characterizes the post-modern turn towards holistic epistemology. Indeed, it emerges as more cognitively respectable than the narrow foundationalism in philosophy that is regularly used both to oppose and to defend faith. Neither taken-for-granted propositions about the order of things, nor an infallible Bible or Church, *really* persuade anyone any more. These are cultural artifacts serving as props in a conservative or else a liberal Christian form of life which commends itself based on the sense of identity it provides, rather than because these foundations are objectively authoritative. It is better to admit it. Faith is of a piece with belief and experience in a form of life, which does a better or worse job of faithfully engaging the subtle complexity of life in the world with the subtle complexity of Bible and Christian tradition. Typically, conservative Christian forms of life betray the world, and liberal forms of Christian life betray Bible and tradition. Abiding faith, however, opens an imaginatively powerful paradigm of mutual encounter, maximizing the transforming engagement between Christ and culture.

For that to be possible the false self that demands control and certainty has to go—the self that excludes others as the regular price of self-definition, living in the desires of other in-group models. Jesus offers an alternative. Consider his parables that upend business as usual. Consider his boundary crossings—those he undertook by boat across that symbolically stormy lake, and those that involved touching outsiders. Chiefly there is his crucifixion, which ever-after makes habitable the place of shame that we fear. All these point to a new self that is God's gift to us in raising Jesus, and pouring out his Spirit in the establishment of a new humanity beyond certainty, anxiety, and violence—the marks of the false sacred.

This is the Church, in which baptism and Eucharist lead us away from individualism to personhood, from the unexamined biological and cultural-structural determinants of normal existence to the super-normal existence of free persons. Normally, we become individuals thanks to the desires of those we emulate, and through those we exclude, sharing in the being of the false God of the false sacred. But "[b]lessed be the God and Father of our Lord Jesus Christ! By his great mercy he has given us a new birth into a living hope through the resurrection of Jesus Christ from the dead" (1 Pet 3:3). This new existence comes from the resurrection and is manifest in new ways of living, beyond the fear for self (ultimately, the fear of death) that sacrifices the other. Finding freedom from this fundamental fear constraining human life makes us live differently and helps us undergo the period of trial that 1 Peter goes on to acknowledge, as our false self is purged away. I decided it was important to add my own testimony to that of James Alison as a witness to the truth of this gift and of this necessarily painful transformation.

This discussion has been a personal one for me, reflecting a journey of discovery. I have learned that belief—even fully-orthodox belief, zealously prosecuted—is not the essence of faith, because the form of life we live will disclose the true *meanings* of our beliefs, and if our form of life does not reflect the mature compassion that comes from sharing Christ's desire, then these beliefs though correct do not add up to genuine faith. This is an old insight, that "faith by itself, if it has no works, is dead" (Jas 2:17). Likewise, I have learned that religious skepticism misses the point, and that its characteristic rationalism should not set the agenda for apologetics. Rather, the key is personal witness—including the theologian's irreplaceable witness to a vigorous paradigm of faith, able to demonstrate powerful engagement between Christ and culture in the realm of ideas. It is Christian witness that leads to conversion, just as participation leads to right knowing in matters of faith. Most of all, I have learned that abiding faith bears the imprint of God's will for Christians and Churches, for the life of the world—not a peevish, defensive or exclusive faith, but a large-souled, compassionate, spiritually mature agency serving God's loving embrace of the world.

Conversion to this sort of faith is more than the resolution of intellectual doubt, and certainly involves more than offering slick arguments to detached skeptics. Rather, it is letting a new self be born, with new eyes and a renewed mind. This is not to deny the place of reasoned argument, but it does require the reasoning mind to come at last to its proper dwelling place in the loving heart, as the servant of an obedient will. This is the form that faith must have if it means abiding in Jesus Christ.

Bibliography

Abraham, William. *The Logic of Evangelism*. London: Hodder & Stoughton, 1989.
Alison, James. *Faith Beyond Resentment: Fragments Catholic and Gay*. London: Darton, Longman & Todd, 2001.
———. *The Joy of Being Wrong: Original Sin Through Easter Eyes*. New York: Herder & Herder, 1998.
———. *Knowing Jesus*. 2nd ed. London: SPCK, 1998.
———. *On Being Liked*. London: Darton, Longman & Todd, 2003.
———. *Raising Abel: The Recovery of the Eschatological Imagination*. New York: Crossroad Herder, 2003.
———. *Undergoing God: Dispatches from the Scene of a Break-In*. London: Darton, Longman & Todd, 2006.
Ault, James M., Jr. *Spirit and Flesh: Life in a Fundamentalist Baptist Church*. New York: Knopf, 2005.
Avis, Paul. *God and the Creative Imagination: Metaphor, Symbol and Myth in Religion and Theology*. London: Routledge, 1999.
Bacon, Francis. *New Atlantis*. London: Haviland, 1627.
Badiou, Alain. *St. Paul: The Foundation of Universalism*. Translated by Ray Brassier. Stanford: Stanford University Press, 2003.
Bainton, Roland H. *Erasmus of Christendom*. London: Collins, 1969.
Balthasar, Hans Urs von. *The Glory of The Lord: A Theological Aesthetics*. Vol 4, *The Realm of Metaphysics in Antiquity* (1967). Translated by Brian McNeil CRV et al. Edinburgh: T. & T. Clark, 1989.
———. *The Glory of The Lord: A Theological Aesthetics*. Vol. 5, *The Realm of Metaphysics in the Modern Age*. Translated by Oliver Davies et al. Edinburgh: T. & T. Clark, 1991.
———. "Theology and Sanctity." In *Explorations in Theology*. Vol. 1, *The Word Made Flesh*. Translated by A.V. Littledale and Alexander Dru, 181–209. 1964. Reprinted, San Francisco: Ignatius, 1989.
Battiscombe, Georgina. *John Keble: A Study in Limitations*. London: Constable, 1963.
Bauerschmidt, Frederick Christian. "Aesthetics: The Theological Sublime." In *Radical Orthodoxy: A New Theology*, edited by John Milbank et al., 201–19. London: Routledge, 1999.
Bauman, Zygmunt. *Consuming Life*. Cambridge: Polity, 2007.
———. *The Individualized Society*. Cambridge: Polity, 2001.

———. *Liquid Fear*. Cambridge: Polity, 2006.
———. *Liquid Love*. Cambridge: Polity, 2003.
———. *Liquid Modernity*. Cambridge: Polity, 2000.
———. *Wasted Lives: Modernity and Its Outcasts*. Cambridge: Polity, 2004.
Beeck, Frans Jozef van. *God Encountered: A Contemporary Catholic Systematic Theology*. Vol. 2/4, *The Revelation of the Glory*. Part IVB, *The Genealogy of Depravity: Living Alive to the Living God*. Collegeville, MN: Liturgical Press, 2001.
Bellah, Robert N. et al. *Habits of the Heart: Individualism and Commitment in American Life*. 2nd ed. Berkeley: University of California Press, 1996.
Beinart, Peter. *The Good Fight: Why Liberals—And Only Liberals—Can Win the War on Terror and Make America Great Again*. New York: HarperCollins, 2006.
Berger, Peter. *The Heretical Imperative: Contemporary Possibilities of Religious Affirmation*. London: Collins, 1980.
Betjeman, John. *Summoned by Bells*. Cambridge, MA: Riverside, 1960.
Bhabha, Homi K. *The Location of Culture*. London: Routledge, 1994.
Blum, Deborah. *Love at Goon Park: Harry Harlow and the Science of Affection*. Cambridge, MA: Perseus, 2002.
Bouma, Gary. *Australian Soul: Religion and Spirituality in the Twenty-first Century*. Melbourne: Cambridge University Press, 2006.
Braaten, Carl, and Robert W. Jenson, editors. *Union with Christ: The New Finnish Interpretation of Luther*. Grand Rapids: Eerdmans, 1998.
Braithwaite, R.B. "An Empiricist's View of the Nature of Religious Belief." In *The Philosophy of Religion*, edited by Basil Mitchell, 72–91. Oxford Readings in Philosophy. Oxford: Oxford University Press, 1971.
Brown, Andrew. "Review of 2007: Press." *Church Times* (December 29, 2007). Online: http://www.churchtimes.co.uk/content.asp?id=48964/.
Brown, Dan. *The Da Vinci Code: A Novel*. New York: Doubleday, 2003.
Bruce, Steve. *God is Dead: Secularization in the West*. Oxford: Blackwell, 2002.
Bultmann, Rudolf. *Theology of the New Testament*. Vol. 1. Translated by Kendrick Grobel. London: SCM, 1952.
Campbell, Colin. *The Romantic Ethic and the Spirit of Modern Consumerism*. York, UK: Alcuin Academics, 2005.
Carrette, Jeremy, and Richard King. *Selling Spirituality: The Silent Takeover of Religion*. London: Routledge, 2005.
Casanova, José. "Secularization, Enlightenment and Modern Religion." In *Public Religions in the Modern World*, 11–39, 235–47. Chicago: University of Chicago Press, 1994.
Certeau, Michel de. *The Mystic Fable*. Vol. 1, *The Sixteenth and Seventeenth Centuries*. Translated by Michael B. Smith. Chicago: University of Chicago Press, 1992.
———. *The Possession at Loudun*. Translated by Michael B. Smith. Chicago: University of Chicago Press, 1996.
Charry, Ellen T. *By the Renewing of Your Minds: The Pastoral Function of Christian Doctrine*. New York: Oxford University Press, 1997.
Coleridge, Samuel Taylor. *Biographia Literaria*. 1817. Reprinted, London: Dent, 1965.
Collins, Paul. "Catholicism and Fundamentalism." In *Between the Rock and a Hard Place: Being Catholic Today*, 178–214. Sydney: ABC Books, 2004.
Conn, Joann Wolski. "Toward Spiritual Maturity." In *Freeing Theology: The Essentials of Theology in Feminist Perspective*, edited by Catherine Mowry LaCugna, 235–59. San Francisco: HarperSanFrancisco, 1993.

Conrad, Joseph. *Heart of Darkness*.1902. Reprinted, London: Penguin, 1973.
Cottingham, John. *The Spiritual Dimension: Religion, Philosophy and Human Value*. Cambridge: Cambridge University Press, 2005.
Countryman, L. William. *The Poetic Imagination: An Anglican Spiritual Tradition*. Traditions of Christian Spirituality. London: Darton, Longman & Todd, 1999.
Cowdell, Scott. *Atheist Priest? Don Cupitt and Christianity*. London: SCM, 1988.
———. *A God for This World*. London: Continuum, 2000.
———. *God's Next Big Thing: Discovering the Future Church*. Melbourne: John Garratt, 2004.
———. "Homosexuality and the Clarity of Scripture: Reflecting with the Archbishop of Sydney." In *Other Voices, Other Worlds: The Global Church Speaks Out on Homosexuality*, edited by Terry Brown, 262–74. London: Darton, Longman & Todd, 2006.
Cozzens, Donald. *Sacred Silence: Denial and Crisis in the Church*. Collegeville, MN: Liturgical Press, 2002.
Cunningham, David S. *These Three Are One: The Practice of Trinitarian Theology*. Challenges in Cotemporary Theology. Oxford: Blackwell, 1998.
Cupitt, Don. "Darwinism and English Religious Thought." In *Explorations in Theology* 6, 42–49. London: SCM, 1979.
———. *The Great Questions of Life*. Santa Rosa, CA: Polebridge, 2005.
———. *Life, Life*. Santa Rosa, CA: Polebridge, 2003.
———. *The Meaning of It All in Everyday Speech*. London: SCM, 1999.
———. *The Sea of Faith: Christianity in Change*. London: BBC Books, 1984.
———. *The Way to Happiness*. Santa Rosa, CA: Polebridge, 2005.
Dawkins, Richard. *The God Delusion*. Boston: Houghton Mifflin, 2006.
Diamond, Malcolm L., and Thomas V. Litzenburg, Jr. *The Logic of God: Theology and Verification*. Indianapolis: Bobbs-Merrill, 1975.
Douglas, Mary. *Natural Symbols: Explorations in Cosmology*. 1970. Reprinted, London: Penguin, 1973.
———. *Purity and Danger: An Analysis of the Concept of Pollution and Taboo*. 1966. Reprinted, London: Routledge, 2002.
Durkheim, Emile. *The Elementary Forms of the Religious Life: A Study in Religious Sociology*. Translated by Joseph Ward Swain. New York: Macmillan, 1915.
Easlea, Brian. *Fathering the Unthinkable: Masculinity, Scientists and the Nuclear Arms Race*. London: Pluto, 1983.
Eco, Umberto. *The Name of the Rose*. Translated by William Weaver. London: Secker & Warburg, 1983.
Evans, C. Stephen. *Faith Beyond Reason: A Kierkegaardian Account*. Reason & Religion. Grand Rapids: Eerdmans, 1998.
Evans, G. R., editor. *The Medieval Theologians*. Oxford: Blackwell, 2001.
Fanon, Frantz. *The Wretched of the Earth*. Translated by Constance Farrington. New York: Grove, 1963.
Finney, John. *Finding Faith Today: How Does it Happen?* London: British and Foreign Bible Society, 1992.
Fleming, Chris. *René Girard: Violence and Mimesis*. Cambridge: Polity, 2004.
Flew, Antony. *God and Philosophy*. London: Hutchinson, 1966.
Foucault, Michel. *Discipline and Punish: The Birth of the Prison*. Translated by Alan Sheridan. London: Penguin, 1977.
———. *Madness and Civilization: A History of Insanity in the Age of Reason*. Translated by Richard Howard. 1967. Reprinted, London: Routledge, 1989.

Fowler, James W. *Stages of Faith: The Psychology of Human Development and the Quest for Meaning.* New York: Harper & Row, 1981.
Frame, Tom. *Anglicans in Australia.* Sydney: University of New South Wales Press, 2007.
Gaita, Raimond. *A Common Humanity: Thinking about Love and Truth and Justice.* Melbourne: Text, 2000.
Geertz, Clifford. "Thick Description: Toward an Interpretive Theory of Culture." In *The Interpretation of Cultures: Selected Essays,* 3–30. New York: Basic Books, 1973.
Giddens, Anthony. *The Transformation of Intimacy: Sexuality, Love and Eroticism in Modern Societies.* Stanford: Stanford University Press, 1992.
Gill, Michael Gates. *How Starbucks Saved My Life.* New York: Gotham, 2007.
Gillespie, Michael Allen. *Nihilism before Nietzsche.* Chicago: University of Chicago Press, 1995.
Girard, René. *Deceit, Desire and the Novel: Self and Other in Literary Structure.* Translated by Yvonne Freccero. Baltimore: Johns Hopkins University Press, 1965.
———. *I See Satan Fall Like Lightning.* Translated by James G. Williams. Maryknoll, NY: Orbis, 2001.
———. *The Scapegoat.* Translated by Yvonne Freccero. Baltimore: Johns Hopkins University Press, 1986.
———. *A Theater of Envy: William Shakespeare.* South Bend, IN: St Augustine's Press, 2004.
———. *Violence and the Sacred.* Translated by Patrick Gregory. Baltimore: The Johns Hopkins University Press, 1977.
Girard, René, with Pierpaolo Antonello and João Cezar de Castro Rocha. *Evolution and Conversion: Dialogues on the Origins of Culture.* London: T. & T. Clark, 2007.
Girard, René, with Jean-Michel Oughourlian and Guy Lefort. *Things Hidden since the Foundation of the World.* Translated by Stephen Bann and Michael Metteer. 1987. London: Continuum, 2003.
Goleman, Daniel. *Emotional Intelligence.* New York: Bantam, 1995.
Green, Garrett. *Imagining God: Theology and the Religious Imagination.* Grand Rapids: Eerdmans, 1989.
Griffin, Susan. *Pornography and Silence: Culture's Revenge against Nature.* New York: Harper & Row, 1981.
Gutierrez, Gustavo. *A Theology of Liberation: History, Politics and Salvation.* Translated by Sr. Caridad Inda and John Eagleson. 1973. Reprinted, London: SCM, 1983.
Hadot, Pierre. *Philosophy as a Way of Life: Spiritual Exercises from Socrates to Foucault.* Translated by Michael Chase. Oxford: Blackwell, 1995.
Hauerwas, Stanley, and William H. Willimon. "The Modern World: On Learning to Ask the Right Questions." In *Resident Aliens: Life in the Christian Colony,* 15–29. Nashville: Abingdon, 1989.
Hawking, Stephen W. *A Brief History of Time: From the Big Bang to Black Holes.* New York: Bantam, 1988.
Hick, John. *An Interpretation of Religion: Human Responses to the Transcendent.* London: Macmillan, 1989.
Hilliard, David. "Un-English and Unmanly: Anglo-Catholicism and Homosexuality." *Victorian Studies* 25 (1982) 181–210.
Huxley, Aldous. *The Devils of Loudun.* London: Chatto & Windus, 1952.
Iacoboni, Marco. *Mirroring People: The New Science of How We Connect with Others.* New York: Farrer, Straus, and Giroux, 2008.

Ind, Jo. *Memories of Bliss: God, Sex and Us*. London: SCM, 2003.
James, Henry. *The Wings of the Dove*. 1902. Reprinted, London: Penguin, 1965.
James, William. *The Varieties of Religious Experience*. New York: Longmans, Green & Co., 1902.
Jantzen, Grace. *Power, Gender and Christian Mysticism*. Cambridge: Cambridge University Press, 1995.
Janz, Paul D. *God, the Mind's Desire: Reference, Reason and Christian Thinking*. Cambridge Studies in Christian Doctrine. Cambridge: Cambridge University Press, 2004.
Jenkins, David. *The Calling of a Cuckoo: Not Quite an Autobiography*. London: Continuum, 2002.
Jones, E. Michael. *Dionysos Rising: The Birth of Cultural Revolution out of the Spirit of Music*. San Francisco: Ignatius, 1994.
———. *Living Machines: Bauhaus Architecture as Sexual Ideology*. San Francisco: Ignatius, 1995.
Kant, Immanuel. *Critique of Pure Reason*. Translated, edited, and with an Introduction by Marcus Weigelt. New York: Penguin, 2007.
Käsemann, Ernst. "The Pauline Doctrine of the Lord's Supper." In *Essays on New Testament Themes*, 108–35. Translated by W. J. Montague. Studies in Biblical Theology 41. London: SCM, 1964.
Keller, Catherine. *God and Power: Counter-Apocalyptic Journeys*, Minneapolis: Fortress, 2005.
Kerr, Fergus. "Thomas Aquinas." In *The Medieval Theologians*, edited by G. R. Evans, 201–19. Oxford: Blackwell, 2001.
Kierkegaard, Søren. *The Concept of Anxiety*. Translated by Reidar Thomte and Albert B. Anderson. Princeton: Princeton University Press, 1980.
Kuhn, Thomas S. *The Structure of Scientific Revolutions*. 3rd ed. Chicago: University of Chicago Press, 1996.
Küng, Hans. *Does God Exist? An Answer for Today*. Translated by Edward Quinn. 1980. Reprinted, Eugene, OR: Wipf & Stock, 2006.
———. *My Struggle for Freedom*. Translated by John Bowden. London: Continuum, 2004.
Lakatos, Imre. "Falsification and the Methodology of Scientific Research Programs." In *The Methodology of Scientific Research Programs: Philosophical Papers*, vol. 1, edited by John Worrall and Gregory Guthrie, 8–101. Cambridge: Cambridge University Press, 1978.
Lakoff, George. *Moral Politics: How Liberals and Conservatives Think*. 2nd ed. Chicago: University of Chicago Press, 2002.
Lash, Nicholas. "Where Does *The God Delusion* Come From?" *New Blackfriars* 88 (2007) 507–21.
LeClercq, Jean, OSB. *The Love of Learning and the Desire for God: A Study of Monastic Culture*. Translated by Catharine Misrahi. 1961. Reprinted, London: SPCK, 1978.
LeDoux, Joseph. *The Emotional Brain: The Mysterious Underpinnings of Emotional Life*. London: Weidenfeld & Nicolson, 1998.
Levinas, Emanuel. "Ethics as First Philosophy" (1984). In *The Levinas Reader*, edited by Seán Hand, 75–87. Oxford: Blackwell, 1989.
Lévi-Strauss, Claude. *The Savage Mind*. The Nature of Human Society Series. Chicago: University of Chicago Press, 1966.
———. *Totemism*. Translated by Rodney Needham. Boston: Beacon, 1963.

Lindbeck, George A. *The Nature of Doctrine: Religion and Theology in a Postliberal Age.* Philadelphia: Westminster, 1984.
Louth, Andrew. *The Origins of the Christian Mystical Tradition: From Plato to Denys.* 2nd ed. Oxford: Oxford University Press, 2007.
Lubac, Henri de. *The Discovery of God.* Translated by Alexander Dru. 1960. Reprinted, Grand Rapids: Eerdmans, 1996.
Lumby, Catharine. "Why Feminists Need Porn." In *Bad Girls: The Media, Sex and Feminism in the 90s,* 94–116. Sydney: Allen & Unwin, 1997.
MacIntyre, Alasdair. *Three Rival Versions of Moral Enquiry: Encyclopedia, Genealogy and Tradition.* Notre Dame, IN: University of Notre Dame Press, 1989.
MacKinlay, Elizabeth. *The Spiritual Dimension of Ageing.* London: Jessica Kingsley, 2001.
MacKinnon, D. M. "The Conflict between Realism and Idealism: Remarks on the Significance for the Philosophy of Religion of a Classical Philosophical Controversy Recently Renewed." In *Explorations in Theology* 5: 151–65. London: SCM, 1979.
―――. "Ethics and Tragedy." In *Explorations in Theology* 5: 182–95. London: SCM, 1979.
Maffesoli, Michel. "The Return of Dionysus." In *Constructing the New Consumer Society,* edited by Pekka Sulkunen et al., 21–37. New York: St. Martin's, 1997.
Maguire, Nancy Klein. *An Infinity of Little Hours: Five Young Men and Their Trial of Faith in the Western World's Most Austere Monastic Order.* New York: Public Affairs, 2006.
Marion, Jean-Luc. *God without Being.* Translated by Thomas A. Carlson. Religion and Postmodernism. Chicago: University of Chicago Press, 1991.
Marshall, Bruce D. "Absorbing the World: Christianity and the Universe of Truths." In *Theology and Dialogue: Essays in Conversation with George Lindbeck,* edited by Bruce D. Marshall, 69–102. Notre Dame, IN: University of Notre Dame Press, 1990.
Martin, David. *On Secularization: Towards a Revised General Theory.* Aldershot, UK: Ashgate, 2005.
Mason, Michael et al. *The Spirit of Generation Y: Young People's Spirituality in a Changing Australia.* Melbourne: John Garratt, 2007.
Matson, Wallace. *A New History of Philosophy.* Vol 2. San Diego: Harcourt Brace Jovanovich, 1987.
Matthew, Iain. *The Impact of God: Soundings from St John of the Cross.* London: Hodder & Stoughton, 1995.
May, Rollo. *The Meaning of Anxiety.* 2nd ed. New York: Norton, 1977.
McIntosh, Mark A. *Mystical Theology: The Integrity of Spirituality and Theology.* Oxford: Blackwell, 1998.
Mehta, Hemant. *I Sold My Soul on eBay: Viewing Faith through an Atheist's Eyes.* Colorado Springs: Waterbrook, 2007.
Merchant, Carolyn. *The Death of Nature: Women, Ecology and the Scientific Revolution.* London: Wildwood, 1982.
Merton, Thomas. *Tears of the Blind Lions.* New York: New Directions, 1949.
Milbank, John. "Only Theology Overcomes Metaphysics." In *The Word Made Strange: Theology, Language, Culture,* 36–52. Oxford: Blackwell, 1997.
―――. *The Suspended Middle: Henri de Lubac and the Debate Concerning the Supernatural.* Grand Rapids: Eerdmans, 2005.
Miller, Alice. *For Your Own Good: Hidden Cruelty in Child-Rearing and the Roots of Violence.* Translated by Hildegarde and Hunter Hannum. 2nd ed. New York: Farrar, Straus, and Giroux, 1984.

Miller, Vincent J. *Consuming Religion: Christian Faith and Practice in a Consumer Culture*. New York: Continuum, 2005.
Mitchell, Basil. *The Justification of Religious Belief*. London: Macmillan, 1973.
Mitchell, Basil, with Antony Flew and R. M. Hare. "Theology and Falsification: A Symposium." In *New Essays in Philosophical Theology*, edited by Antony Flew and Alasdair MacIntyre, 96–108. London: SCM, 1955.
Montaigne, Michel de. "Of Presumption." In *The Essays of Montaigne*. Vol. 2. Translated by E. J. Trechmann, 83–84. London: Oxford University Press, 1927.
Moore, Robert, and Douglas Gillette. *King, Warrior, Magician, Lover: Rediscovering the Archetypes of the Mature Masculine*. San Francisco: HarperSanFrancisco, 1990.
Morris, Colin. *The Discovery of the Individual 1050–1200*. London: SPCK, 1972.
Morton, Tom. "Manufacturing Ancient Hatreds." *Griffith Review* 7 (2005) 222–25.
Murphy, Nancey. *Beyond Liberalism and Fundamentalism: How Modern and Postmodern Philosophy Set the Theological Agenda*. Valley Forge, PA: Trinity, 1996.
Nandy, Ashis. *The Intimate Enemy: Loss and Recovery of Self under Colonialism*. New Delhi: Oxford University Press, 1983.
Newman, John Henry. *A Grammar of Assent*. 1870. Reprinted, New York: Doubleday, 1955.
Niebuhr, Reinhold. *The Irony of American History*. New York: Scribners, 1952.
Nietzsche, Friedrich. *On the Genealogy of Morals*. Translated by Douglas Smith. Oxford: Oxford University Press, 1996.
Nussbaum, Martha C. "Love's Knowledge." In *Love's Knowledge: Essays on Philosophy and Literature*, 261–85. New York: Oxford University Press, 1990.
Orwell, George. *Shooting an Elephant and Other Essays*. London: Penguin, 2003.
Oughourlian, Jean-Michel. *The Puppet of Desire: The Psychology of Hysteria, Possession and Hypnosis*. Translated by Eugene Webb. 1982. Reprinted, Stanford: Stanford University Press, 1991.
Pascal, Blaise. "Memorial." In *Pascal: Selections*, edited by Richard H. Popkin, 69–70. The Great Philosophers. London: Macmillan, 1989.
———. *Pensées*. Edited and translated by A. J. Krailsheimer. London: Penguin, 1976.
Phillips, D. Z. "Religious Belief and Language Games." *Ratio* 12 (1970) 26–46.
Pickering, W. S. F. *Anglo-Catholicism: A Study in Religious Ambiguity*. London: SPCK, 1989.
Pickstock, Catherine. *After Writing: On the Liturgical Consummation of Philosophy*. Oxford: Blackwell, 1998.
Placher, William C. *The Domestication of Transcendence: How Modern Thinking about God Went Wrong*. Louisville: Westminster John Knox, 1996.
Pohier, Jacques. *God—In Fragments*. Translated by John Bowden. New York: Crossroad, 1986.
Polanyi, Michael. *Personal Knowledge: Towards a Post-Critical Philosophy*. Chicago: University of Chicago Press, 1962.
Polkinghorne, John. *Science and Providence: God's Interaction with the World*. London: SPCK, 1989.
Popper, Karl. *The Logic of Scientific Discovery*. New York: Harper, 1965.
Porter, Muriel. "Beyond the Cathedral Doors." *Griffith Review* 7 (2005) 178–84
———. *The New Puritans: The Rise of Fundamentalism in the Anglican Church*. Melbourne: Melbourne University Press, 2006.

Porter, Roy. *Flesh in the Age of Reason: How the Enlightenment Transformed the Way We See Our Bodies and Souls*. London: Penguin, 2004.

Putnam, Robert D. *Bowling Alone: The Collapse and Revival of American Community*. New York: Simon & Schuster, 2000.

Quine, W. V. "Two Dogmas of Empiricism." In *From a Logical Point of View*, 20–46. Cambridge: Harvard University Press, 1953.

Rahner, Karl. *Foundations of Christian Faith: An Introduction to the Idea of Christianity*. Translated by William V. Dych. London: Darton, Longman & Todd, 1978.

Ramsey, Arthur Michael. *The Gospel and the Catholic Church*. London: Longman, Green & Co., 1936.

Reno, R. R. "*Pro Nobis*: Words We do Not Want to Hear." In *In the Ruins of the Church: Sustaining Faith in an Age of Diminished Christianity*, 47–61. Grand Rapids: Brazos, 2002.

———. *Redemptive Change: Atonement and the Christian Cure of the Soul*. Theology for the Twenty-first Century. Harrisburg, PA: Trinity, 2002.

Rivera, Mayra. *The Touch of Transcendence: A Postcolonial Theology of God*. Louisville: Westminster John Knox, 2007.

Rizzolatti, Giacomo, and Corrado Sinigaglia. *Mirrors in the Brain: How Our Minds Share Actions, Emotions, and Experience*. Translated by Frances Anderson. Oxford: Oxford University Press, 2008.

Robinson, Geoffrey. *Confronting Power and Sex in the Catholic Church: Reclaiming the Spirit of Jesus*. Melbourne: John Garratt, 2007.

Rohr, Richard. *Adam's Return: The Five Promises of Male Initiation*. New York: Crossroad, 2004.

Rowell, Geoffrey. *The Vision Glorious: Themes and Personalities in the Catholic Revival in Anglicanism*. Oxford: Oxford University Press, 1983.

Ryle, Gilbert. *The Concept of Mind*. London: Hutchinson University Library, 1949.

Sabbah, Fatna A. *Woman in the Muslim Unconscious*. Translated by Mary Jo Lakeland. Athene. London: Pergamon, 1984.

Said, Edward. *Orientalism*. 1978. 25th anniversary ed. New York: Vintage, 1994.

Sanders, E. P. *Paul and Palestinian Judaism: A Comparison of Patterns of Religion*. London: SCM, 1977.

Saul, John Ralston. *Voltaire's Bastards: The Dictatorship of Reason in the West*. London: Penguin, 1993.

Schad, John. *Queer Fish: Christian Unreason from Darwin to Derrida*. Brighton, UK: Sussex Academic, 2004.

Scheler, Max. *Ressentiment*. Translated by Lewis B. Coser and William W. Holdheim. Marquette Studies in Philosophy. Milwaukee: Marquette University Press, 2003.

Schillebeeckx, Edward. *The Eucharist*. Translated by N. D. Smith. London: Sheed & Ward, 1968.

Schleiermacher, Friedrich. *On Religion: Speeches to its Cultured Despisers*. 3rd ed. Translated by John Oman. 1958. Reprinted, Louisville: Westminster John Knox, 1994.

Schmemann, Alexander. *The World as Sacrament*. New York: Herder & Herder, 1965.

Schweitzer, Albert. *The Mysticism of Paul the Apostle*. Translated by William Montgomery. London: A. & C. Black, 1931.

———. *Out of My Life and Thought: An Autobiography*. Translated by C.T. Campion. New York: Mentor, 1953.

———. *The Quest of the Historical Jesus: A Critical Study of Its Progress from Reimarus to Wrede*. Translated by William Montgomery. London: A. & C. Black, 1910.
Sennett, Richard M. *The Corrosion of Character: The Personal Consequences of Work in the New Capitalism*. New York: Norton, 1998.
Sheldrake, Rupert. *The Rebirth of Nature: The Greening of Science and God*. London: Rider, 1991.
Shelley, Mary. *Frankenstein: Or, the Modern Prometheus*. 1818. New ed. Edited by M. K. Joseph. Oxford World's Classics. Oxford: Oxford University Press, 2008.
Shogimen, Takashi. "Academic Controversies." In *The Medieval Theologians*, edited by G. R. Evans, 233–49. Oxford: Blackwell, 2001.
Sickels, Eleanor M. *The Gloomy Egoist: Moods and Themes of Melancholy from Gray to Keats*. New York: Columbia University Press, 1932.
Singer, Peter. *Animal Liberation: A New Ethic for Our Treatment of Animals*. New York: Avon, 1975.
Skinner, John. *Hear Our Silence: A Journey into Prayer*. Leominster, UK: Gracewing, 2003.
Slee, Nicola. *Women's Faith Development: Patterns and Processes*. Explorations in Practical, Pastoral and Empirical Theology. Aldershot, UK: Ashgate, 2004.
Sloterdijk, Peter. *Critique of Cynical Reason*. Translated by Michael Eldred. Theory and History of Literature. Minneapolis: University of Minnesota Press, 1987.
Smith, Wilfred Cantwell. *Towards a World Theology: Faith and the Contemporary History of Religion*. Philadelphia: Westminster, 1981.
Springsted, Eric O. *The Act of Faith: Christian Faith and the Modern Self*. Grand Rapids: Eerdmans, 2002.
Sternberg, Esther M. *The Balance Within: The Science Connecting Health and Emotions*. New York: Freeman, 2000.
Stratton, David, and Margaret Pomeranz. "Into Great Silence." Online: http://www.abc.net.au/atthemovies/txt/s1910423.htm.
Tanner, Kathryn. *Theories of Culture: A New Agenda for Theology*. Guides to Theological Inquiry. Minneapolis: Fortress, 1997.
Taylor, Charles. *A Secular Age*. Cambridge, MA: Belknap, 2007.
———. *Sources of the Self: The Making of the Modern Identity*. Cambridge: Harvard University Press, 1989.
Tilley, Terrence W. *Inventing Catholic Tradition*. Maryknoll, NY: Orbis, 2000.
Tincq, Henri, with René Girard. "'What Is Occurring Today Is Mimetic Rivalry on a Planetary Scale': René Girard on September 11." Online: http://www.morphizm.com/politix/girard911.html.
Toulmin, Stephen. *Cosmopolis: The Hidden Agenda of Modernity*. Chicago: University of Chicago Press, 1990.
Tracy, David. *The Analogical Imagination: Christian Theology and the Culture of Pluralism*. London: SCM, 1981.
Turgenev, Ivan. *Fathers and Sons*. 1861. Translated by Rosemary Edmonds. London: Penguin, 1965.
Turner, Denys. *The Darkness of God: Negativity in Christian Mysticism*. Cambridge: Cambridge University Press, 1995.
Underhill, Evelyn. *Mysticism: A Study in the Nature and Development of Man's Mystical Consciousness*. London: Dent, 1911.
———. *The Mystic Way: A Psychological Study in Christian Origins*. London: Dent, 1929.
Vattimo, Gianni. *After Christianity*. Translated by Luca D'Isanto. Italian Academy Lectures. New York: Columbia University Press, 2002.

———. *Belief.* Translated by Luca D'Isanto and David Webb. Stanford: Stanford University Press, 1999.
Watts, Fraser, and Mark Williams. *The Psychology of Religious Knowing.* Cambridge: Cambridge University Press, 1988.
Waugh, Evelyn. *Brideshead Revisited.* 1945. Reprinted, London: Penguin, 1982.
Webber, Robert E. *Ancient-Future Faith: Rethinking Evangelicalism for a Postmodern World.* Grand Rapids: Baker, 1999.
Weber, Max. *The Protestant Ethic and the Spirit of Capitalism.* Translated by Talcott Parsons. 1958. Reprinted, Mineola, NY: Dover, 2003.
Webster, John. *Holiness.* London: SCM, 2003.
Werpehowski, William. "Ad Hoc Apologetics." *Journal of Religion* 66 (1986) 282–301.
Wilding, Michael. "Something Better: Fundamentalism, Revolution, Loss of Faith and the Future." *Griffith Review* 7 (2005) 213–21.
Williams, Rowan. *Lost Icons: Reflections on Cultural Bereavement.* Edinburgh: T. & T. Clark, 2000.
———. *On Christian Theology.* Challenges in Contemporary Theology. Oxford: Blackwell, 2000.
———. *The Wound of Knowledge: Christian Spirituality from the New Testament to St John of the Cross.* London: Darton, Longman & Todd, 1979.
Winch, Peter. "Understanding a Primitive Society." In *Ethics and Action*, 8–49. London: Routledge & Kegan Paul, 1972.
Winton, Tim. "The Turning." In *The Turning*, 133–61. Sydney: Pan Macmillan, 2004.
Wittgenstein, Ludwig. "Ethics, Life and Faith." In *The Wittgenstein Reader*, edited by Anthony Kenny, 287–305. Oxford: Blackwell, 1994.
———. *On Certainty.* Edited by G. E. M. Anscombe and G. H. von Wright. Translated by Denis Paul and G. E. M. Anscombe. 1969. Reprinted, New York: Harper & Row, 1972.
———. *Philosophical Investigations.* Translated by G. E. M. Anscombe. 2nd ed. New York: Macmillan, 1958.
Wolin, Richard. *The Seduction of Unreason: The Intellectual Romance with Fascism from Nietzsche to Postmodernism.* Princeton: Princeton University Press, 2004.
Wuthnow, Robert. *Christianity in the Twenty-first Century: Reflections on the Challenges Ahead.* New York: Oxford University Press, 1993.
Wynn, Mark R. *Emotional Experience and Religious Understanding: Integrating Perception, Conception and Feeling.* Cambridge: Cambridge University Press, 2005.
Wyschogrod, Edith. *Saints and Postmodernism: Revisioning Moral Philosophy.* Religion and Postmodernism. Chicago: University of Chicago Press, 1990.
Yeats, William Butler. "The Second Coming." In *Michael Robartes and the Dancer* (1921). Accessed in *Yeats: Selected Poetry*, 99–100. London: Pan, 1974.
Zaehner, R. C. *Mysticism, Sacred and Profane: An Inquiry into Some Varieties of Praeternatural Experience.* Oxford: Clarendon, 1957.
Zizioulas, John. *Being as Communion: Studies in Personhood and the Church.* Contemporary Greek Theologians. Crestwood, NY: St. Vladimir's Seminary Press, 1997.

Index

Abelard, Peter, 52–53
Abraham and Isaac, 108
Abraham, William, 163, 211
Acts of the Apostles
   2:1–11, 109
   9, 182
Advertising, 25, 29
Affect, 93–94, 125, 126, 127, 131–34 passim, 151, 160
Ahaz (king of Judah), 108
AIDS, 29
Alexander of Hales, 53
Alison, James, ix, 4, 79, 146, 187–88, 192–203, 208, 211
Alocoque, Margaret Mary, 195
America (*see* United States of America)
Analogy, Doctrine of, 51, 55, 60–62
Anges, Mother Jeanne des, 84–85
Anglicanism (*see also* Anglo-Catholicism), 12, 13, 16, 41, 63, 68, 88, 97–98, 169, 173, 174, 191–92
Anglo-Catholicism, 12–15, 88, 97–98, 100, 135, 139, 171
Anthropology, 18–19, 179, 206
Anti-Semitism, 72, 93
Antonello, Pierpaolo, 214

Anxiety, 1, 2, 4, 22, 99, 105, 107, 177, 179, 180, 189–97 passim, 201
Apocalypse Now (film), 111
Apocalyptic, 59, 71, 73, 111, 113, 115, 117, 181
Aquinas, Thomas, 49, 50, 52–58 passim, 122, 125, 127. 166
Aristotle, 53, 106, 128, 166
Arnold, Matthew, 44
As It Is in Heaven (Swedish film), 29
Asylum seekers, 84, 88
Athanasius, 123
Atheism, 2, 16, 32, 41–46, 62, 68–69, 82, 148–49, 205
Augustine of Hippo (and Augustinianism), 50, 55, 107, 125, 126, 127, 166, 171
Ault, James M., 33, 211
Austen, Jane (*Pride and Prejudice*), 70
Australian spirituality, 38, 46
Averroism, 53
Avis, Paul, 169, 170, 172, 211

Babel, 108
Baby-Boomer generation, 20–21
Bacon, Francis, 94, 169, 211
Badiou, Alain, 117–18, 123, 211
Bainton, Roland, 10, 211

Balthasar, Hans Urs von, 49, 52, 55, 57, 59, 61, 128, 175
Baptism, 104, 109, 111, 114, 123–26 passim, 132, 144, 206, 208
Barth, Karl, 136
Basil of Caesarea, 124
Bataille, Georges, 72
Battiscombe, Georgina (*John Keble*), 13, 211
Bauerschmidt, Frederick Christian, 156, 211
Bauhaus architecture, 71
Bauman, Zygmunt (and liquid modernity), 25–31 passim, 35, 86–87, 88, 211–12
Beck, Ulrick, 26
Beeck, Frans Josef van, 197, 212
Beinart, Peter, 181, 212
Being, 50–58 passim,
Bellah, Robert, 39, 152, 212
Benedict of Nursia, 124, 131
Benedict XVI, Pope, 34
Bentham, Jeremy, 169
Berg, Alban (opera: *Lulu*), 71
Berger, Peter (*The Heretical Imperative*), 32, 212
Bernard of Clairvaux, 126, 127
Bernini, Giovanni, 35–36
Betjeman, John, 98, 212
Bhabha, Homi, 89–90, 212
Bible, 51, 52, 55, 62, 64, 125–29 passim, 139, 140, 144, 150, 163, 164, 169, 171, 175, 178, 186, 188, 194, 207
Big Brother, 29–30
Blanchot, Maurice, 72
Blum, Deborah, 93, 212
Bodily knowing (and wellness), 14, 151–52, 190
Bolshevism, 71–72
Bonaventure, 53, 127
Bonhoeffer, Dietrich, 176
Book of Daniel, The (NBC series), 182

Bosch, Hieronymus (painting: "The Garden of Earthly Delights"), 131
Bossy, John, 21
Bouma, Gary, 38, 212
Bowlby, Peter, 93
Braaten, Carl and Robert W. Jenson (*Union With Christ*), 135, 212
Braithwaite, R. B., 162, 212
Bridget Jones' Diary, 70
Brown, Andrew, 43, 212
Bruce, Steve, 32, 34, 43, 46, 212
Brueghel, Pieter (the Elder), 87
Bultmann, Rudolf, 3, 113–17, 119, 122, 134, 156, 212
Burke, Gregory, 105

Cajetan, Cardinal (Thomas de Vio), 60–61
Calvin, John, 57, 74
Cambridge Platonists, 23
Campbell, Colin, 24, 212
Capitalism (and market economy), 10, 16, 70, 98–99, 99–100
Career, the, 27–28
Carrette, Jeremy and Richard King, 40–41, 212
Casanova, José, 15–16, 212
Catechumenate, 162–63
Catholic Christianity (and Roman Catholicism), 2, 12–15 passim, 34–35, 60–63, 68, 84–85, 150, 155, 171–72, 185–86, 188–89
Certainty (and uncertainty), 1, 2, 3, 4, 35, 47, 48, 49, 65–74, 105, 107, 124, 130, 137, 177, 179, 180, 189, 197–98, 201, 208
Certeau, Michel de, 3, 85, 129–31, 212
Cervantes, Miguel de, 79
Charles I of England, 62
Charry, Ellen T., 3, 118–20, 123, 124, 125, 212
Child Rearing, 99
Choice (in sociology), 17, 31, 35, 59
Christ (*see* Jesus Christ)

Church (and ecclesial existence), 2, 4, 104, 109, 126, 133, 139, 141, 149, 189–204 passim, 207, 208
Churchgoing, decline in, 16
Classical Antiquity, 49
Cloud of Unknowing, The, 132
Cognitive-Propositional faith, 150–54, 158, 159–60
Cold War, 73, 82, 83, 94–95, 181
Coleridge, Samuel Taylor, 170, 212
Collins, Paul, 34, 212
Colonial experience (and post-colonialism), 2, 16, 84, 89–93, 96–98, 99, 136, 179, 185, 206
Colossians
3:3, 133
Community (and loss of community), 2, 9, 11, 19–22, 26, 38, 128
Conn, Joann Wolski, 202, 212
Conrad, Joseph (*Heart of Darkness*), 111, 213
Conservative Christianity, 32–36
Consumer Culture (and consumer spirituality), 2, 9, 14, 16, 18, 22–46, 48, 86–87, 100, 103, 107, 108, 205, 206
Control, 3, 47, 48, 49, 66–71, 74, 83–100 passim, 104, 128, 129, 136, 177, 197–98, 206, 208
Conversion, 3, 104, 141–45, 167, 173, 195, 208
Copernican Revolution, 63
1 Corinthians
1:8, 114
4:15–18, 121
4:20, 110
6:9–10, 110
10:1–6, 111
10:12, 114
11:1, 121, 175
15:50, 110
15:58, 114
16:13, 115

2 Corinthians
1:21, 115
5:11–14, 194
5:17, 110, 175
Corpus Christi (and Blessed Sacrament), 13
Cosmology, 62–65, 77, 123
Cosmopolis (*see* Toulmin, Stephen)
Cottingham, John, 158, 159, 213
Counter Reformation, 58, 69
Countryman, William, 169, 212
Cowdell, Scott, ii, 45, 69, 97, 149, 162, 184, 200–201, 213
Cozzens, Donald, 34, 213
Creation Narrative (Elohist), 144, 198
Creation science, 150
Cross, the, 118, 176
Cultural-Linguistic faith (*see* Form of Life, Christianity as a)
Culture, 76–78, 80
Cunningham, David, 181, 191, 213
Cupitt, Don, 44–46, 156, 162, 213

D'Alembert, Jean le Ronde, 68
Da Vinci Code, The, 42, 212
Dante Alighieri, 64
Darjeeling Limited, The (film), 37
Darkness of God, 105, 124, 125, 126, 129, 133, 134, 158
Darwin, Charles (and Darwinian evolution), 42, 149
Dawkins, Richard, 8, 41–46, 147–49, 150, 155, 159, 213
de Lubac, Henri (*see* Lubac, Henri de)
Deists, 68
Denys the Carthusian, 128
Depression, Great, 71
Descartes, René (and Cartesianism), 50, 60, 61, 65–67, 71, 84, 106, 149, 169, 190
Desire (*see* Mimesis)
Deviance 2, 84–88,
Diamond, Malcolm L. and Thomas V. Litzenburg, 148, 213

Diderot, Denis, 68
Differentiation (in sociology), 16
Dionysian, 71, 73, 81
Dionysius the Areopagite (Pseudo-Denys), 125
Donne, John (poem: "An Anatomy of the World"), 62, 64, 65, 71
Dostoyevsky, Fyodor, 79
Douglas, Mary, 18–19, 76–78, 213
Duomo, the (Florence Cathedral), 21
Durkheim, Emile, 76, 213

Easlea, Brian, 94, 213
Eckhart, Meister, 126, 132
Eco, Umberto (*The Name of the Rose*), 54, 58, 213
Einstein, Albert, 71
Emerson, Ralph Waldo, 24
Emotion (vs. reason; *see also* Affect), 67, 126, 138, 151, 160
Empiricism, 56, 131, 163–69
Encyclopedists (*Philosophes*), 68, 169
Enlightenment, 68–71, 73, 86, 129, 148, 149, 151, 154, 162, 206
Environmental Movement (and climate change), 3, 22–23, 30
Ephesians, Letter to the (and Deutero-Pauline themes), 119–20, 134
Ephesians
  4:1, 119
  4:11–16, 119
  4:17b, 119
  5:1–2a, 121
  5:19–20, 120
  5:21—6:9, 120
  6:19–22, 120
Epicureans, 106
Episcopacy, 120
Erasmus, 9–10, 63
Eucharist (and Eucharistic existence), 1, 2, 21, 50, 60, 109, 111, 112, 114, 123–26 passim, 132, 139, 144, 188–89, 206, 208

Evangelicalism, 42, 139, 141, 163, 182
Evans, C. Stephen, 150, 213
Evans, G. R., 213
Existentialism, 22, 71, 113–17 passim, 134, 156
Experience, religious, 132–34, 142, 154–58, 176
Experiential-Expressive faith, 154–58, 160
Ezekiel
  37, 109

False Sacred, 2, 48, 75–100, 128, 177, 178, 185, 204, 206, 207, 208
Fanon, Frantz, 89, 94, 97, 213
Fascism, 72
Fashion, 24
Fathers (of the Church), 1, 106, 107, 123–26, 133, 134, 137, 206
Feeding of the Multitude, Jesus's (Matthew 14), 144
Feminism (and feminist theology), 3, 95–96, 136, 179, 206
Feudalism (*see also* Monarchy) 52
Feuerbach, Ludwig, 170, 180
Fichte, Johann Gottlieb, 71
Fideism, 51, 104, 150, 161, 175, 183
Finney, John, 141, 213
Flaubert, Gustav, 79
Fleming, Chris, 78, 213
Flew, Anthony, 166, 213
Fordist economy and production 22, 25, 70, 99
Foreignness, 2, 83, 87–98,
Form of Life, Christianity as a (and Cultural-Linguistic faith), 140, 144, 147, 157, 160–63, 175, 185, 186, 207, 208
Foucault, Michel, 2, 60, 64, 70, 84–88, 133, 206, 213
Founding Murder, 81, 82
Fowler James (*see also* Stages of Faith) 152–53, 214
Frame, Tom, 2, 214

Franciscan Movement (and Francis of Assisi), 52–58 passim, 126, 127
Franklin, Benjamin, 10, 24
French Revolution, 23, 67–68, 86
Freud, Sigmund, 71, 78, 87, 145, 155
Fundamentalism, 32–36, 38, 55, 168–69, 197–98

Gaita, Raimond, 195, 214
Galatians
   2:19–20, 110
   3:26–28, 110
   3:26—4:20, 118
   4:6, 110
   5:1, 115
   5:21, 110
   5:24–25, 110
   6:14, 110, 118
Galileo, 16, 63
Geertz, Clifford, 161, 214
Generations X and/or Y, 19–21, 35–36, 37, 38
Genesis
   1:2, 109
   8:1–11, 145
   11:1–9, 109
   22:1–19, 108
   28:16, 12
Gerasene Demoniac, 199
Giddens, Anthony 28–29, 214
Gill, Michael Gates (*How Starbucks Saved My Life*), 28, 214
Gillespie, Michael Allen, 53, 54, 57, 71, 214
Gilson, Etienne, 50
Girard, René (and Girardian theory), ix, 2, 3, 4, 78–83, 90–93, 97, 104, 117–22 passim, 134, 137, 145–47, 150, 166, 172, 179, 183, 184, 187, 190, 194–200 passim, 206, 214, 219
Global economy (and Globalization), 16, 22, 23, 25, 33, 40, 84, 100, 179, 205

Glorious Revolution, 66
Goethe, Johann Wolfgang von, 44
Goleman, Daniel, 151, 214
Goya, Francisco, 88
Grandier, Urbain, 84–85
Green, Garrett, 3, 169, 170, 172, 174–76, 214
Gregory of Nyssa, 124, 129
Gregory of Rimini, 57
Griffin, Susan, 95–96, 214
Gropius, Walter, 71
Gutierrez, Gustavo, 91, 214

Hadewijch of Antwerp, 127
Hadot, Pierre, 106, 214
Harlow, Harry, 93
Hauerwas, Stanley, 136, 162, 214
Hawking, Stephen (*A Brief History of Time*), 42, 214
Hegel, Georg Friedrich, 170, 180
Heidegger, Martin, 72, 184
Henry IV of France, King (Henry of Navarre), 62, 63, 65
Henry of Ghent, 54
Herod's Banquet (Matthew 14), 144
Hick, John, 155, 214
Hilliard, David, 98, 214
Hillsong Church (Sydney), 35
Hitler, Adolf, 99
Hobbes, Thomas, 63, 169
Holbach, Paul Henri Baron d', 68
Holkot, Robert, 57
Homosexuality, 88, 91, 96–98, 182, 187–88, 199
Hooker, Richard, 169
Huddlestone, Trevor, 98
Huguenots, 62, 84
Hume, David, 10–11
Hus, Jan, 59, 130
Huxley, Aldous, 85, 214

Iacoboni, Marco (and mirror neurons), 79, 214

Imagination (*see* Paradigmatic Imagination)
Incarnation, 123, 125, 186, 187
Ind, Jo, 151, 215
Individual(ism), 25, 50, 69, 116, 127, 189–97 passim
Individualized Faith, 1, 3, 10, 11–15, 19, 22, 47, 58, 100, 205, 206
Interdividual Psychology (*see also* Mimesis), 78, 79, 90, 92, 104, 120, 121, 145–47, 189–90, 196
Into Great Silence (German film; and Carthusian monasticism), 7–11 passim, 47
Isaiah
  7, 108
Islam, 33, 83, 95, 181

James, Letter of
  2:17, 208
James, Henry (*The Wings of the Dove*), 193–94, 215
James, William, 132, 215
Jantzen, Grace, 3, 125–29 passim, 133, 215
Janz, Paul, 156, 184, 185, 215
Jenkins, David, 3, 35, 138–40, 141, 145, 146, 147, 157, 168, 176, 215
Jesus Christ, 1, 57, 74, 104, 105, 109–22 passim, 134, 138, 139, 143, 144, 145, 147, 149, 175, 180, 182, 187–88, 194, 195, 196, 198, 206–9
John
  4:5–42, 112
  6:25–40, 112
  9:1–35, 113
  15:5a, 109
  20:23, 109
John of the Cross, 105, 124, 129, 133, 158
John the Baptist (assassination; *see also* Feeding of the Multitude), 144
John, St. (and John's Gospel) 107, 109, 112, 206

Jonah, 143
Jones, E. Michael, 71, 215
Julian of Norwich, 127
Jung, Carl Gustav, 72

Kant, Immanuel, 131, 135, 215
Käsemann, Ernst, 115, 215
Katrina, Hurricane, 30
Keble, John, 12–13, 135
Keller, Catherine, 73, 74, 181, 197–98, 215
Kenosis, 184
Kerr, Fergus, 51, 215
Kierkegaard, Søren, 22, 43, 45, 71, 149, 162, 176, 180, 189, 215
Kipling, Rudyard, 91, 96
Kuhn, Thomas (and paradigms), 3, 151, 165–69, 176, 215
Küng, Hans, 34–35, 58, 155, 215

La Mettrie, Julien, 68
Labadie the Nomad, 130
Lakatos, Imre, 168, 215
Lakoff, George, 99, 215
Lash, Nicholas, 41, 215
Latin Mass, 34
Law, Jewish, 118, 122
Le Clerq, Jean, 124, 215
LeDoux, Joseph, 151, 215
Lefort, Guy, 214
Leibniz, Gottfried Wilhelm, 65–67
Lenin, Vladimir Ilych, 71–72
Levinas, Emanuel, 192, 193, 215
Lévi-Strauss, Claude, 76–78, 215
Liberation Theology, 91, 136
Lindbeck, George, 3, 150–63 passim, 176, 185, 216
Liturgy, 107, 109, 122, 124, 125–29 passim, 133, 135, 139, 163, 194
Locke, John, 70, 71, 106, 112, 169
Logical Positivism, 71
Loudun, possession at, 84–85, 91, 130
Louis XIV of France, King (the Sun King), 67–68

Louth, Andrew, 3, 106, 123–26 passim, 129, 133, 216
Loyola, Ignatius (and Ignatian Exercises, The), 61, 69
Lubac, Henri de, 99, 216
Luckmann, Thomas, 16
Luke
  4:1–13, 109
  7:36–50, 145
  9:28–36, 109
Lumby, Catharine, 95, 216
Luther, Martin, 9, 57, 128, 130, 135, 176
Lyotard, Jean-Francois (and the sublime), 155–56

MacIntyre, Alasdair, 119, 168, 216
MacKinlay, Elizabeth (and ageing; see also Stages of Faith), 154, 216
MacKinnon, D. M., 4, 180–81, 184, 216
Madness, 87–88
Madness of King George, The (film), 87
Maffesoli, Michel, 26, 216
Maguire, Nancy Klein (*An Infinity of Little Hours*), 7, 216
Managerialism, 28, 38
Manhattan Project, 94–95
Marion, Jean-Luc, 188–89, 216
Mark
  1:12–15, 109
  5:1–20, 199
  9:2–13, 109
Marriage, 29, 139
Marshall, Bruce, 186, 216
Marsilius of Ficino, 60
Martin, David, 36, 216
Marx, Karl (and Marxism), 23, 44, 62, 70, 170, 180
Mason, Michael (*The Spirit of Generation Y*), 38, 46, 216
Materialism (philosophical, see also Marxism), 68–71
Matson, Wallace, 164, 216

Matthew
  1:22–23, 108
  2, 109
  4:1–11, 109
  14, 143, 144–45
  17:1–8, 109
Matthew, Iain, 158, 216
May, Rollo (*The Concept of Anxiety*), 22, 216
McIntosh, Mark, 3, 50, 106, 127, 131, 192, 193, 216
Mechtild of Magdeburg, 127
Mehta, Hemant (*I Sold My Soul on eBay*), 44, 216
Merchant, Caroline, 94, 216
Merton, Thomas (poem: "The Quickening of St. John the Baptist"), 8, 216
Metaphysics, 3, 22, 183–87
Middle Ages, 1, 2, 3, 8, 15, 17, 48–60, 64, 69, 71, 100, 107, 122, 126–30, 137, 184, 206, 207
Middle Classes, 24
Milbank, John, 51, 53, 54, 62, 216
Miller, Alice, 99, 216
Miller, Vincent J., 24, 36, 37–38, 217
Milton, John, 169
Mimesis (and desire; see also Girard, René), 78–83 passim, 85, 91, 100, 104, 119–22 passim, 134, 137, 145–47 passim, 167, 172, 179, 187, 194
Mirecourt, Jean de, 57
Mirror Neurons, 79
Mitchell, Basil (and cumulative cases), 156, 166–67, 168, 217
Modernity, Western, 1, 2, 3, 9, 18, 22, 25, 33, 46, 48, 62–74, 77, 82–100, 103, 104, 107, 108, 115, 122, 125, 127, 128, 136, 137, 152, 169, 170, 176, 177, 179, 184, 190–92, 196, 203, 205
Monarchy (*see also* Feudalism) 67–68, 70

Monasticism, 7–11, 47, 124, 128
Montaigne, Michel de, 49, 63–64, 66, 73, 217
Montesquieu, Baron de, 68
Moore, Robert and Douglas Gillette, 154, 217
Morris, Colin, 51, 217
Morton, Tom, 33, 217
Murphy, Nancey, 3, 164, 166, 168, 217
Mysticism, 1, 3, 103–34, 207
Mythology, 78

Nandy, Ashis, 91–92, 96–97, 217
Nantes, Edict of, 62
Nation State, 16, 30, 128, 206
Natural Order, 53, 94–95, 112
Nazism, 72, 93
Neale, John Mason, 135
Neo-Liberalism, 40
New Social Movements, 73
New Testament (and NT studies) 1, 112, 126
New-Age Spirituality, 11–15 passim, 37
Newman, John Henry, 3, 135, 169–74, 175, 176, 186, 217
Newton, Isaac, 63, 65–71 passim, 173
Nicene Creed, 123
Niebuhr, Reinhold (*The Irony of American History*), 73, 217
Nietzsche, Friedrich, 22, 43–44, 45, 71, 159, 179, 184, 217
Nihilism, 17, 49, 71–72
Noah's Dove, 145
Nominalism, 2, 52–58, 61, 71, 122, 127, 133
Northern Ireland (the Troubles) 83
Nouvelle Theologie, 61
Novel, the, 70
Nussbaum, Martha ("Love's Knowledge"), 151, 217

Ockham, William of, 54–58 passim
Olivi, Peter John, 58

Opus Dei, 34
Orient (*see also* Other, the), 88–89
Origen, 123, 175
Orwell, George ("Shooting an Elephant"), 30, 84, 91–93, 96, 217
Other, the, 2, 83–100 passim, 107, 129, 131, 133, 179, 195–96
Oughourlian, Jean-Michel, 146, 214, 217

Pailin, Michael (BBC comedy series: *Ripping Yarns*), 96
Paley, William, 173
Papacy (and papal power, infallibility), 58–60, 128, 171, 176
Paradigmatic Imagination (and pattern recognition), 3, 138, 163–76, 183
Participatory Knowing, 3, 106, 107, 124, 126, 138, 163, 208
Pascal, Blaise, 69, 149, 157, 217
Paul, St. (and Pauline mysticism), 3, 107, 109–22, 123, 133, 134, 137, 145, 175, 182, 191, 194, 206
Pearson, Christopher, 34
Pentecost, 108
Pentecostalism, 32, 35–36, 85, 160
Performativity (and rhetoric), 117–22 passim
1 Peter
3:3, 208
Philippians
1:27, 115
3:1–11, 110
3:12, 114
3:17, 121
3:21, 122
4:1, 115
Phillips, D. Z., 162, 217
Philo, 123, 124
Physics, 65–66
Pickering, W. S. F. (*Anglo-Catholicism*), 98, 217

Pickstock, Catherine, 56, 59, 188–89, 217
Pietism, 110, 111, 114, 127, 154, 160
Placher, William, 51, 60, 217
Plato (and the Forms), 52–53, 106, 123, 125, 127
Plotinus (and Neo-Platonism) 123, 125
Pobee, John, 191
Pohier, Jacques, 34–35, 203–204, 217
Polanyi, Michael, 151, 217
Polkinghorne, John, 149, 217
Popper, Karl, 151, 217
Porete, Marguerite, 129
Pornography, 95–96
Porter, Muriel, 35, 217
Porter, Roy (*Flesh in the Age of Reason*), 151, 218
Post-Liberal Theology, 162, 185, 186
Post-Modernity (and late-modernity), 2, 3, 4, 22, 26, 27, 49, 73, 77, 103, 136, 137, 179, 182, 192
Power (divine, social and ecclesial) 58–60, 61, 84–88 passim, 127, 128, 176, 179, 181, 193, 198
Prayer, 139, 160
Pre-modern culture, 13, 31, 125, 126
Priestley, Joseph, 68
Prison, the, 86
Privatization (in sociology), 16
Problem of Evil, 148, 180
Proust, Marcel, 79
Psalms
   22, 157
   34:8, 103
   77, 157
Puritanism, 10, 23–24, 33, 70, 74
Pusey, Edward Bouverie, 135
Putnam, Robert D., 20–21, 218

Queer Theory (*see also* Homosexuality), 3, 98

Quine, Willard V. ("Two Dogmas of Empiricism"), 3, 164–65, 168, 218

Rabelais, François, 63
Radical Orthodoxy, 17, 49
Rahner, Karl, 155, 218
Ramsey, Arthur Michael, 60, 218
Realism (foundationalism; and anti-realism), 52–53, 156, 164–65, 175, 180, 184
Reality Television, 29–30
Reason (and rationalism), 3, 104, 106, 114, 124, 126, 127, 130–36 passim, 138, 147, 148–54, 161, 163, 165, 168, 169, 172, 179, 183, 185, 209
Reformation, Protestant, 9–10, 16, 57, 64, 100, 115, 116, 129, 130
Reincarnation, 46
Relativism (and pluralism), 12, 31–32, 133, 155, 179, 201
Renaissance, 62–65, 66, 69, 79
Reno, Russell R., 159, 191, 218
Ressentiment, 43, 159
Restoration England, 67
Resurrection, 122, 183, 187, 192, 208
Revelation, Book of, 21, 178
Richardson, Samuel (*Pamela* and *Clarissa*), 70
Richelieu, Cardinal, 85
Ritual, 76, 81, 85
Rivera, Mayra, 180, 218
Rizzolatti, Giacomo and Corrado Sinigaglia (*see also* Mirror Neurons), 79, 218
Robinson, Geoffrey, 34, 218
Rocha, João Cezar de Castro, 214
Rohr, Richard (and masculinity; *see also* Stages of Faith) 153–54, 218
Rolle, Richard, 127
Romans
   1–3, 118
   6:10–11, 110
   7:4, 110

Romans (*continued*)
   7:4–5, 111
   8:1–2, 9–11, 110
   12:2, 175
   14:17, 110
Romanticism (and romantic movement; romantic expressivism), 23, 24, 38, 42, 44, 70, 127, 131, 154–55, 170, 190, 192
Roscelin, 52
Rousseau, Jean-Jacques, 68
Rowell, Geoffrey (*The Vision Glorious*), 135, 218
Ryle, Gilbert (and linguistic behaviourism), 190, 218

Sabbah, Fatna, 95, 218
Sacrifice, 145, 178
Said, Edward, 88–89, 218
Saints, 107, 122, 128, 192–97
Sanders, E. P., 3, 115–17, 122, 218
Satan, 80
Saul, John Ralston, 69, 218
Scapegoat, 2, 80, 83, 85, 86, 187, 206
Schad, John, 88, 98, 218
Scheler, Max, 43, 159, 218
Schelling, Friedrich William, 131
Schillebeeckx, Edward, 188, 218
Schleiermacher, Friedrich, 154–55, 218
Schmemann, Alexander, 203, 218
Schmutz, Jacob, 53
Scholasticism, 3, 60–62, 69, 128, 129, 171
Schweitzer, Albert, 3, 109–13, 116, 122, 136, 218–19
Science and Religion, 3, 53, 138, 148–49
Scotus, Duns, 54, 60–61
Scrooge, Ebenezer, 8
Secularization (and secularity), 2, 9, 11–19, 21, 48, 55, 60, 107

Self, 4, 9, 13, 19, 70, 88–92 passim, 104–7 passim, 115, 185, 189–97 passim, 205, 208
Sennett, Richard M., 28, 219
Sexuality 28–29, 78, 80, 82, 168, 203
Shakespeare, William 49, 59, 63, 79
Shame, 146
Sheldrake, Rupert, 94, 219
Shelley, Mary (*Frankenstein*) 95, 219
Shogimen, Takashi, 58, 219
Sickels, Eleanor, 23, 219
Sin, 113–17 passim, 118, 122
Singer, Peter (*Animal Liberation*) 93–94, 219
Skepticism, Religious, 3, 4, 15, 42, 69, 106, 107, 112, 127, 137, 148–49, 157, 158–60, 162, 170, 176, 200–201, 209
Skinner, John (*Hear Our Silence*) 7, 219
Slee, Nicola (and women's faith; *see also* Stages of Faith), 153, 219
Sloterdijk, Peter, 14–15, 42, 219
Smith, Wilfred Cantwell, 155, 219
Song of Songs, 128, 145
Spirit, 104, 108, 110, 119, 124, 125, 179, 183, 208
Spiritual Maturity, 197–203, 209
Springsted, Otto, 108, 111, 112, 113, 125, 219
Stages of Faith, 152–54
Stalin, Josef (and Stalinism), 70, 71–72
State Churches, 16
Stein, Edith, 192
Stendhal, 79
Sternberg, Esther, 151–52, 219
Stratton, David, 8, 11, 219
Suarez, Francisco (and Spanish Jesuits), 60–61, 129

Tanner, Kathryn, 185, 219
Taylor, Charles, 10–11, 13, 14, 17–18, 20, 42, 44, 49, 64, 69, 106, 152, 219

Teresa of Avila, 129
Thatcher, Margaret, 140
1 Thessalonians
   1:6–7, 121
   2:12, 110
   3:13, 115
   5:23, 115
Thirty-Years War, 62, 65, 66, 84–85, 130, 154
Thoreau, Henry David, 24
Tilley, Terrence, 185–86, 219
Timothy (Paul's protégé), 121
Tincq, Henri, 83, 219
Titanic, 30, 72
Toulmin, Stephen (and Cosmopolis), 2, 49, 50, 59, 62–74, 78, 82, 83, 84–88 passim, 105, 107, 118, 126, 129, 130, 177, 179, 181, 182, 206, 219
Tracy, David, 117, 219
Transignification, 188
Transubstantiation, 188–89
Trent, Council of, 61, 130, 187
Tribal Faith, 1, 3, 10, 11–15, 22, 100, 205
Trinity, 4, 124, 125, 181, 184, 191, 197
Trotsky, Leon, 71
Turgenev, Ivan (*Fathers and Sons*), 71, 219
Turner, Denys, 3, 105, 128, 132

Underhill, Evelyn, 132, 219
Uniqueness and Finality of Christ, 182–83, 201
United States of America, 20–21, 33–34, 73–74, 83, 86, 181, 197–98
Univocity (of being, in metaphysics), 50, 55, 60–62
Unreason, 87, 98
Urban Western Life, 19–22
Usus Pauper, 58

Van Gogh, Vincent, 88
Vatican II, 34, 135, 155, 188

Vattimo, Gianni, 3, 184, 219–20
Versailles, 68
Victims, 48, 81–100 passim, 145–47, 180, 192, 200–201, 206
Violence, 1, 2, 4, 49, 80, 83–100 passim, 105, 177, 178, 197–98
Voltaire, François Marie Arouet de, 68

Walking on the Sea, Jesus (Matthew 14), 143, 144–45
War on Terror, 83, 181
Watts, Fraser and Mark Williams, 151, 220
Waugh, Evelyn (*Brideshead Revisited*), 160, 220
Webber, Robert E., 163, 220
Weber, Max, 10, 22–24 passim, 220
Webster, John, 197, 220
Weil, Simone, 192, 195
Werpehowski, William, 186, 220
Wilde, Oscar, 84, 91, 96–97, 98
Wilding, Michael, 33, 220
Williams, Rowan, 4, 21, 55, 62, 133, 134, 180–204 passim, 220
Willimon, William, 162, 214
Winch, Peter, 161, 220
Winton, Tim ("The Turning"), 3, 141–45, 157, 167, 176, 220
Witchcraft, 77–78
Wittgenstein, Ludwig (and language games), 3, 45, 161–63, 167, 176, 190, 220
Wolin, Richard, 73, 220
Woolf, Virginia (and Bloomsbury Set), 96–97
World Trade Centre (9/11), 83, 207
World War I, 72–74
World War II, 72, 82
Wuthnow, Robert, 33, 220
Wycliff, John, 59
Wynn, Mark R., 151, 220
Wyschogrod, Edith, 3, 192–97, 220

Yeats, William Butler (poem: "The Second Coming"), 71, 220

Zaehner, R. C., 133, 220
Zizioulas, John, 4, 196–97, 220

www.ingramcontent.com/pod-product-compliance
Lightning Source LLC
Chambersburg PA
CBHW020407230426
43664CB00009B/1215